STAYING THE COURSE AS A CIO

Founded in 1807, John Wiley & Sons is the oldest independent publishing company in the United States. With offices in North America, Europe, Asia, and Australia, Wiley is globally committed to developing and marketing print and electronic products and services for our customers' professional and personal knowledge and understanding.

The Wiley CIO series provides information, tools, and insights to IT executives and managers. The products in this series cover a wide range of topics that supply strategic and implementation guidance on the latest technology trends, leadership, and emerging best practices.

Titles in the Wiley CIO series include:

Transforming IT Culture: How to Use Social Intelligence, Human Factors, and Collaboration to Create an IT Department That Outperforms by Frank Wander

Unleashing the Power of IT: Bringing People, Business, and Technology Together by Dan Roberts

The U.S. Technology Skills Gap: What Every Technology Executive Must Know to Save America's Future by Gary J. Beach

Architecting the Cloud: Design Decisions for Cloud Computing Service Models (SaaS, PaaS, and IaaS) by Michael Kavis

Staying the Course as a CIO: How to overcome the trials and challenges of IT Leadership by Jonathan Mitchell

STAYING THE COURSE AS A CIO

HOW TO OVERCOME THE TRIALS AND CHALLENGES OF IT LEADERSHIP

Dr Jonathan M Mitchell

WILEY

This edition first published 2015
© 2015 Jonathan Mitchell

Registered office
John Wiley & Sons Ltd, The Atrium, Southern Gate, Chichester, West Sussex, PO19 8SQ,
United Kingdom

For details of our global editorial offices, for customer services and for information about how to apply
for permission to reuse the copyright material in this book please visit our website at www.wiley.com.

Wiley publishes in a variety of print and electronic formats and by print-on-demand. Some material
included with standard print versions of this book may not be included in e-books or in print-on-
demand. If this book refers to media such as a CD or DVD that is not included in the version you
purchased, you may download this material at http://booksupport.wiley.com. For more information
about Wiley products, visit www.wiley.com.

Designations used by companies to distinguish their products are often claimed as trademarks. All
brand names and product names used in this book are trade names, service marks, trademarks or
registered trademarks of their respective owners. The publisher is not associated with any product or
vendor mentioned in this book.

Limit of Liability/Disclaimer of Warranty: While the publisher and author have used their best
efforts in preparing this book, they make no representations or warranties with respect to the accuracy
or completeness of the contents of this book and specifically disclaim any implied warranties of
merchantability or fitness for a particular purpose. It is sold on the understanding that the publisher is
not engaged in rendering professional services and neither the publisher nor the author shall be liable
for damages arising herefrom. If professional advice or other expert assistance is required, the services
of a competent professional should be sought.

Library of Congress Cataloging-in-Publication Data
Mitchell, Jonathan M., 1961–
    Staying the course as a CIO : how to overcome the trials and challenges of IT leadership/
Dr. Jonathan M. Mitchell.
        pages cm.—(The Wiley CIO series)
    Includes bibliographical references and index.
    ISBN 978-1-118-96887-1 (hardback)
    1. Chief information officers. 2. Information technology—Management. I. Title.
    HD30.2.M577 2015
    658.4′038—dc23
                                                                    2014025612

A catalogue record for this book is available from the British Library.

ISBN 978-1-118-96887-1 (hardback)
ISBN 978-1-118-96884-0 (ebk)
ISBN 978-1-118-96886-4 (ebk)

Cover image: © Jonathan Mitchell
Cover design: Wiley

Set in 10/12 pt Janson Text LT Std by Aptara Inc., New Delhi, India
Printed in Great Britain by TJ International Ltd, Padstow, Cornwall, UK

TABLE OF CONTENTS

INTRODUCTION

D o you want to be a great IT leader? Why not? For those in corporate or public sector life, becoming a Chief Information Officer, a Senior Vice President or perhaps even a Chief Digital Officer in a large organisation is seen by many—quite rightly—to be the very pinnacle of achievement in the world of Information Technology. Today, an increasing number of IT leaders have become Board or Executive Team members in their companies. Almost all exert high levels of power and influence. However, the life expectancy of this corporate rainmaker is shockingly short. IT leaders often seem to enjoy a span no longer than a mayfly as they flutter away in the turbulent waters of the corporate pond. Few seem to stay the course for much longer than a couple of years and it is rare to find anyone making it to half of a decade or more. Some organisations even change their CIO every year. And most of the endings are not happy ones either. Very often something, or more commonly a whole bunch of somethings, goes horribly wrong and the reign of the noble IT leader comes to an abrupt and brutal end. In some cases the disaster takes the form of a slow-motion train wreck. With growing inevitability, it can be months before the inadvertent act of hara-kiri is finally completed and the inevitable mushroom cloud of dust and the smell of doom imperiously rise from the tangled mass of mangled locomotives, twisted rails and spilt cargo. More often however, the end is quicker and much more sinister. Whispered rumours around the water-cooler are shortly followed by a curiously empty executive office and a bland corporate announcement referencing "Special Projects" or some similar metaphor. It's all very sad. After all, the incumbent had probably spent twenty years or more of their life assiduously building their career and preparing for this great opportunity. Who would have thought it would end with little more than a cardboard box full of belongings, a tearful goodbye from their executive assistant and a lonely trip down the service elevator? The displaced IT leader will be wondering what happened and what, if anything, they could have or should have done. They will also believe that life in the IT industry is unfair, which of course is also true.

What this IT leader and many more before them may not have fully appreciated is that the IT industry is riddled with a bewildering arrangement of trials and challenges. Each of these horrors has been carefully designed by Mother Nature to cause you the maximum amount of pain, suffering and even career death. There are however, a few, sparse straws of hope onto which you can clutch. As you contemplate the vistas of vicissitude ahead of you, be aware that others have gone before and some have even stayed the course. The very few wise, battle-scarred warriors who have lived to tell their tale know that these same horrors appear again and again with relentless regularity. It doesn't matter which business or public sector organisation you work in. It doesn't even matter whether you are trying to run a relatively small IT function on a single site or a complex enterprise scattered across far distant geographies. Suffering is pandemic at least as far as leadership in IT is concerned.

In this book, we will examine some of the worst trials and challenges you might well run into on your quest to be a world-class IT leader. Some you may be able to side-step and we will look at various methods of fancy footwork you might employ. But unfortunately many will already have a firm missile lock and you will have to endure some pain as well as dealing with the aftermath. Only the most careful attention before, during and after the event will give you any chance of staving off disaster. A strong constitution is also required. I was once given an indispensable piece of advice by a wonderful lady aviator who taught me how to fly (few are immune from their mid-life crisis). "What should I do if things go wrong up there?" I asked. She broke into a broad smile, laughed and said. "Panic slowly of course".

Dr Jonathan Mitchell
Ashbourne
Derbyshire
UK

CHAPTER 1

Dislocated Stakeholders

"Where is the 'any' key?"
(Homer Simpson, in response to the message, "Press any key")

Stakeholders, as one of my colleagues once said to me, "should be tied to one". He was definitely in the "Joan of Arc" school of stakeholder management. "It's all very good when they are feisty and swashbuckling," he continued, "but when they start to get irritating, you should tie 'em to a pole and light a bonfire." This approach has obvious attractions, but there are few people who can avoid the scourge of the irritating stakeholder whose mission in life is to make your life a misery. King Henry VIII, the sixteenth-century King of England, was one of the few heroes of history who was able to buck the trend. As most British schoolchildren will know, Old Henry had a penchant for doing his own thing. It was never a good idea to be his wife when he got bored (which happened at least five times it seems). Kings in olden days generally didn't have that many stakeholders to worry about especially if they had bags of charisma and a large, loyal army at their disposal. Henry therefore pushed the boundaries of his not inconsiderable power to the limits. During his reign he worked his way through six wives, as well as starting a war with France (which is something every good British monarch feels they have to do). He also created the Royal Navy (Loades, 2009) and is even thought by some to have written the quintessential English song *Greensleeves* (Trow, 2010). Henry was certainly a colourful and decisive monarch and he knew how to please a crowd. When he became King at the tender age of 17, one of the very first things he did was to order the execution of the two men his father had employed to collect heavy taxes from the fair folk of England. All but two people in the land thought that this was a great idea. He was also fond of hunting, gambling and dancing. It is said that he only spent an hour a day on government business (Spartacus Educational, 2013).

Perhaps Henry's biggest moment in history came when he decided to divorce his first wife, Catherine of Aragon. Popular culture suggests that Henry grew bored of Catherine. Knowing the response he'd get from Pope Clement (who wasn't much of a fan of divorces, especially when they involved Catholic Queens), he apparently decided that he would stick his fingers up at the Catholic Church and invent a whole new religion. This we now know today as protestant Anglicanism. While it is true that Henry was eventually excommunicated by the Pope, the divorce from Catherine was probably only one symptom of Henry's problems with his stakeholders (Weir, 2002). Henry was a fiercely independent chap by all accounts and his motives and methods were devious—at least when it came to finding ways that allowed him to operate in a completely unconstrained fashion. He was also thought to be a good Catholic, but Henry just couldn't live with the concept of an old guy with a beard in far-off Italy telling him what to do. Between 1532 and 1537, he instituted a number of statutes that dealt with the relationship between himself and the pope. For example, in 1534 he mandated that the clergy could only elect bishops nominated by him. For an encore he then declared that the King was the only "Supreme Head on Earth of the Church of England". So there! All in all, Henry must have been a very fine megalomaniac even if he did over-eat a bit as he grew older.

We, unfortunately, do not have the freedom of action enjoyed by people such as good King Henry, or any other historical giants for that matter. We therefore need to understand the identity and motivations of the stakeholders who hold influence over all that we do (at least in the work place context). Tudor-style, summary execution is frowned upon today. This means that it is a relatively unlikely outcome if you do somehow become detached from your stakeholders. But be warned, there are plenty of other nefarious and deeply unpleasant methods of punishment available to people in corporate life today. Dislocation is painful and if you do not rapidly connect things back together properly, then they will become detached forever and it won't be long before someone decides to put the pieces in the air-lock so that they can be blasted out into space.

So who are our stakeholders and what do they want?

Wooden Poles with Holder

In its simplest sense, a stakeholder is a person, group or organisation that has interest or concern in an organisation (Business Dictionary, 2013). The days when people felt they needed to carry wooden poles around with them disappeared with the wizards of Middle Earth. Stakeholders also have nothing to do with vampires, though if you do unhappily have a vampire infestation on your hands, driving wooden sticks through the hearts of the un-dead while they sleep in their coffins is widely considered an effective pest control measure. These days life is much easier. Modern vampires tend to be good-looking teenagers with a conscience. It was never like that in Bela Lugosi's day.

"We don't vanquish vampires so don't call us stakeholders!"
Jackie Sadek

So while a few of our stakeholders may be brandishing wooden sticks, more often their weapon of choice is the pointed word. And you will find plenty of those out there—both words and people. There are of course, a wide range of different stakeholders who are affected by IT. In fact, pretty much everyone in the company, together with all your suppliers and customers, receive the delicate ministrations of your organisation in some form or other. Figure 1.1 shows some of the major stakeholders you will encounter. The strong arrows show the strong connections while the dotted arrows represent a looser stakeholder engagement. There may be some corporate outward-looking IT functions which have very intimate relations with customers and suppliers but for most of us, it is the Board of Directors and the leadership of the company, our beloved middle managers and the common or garden users who will demand most of the management time of an IT leader. We should look at each in turn.

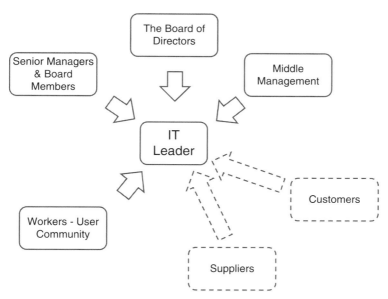

Figure 1.1 The CIO's Major Stakeholders

Because They're Worth It?

Let us look first at our user community, or to use a better term—the workers. They are the most voluminous group of your stakeholders and they are comprised of real people doing real jobs. Workers are really cool people. They actually get to do stuff other than emails and meetings. On occasions, what they do get up to can even be useful to the company. It doesn't matter whether they are on the floor of a factory bending metal, or in an office creating what I believe is known these days as "intellectual property"; these people are precious and you have to look after them as best as you can. However, as far as a voice in IT is concerned, most of these folks will strictly be in the silent majority category.

> **"Every day I get up and look through the Forbes list of the richest people in America. If I'm not there, I go to work."**
> *Robert Orben*

That said, the needs of the many are simple and straightforward—at least from their perspective. When I've spoken to computer users over the years about their requirements, the answers they give me are fairly consistent. I'm sure it will be the same for you. These good folk will want the latest models of phones and tablet computers and they will want to change them as frequently as they change their socks. They believe they cannot live without the most powerful laptops and personal computers known to man. They will also want to store infinite amounts of email in their inboxes and send and receive massive PowerPoint files that run into terrorbytes. They will demand full and unfettered access to the Internet, so that they can use whatever social media, home banking or any other e-commerce sites take their fancy. Some will want you to fund small pet projects because they naively believe that technology will make their working lives easier. Finally, everyone wants a helpdesk that is instantly answered by a beautiful, courteous person who has bucket loads of empathy to hand. Some may even want these people to solve their problems.

While such requests are easy to understand, responding to them sensitively can be tricky. Many IT leaders faced with the enormity of the task just throw up their hands and subscribe to the pleasing mantra "The only good user is a dead user". The security needs of your network will of course, horribly constrain the things that you can do for them, but it is pointless explaining this to anyone. They won't understand and they won't care. Why should they? Your users will just see a computer that's much the same as the one they have at home, except that this machine is probably older and of course they can't change their wallpaper or replace the arrow cursor with a banana that peels itself. When people come to work, they will demand and expect all the freedoms they enjoy on their virus-laden, spyware-riddled, zombie-bot, home computers, smartphones and tablets. However, despite all the corporate problems, allowing "reasonable personal use" on company computers is a policy you should strongly consider championing. It is a winning (if sometimes painful) strategy. It is particularly helpful if you want to promote computer literacy amongst your workforce. There are of course always unexpected and sometimes unpleasant things that can happen when you give human beings a bit of freedom. Kings worked this out pretty early on, which is why they were so fond of the operating system we know as Feudalism. Basically, they got to be the Lords while the rest of us were "vassals" and had to do what we were told (Abdy, 2012). Back here in the twenty-first century corporate life is slightly more egalitarian. This new freedom allows any miscreants to get up to amazing things. I have seen some horror stories that would make Mary Shelley blush.

Some years ago I recall that we lost a complete night's worth of backups in a data centre I was managing. This was because a computer operator spent his entire shift downloading gigabytes of video files of his favourite soccer team—it was Manchester United as it turns out. The network was so overloaded that all the applications eventually timed themselves out and backed out of the rather important job of backing things up. Imagine people running all around the computer room like headless chickens. Meanwhile the operator in question, oblivious to the chaos he had caused, quietly sat in the corner of the office repeatedly watching videos of his favourite stars with spray tans and hair transplants kicking a ball and waving garish trophies around.

Then there was the time when we found an employee who clearly didn't like his job. He spent every single minute of every working day surfing the Internet. He usually started five minutes after he had clocked in and continued until he stopped for lunch. Forty-five minutes later he was at it again, only to finish five minutes before he clocked out. This went on for weeks on end. When we looked at the usage logs, we could even calculate how long it took for cups of coffee to pass through his system. Before you think "too much information", let me reassure you that we could work it out quite simply from the breaks he had taken in between surfing sessions. It was about an hour and half if you are interested. The incandescent HR Director wanted to fire the individual. He was not amused by my suggestion that we put the employee's name forward for some kind of Guinness Book of World Records nomination. Clearly supervision and motivation had failed this person in abundance in his day job, but I certainly couldn't have surfed with anything like the dedication he showed. The individual's manager was the one who ended up with the biggest rocket however. He was told in no uncertain terms that from now on he was expected to harness the dogged conscientiousness of his loyal employees.

My all-time favourite "user howler of the century" story however, happened shortly after the 9/11 terrorist attack in New York. A Middle East-based employee, appalled by what he had seen, decided to send an email to every other employee in the company. He wanted to tell everyone that people in his part of the world condemned the terrorist action. His plan was to express solidarity with his colleagues in North and South America, Europe, Asia, Africa, Australasia and even a polar station in Antarctica. Normal controls within the network meant that our intrepid hero was not able to simply send an email to the 105,000 employees on the payroll at that time. Bulk emailing was both discouraged and curtailed by company policy. Nevertheless, undeterred by such a flimsy set of obstacles, our hero spent many, many hours and probably several days putting together a dazzling number of distribution lists. The size of each was carefully crafted so that it slipped just under the "number of recipients" restrictions that the computer administrators had put in place. The results were spectacular. Sending off his emails in batches, the disaster unfolded with delicious slowness. First, local servers became clogged, after which regional servers started to choke. Within a couple of hours network diagrams at Network High Command began to glow with angry tones of red. The "Clark Kents" at Network crisis control struggled into nearby telephone boxes to don their "Superman" outfits. In the command centre confused reports suggested that a virulent virus was spreading uncontrollably across the globe. Blizzards of sandy emails marched across North Africa scattering bloated, overfilled, groaning mailboxes before them. Even Field Marshal Rommel and his Afrika Korps would have been impressed as first Egypt and then Tunisia ground to a halt. It took several more hours of headless chicken antics before the panicky network team had calmed down enough to diagnose the problems in the Middle East region. Network traffic was eventually throttled back and re-routed via various improbable countries. The over-impressively large "world domination" screens covering the walls of the Crisis Command Centre began to turn amber and eventually, to everyone's relief, they settled to a soothing, verdant green. Later that day, most of the offending messages had been identified and a mass deletion process was underway. The countries initially affected found their computer systems disrupted for a few days, but the damage was, to be fair, fairly limited. It did take some time however, to persuade the authorities that we did not have another terrorist on our hands. Happily, our employee with a conscience was neither shot nor disciplined nor was he even sent to an American holiday camp on a Caribbean island. Everyone lived happily ever after, except perhaps the network manager, who I am told is responding well to medication.

All this goes to show that everything has its price. Indeed the price of electronic freedom can be very expensive for its custodians. But it is still nonetheless a recommended course of action for the avant-garde IT leader. You will be fine as long as you are the type of person who is not easily surprised by the wit and wisdom of man or woman.

If you consider the business applications that people use in their day-to-day jobs, however, the situation is not good. This is because the views and opinions of actual workers are rarely considered by their leadership when new computer applications are conceived, developed and introduced on their behalf. The average worker must have the patience of a saint when you consider what their senior colleagues have done for them. Many applications designed to help them do their jobs more efficiently don't generally help them one little bit. Indeed, the programs have probably been horribly customised by colluding tribes of middle managers and analysts aided and abetted by geeks from the IT department. The "cool" ideas of the geeks and a range of unsatisfactory committee-spawned, camel-like design compromises may render the application completely unusable. You don't have to look far in the trade press for lurid examples of new processes and systems which have caused untold misery to all concerned. Some shock, horror, noun-stack nightmares even make it to the national newspapers, such as the demise of the UK National Health Service project (*Daily Mail* - £12bn NHS computer system is scrapped, 2011). Some conspiracy theorists out there may even believe that programmers' tool- kits come with all these handy features built-in (Figure 1.2).

> **"So much of what we call management consists in making it difficult for people to work."**
> *Peter F. Drucker*

But there is some good news out there. There are some ways for you to calibrate yourself with the datum of reality in the work place. Some companies are really very good at it. A colleague of mine who worked for a large supermarket chain in Europe described to me a fantastic model that I would recommend to anyone. Each year, all the senior managers and executives of the company up to and including the Chief Executive are obliged to spend more than a week of their time carrying out relatively unskilled tasks in the company's retail outlets or distribution centres. Some even got to meet real customers. This laudable act was intended to keep the feet of the anointed firmly on the ground. It also gave the executives a chance to understand what working at the sharp end was really like. Finally it was a great morale booster for the checkout staff as they watched their hapless leaders struggle to weigh a pound of apples or puzzle over the pricing of a kumquat.

When my friend returned from his short sabbatical, I quizzed him on his experiences. First of all, I noticed that he was limping and he had a bandaged hand. "It's a lot more physical than you would expect", was his response when he noticed me staring. "What did you learn?" I asked. He narrowed his eyes and looked at me threateningly. "Doors!" he cried, "I never realised how impossible doors can be." I was taken aback. The only software package I had heard of that had "doors" in the name had nothing to do with retail

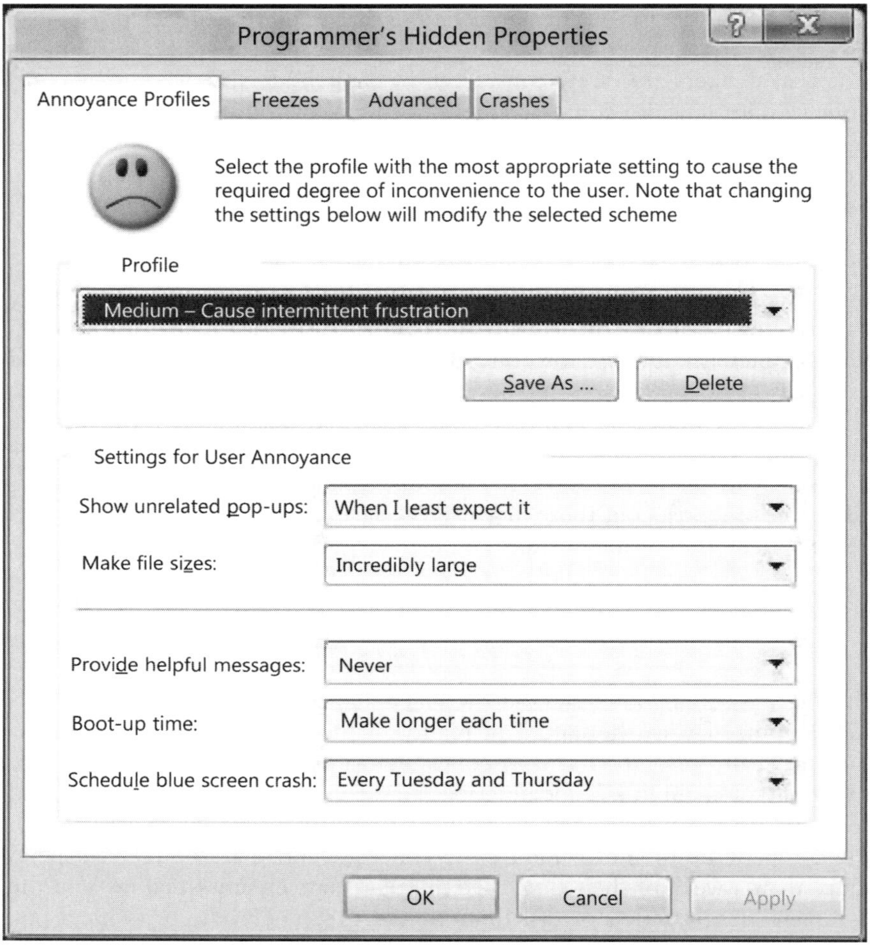

Figure 1.2   How to Win Friends and Influence People?

warehousing. "Well" he continued, "the way that my people designed the warehouse systems means that anyone using it had to walk through at least three doors for every single transaction they did. That's how I damaged my hand. Someone was coming the other way at just the wrong time." With rising emotion he continued. "When I get back to the office the very first thing I'm going to do is to remove all the doors in our warehouses and make a great big bonfire with them. Then I'll make the project team redesign their system from scratch. This time we will really make sure that things work smoothly and reliably. Finally, we'll put the implementation team to work in the warehouse in real life for a good few weeks. When they complain, we'll make them work a few weeks more. That'll teach them." With a disturbing glint in his eye, he hurried off. It had definitely been a formative experience.

**"Great Spirit, grant that I may not criticize my neighbour until
I have walked a mile in his moccasins."**
Native American Prayer

On the other side of the coin, an example of how to do this "process thing" really well also occurred in a warehousing project. The particular warehouse in question was critical to the company as it shipped over £120m of material and spares each week. The project team had found out that there was an industry-leading package to do this type of work, but unlike everyone else in the industry they curiously decided to use the package as it was designed. After they had installed their un-customised software, they took over a small warehouse building where a simulation of the proposed system was built. Each process was developed and tested exhaustively. Many, many members of the real workforce were intimately involved throughout the whole exercise. When the team was satisfied that it would all work, they proceeded to the implementation phase. They then carried out three full dress rehearsals with real data before the system went live. The last of these involved complete and full parallel running of both the old and the new systems. This was done with production data from the full, burgeoning databases of dirty data that comprise "real life" usage. This approach meant that each transaction had to be carried out twice, once in each system. They had, of course, to roster two sets of shift teams (comprising hundreds of people in each) to adequately staff the expensive parallel operation.

When the system did go live, it was notable that performance metrics did not fall away as expected—in fact they improved. A few very minor glitches did appear in the days that followed (largely through data integrity issues), but the project team and the workforce swiftly dealt with each of them without undue impact. The parallel running regime meant that customers would not have been impacted anyway. In fact, the cunning inventory-building program that the Stalinist project manager had introduced in the preceding weeks to buffer the inevitable unexpected problems meant that he was well insulated from any transition glitches. The project team also stayed in place, watching as well as participating. After three weeks and one full business cycle of live use had passed, a number of improvements were identified together with one or two minor howlers that needed to be corrected. These were swiftly implemented, regression tested and released. The result was a happy workforce that was considerably more productive than they had previously been. Unlike most IT projects however, the celebrations only started once the new warehouse was stable and transacting at the higher volumes stated in the business plan, rather than when the code was "delivered". The key point here is that it was the business outcome that was celebrated, not the IT project.

The outdated concept of projects being celebrated when they go live, rather than waiting until they have actually delivered benefit to the organisation is a nasty and dangerous practice. It should be consigned to a list of "bad things we promise we will not do any more". Imagine a situation where a surgeon and his team down tools, whoop with joy, crack open the champagne and start celebrating a few moments after they'd cut out your tumour? Mercifully for us, they do bother to sew us back up again. They also continue to monitor us with professional aftercare to make sure the problem really has gone away. We really could do with a great deal more of that sort of TLC in the IT world. Any IT project teams who toss a lemon of a project over the fence onto the heads of the defenceless user community and run away deserve everything that they get. Having a warehouse door slammed in their face would be a good start.

The Joys of Middle Management

Just who are the middle managers in an organisation? What do they do, where do they come from and why are there so many of them? Well, we could enjoyably argue about the definition until the end of time, especially if we let any middle managers join in the discussion. However, let's just for the purposes of this debate define them as people in the organisation who report to a manager, but also have managers working for them. In other words, they are not directly connected either to any real work that goes on, nor to the leadership who are making strategic decisions at the top. This insulation from reality means that these creatures can sometimes live in a strange and wondrous world of their own, where the skills of managing meaningless meetings and enduring endless emails have risen to the status of high art.

> "Meetings are indispensable when you don't
> want to do anything."
> *John Kenneth Galbraith*

Much fun is poked at middle managers, and they are often parodied as being faintly ridiculous. However, they are creatures of nascent danger to any IT leader. This is not because they are bad people, but because they are managers. As managers, they will feel that they are able to make things happen, not only on their patch but elsewhere in the organisation as well.

Middle managers who use computers often feel that they have a right to both demand and get a shiny new software application to help them do their job. This "right of entitlement" is an unusual concept in corporate life that seems unique to IT. Managers certainly won't dare ask for new carpets or large office plants. The management grading system has taken care of that. Woe betide you if you are a grade 17 manager asking for some grade 19 foliage. But ask these people about computers and they will become deeply agitated about their urgent need for an expensive new departmental application that could cost millions. Managers will also fervently believe that their application must be grotesquely customised to meet their every whim. Whether you like it or not, most of the impetus for new IT investments in your company will come disproportionately from the middle management. My own personal record was to discover nearly 700 active IT projects in an organisation of only 40,000 people. With a project budget of a mere £20m, this meant that each project was spending £28,571.42 each year. It's hardly surprising that few were ever finished.

> **Q. "How can you tell the difference between a Middle Manager and a Senior Manager?"**
>
> **A. "The Middle Manager always thinks he needs more resources and more people to get things done. The Senior Manager is just the opposite—he thinks he is expending too much resource with too many people."**
> *Anon.*

Is this a bad thing? Well, it need not be so, but certain obstacles get in the way of having an effective middle management community living in a utopian harmony of peace and love with the IT organisation. Here are some of them.

Layers and Spans

As I've already suggested, there are often quite large numbers of middle managers in any large corporate organisation. This is because most companies base their operating models on pyramidal organisational structures. The structures are generated through work breakdown models, often based on function or geography. A company might break itself up into several divisions (such as R&D, Product Development, Sales and Marketing, Production & Distribution etc.). Each of these divisions can then be further broken down into smaller units. Sales and Marketing for example, could be divided geographically into regions (such as North America or Europe), and then subsequently decomposed further into country organisations and perhaps finally into sales territories. In this model, significant numbers of middle managers are created as the organisation unfolds layer by layer.

The upshot of all this is that if you are not careful, then you can end up with an alarming number of levels in an organisation. There may also be quite

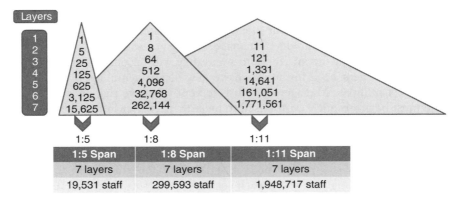

Figure 1.3   The Relationship between Management Span and Organisational Size

impressive numbers of people who are "managing" things rather than "doing" things. The average number of people who report to each of these supervisors dictates both the number of middle managers and the number of hierarchical layers in the company. Many organisations do not pay attention to this important detail. As a result they can quickly become overwhelmed with barbarian hordes of middle managers swarming around the halls and offices.

Figure 1.3 shows what happens if an organisation unfolds with reporting lines of 1:5, 1:8 and 1:11. In effect, each layer of the organisation will have 5, 8 or 11 people reporting to each manager at each level of the company.

If you compare the three models, you will notice that the 1:5 model requires seven levels of management structure to accommodate a mere 19,531 managers and staff. However, the same number of levels would support 299,593 people in the 1:8 ratio. But if you structure your organisation at 1:11, then a staggering 1,948,717 can be accommodated. The number of managers in an organisation is often an unintended side-effect of the reporting spans you choose. For example, even in a medium-sized company of 20,000 people, the spans make a huge difference. In the 1:5 model above, 3,906 managers are required to man such a company, whereas the 1:11 model will only deploy 1,464 supervisors. If it costs $80,000 to employ a manager, then the extra 2,442 managers required in the 1:5 span organisation will add nearly $200m of operating cost to the company. So if you ever wondered why management consultants are always banging on about layers, spans and flatter structures then this is the reason why. One organisation where I worked operated with an average management to staff ratio of 1:5½. Under cover of the 2008 recession, we ran a program which consultants would call "delayering" the company. We tasked each part of the organisation to make structural alterations to their reporting lines so that the management/staff ratio moved towards a target of 1:8. This had a startling impact. We found that we were able to remove nearly 2,500 managerial and clerical posts out of a white collar workforce of 19,800 without causing major disruption to the business. This saved more than £120m of annual operating costs. In comparison, to achieve £120m of profit, the company would have to sell nearly £1.5 billion of equipment and services (which was never going to be easy in the deepest recession in living memory).

> **"If sufficient number of management layers are superimposed on top of each other, it can be assured that disaster is not left to chance."**
> *Norman Augustine*

Short organisational spans of five or less reports per manager lead to towering management structures comprised of many layers, populated by very large numbers of managers. Furthermore each manager will also have rather less responsibility and rather more time on their hands compared to their counterparts in flatter structures. Should you belong to such a low-span company, then you can probably look forward to a great deal of middle management attention. There is also likely to be heavy demand for lots of new computer systems. Now might be a good time to undertake a quick analysis of the structure of the company to identify the low-span zones. There's a very good chance that these are the areas where most of the pent-up demand for new projects, systems and services are coming from. Conversely, a line manager with fifteen reports is likely to be far too busy to be thinking about trivial things like IT. He or she will be focussed on the important job of keeping their head above the ever rising waters. However, should a heavily loaded manager ever get very passionate about wanting some electronic assistance then there is likely to be a very good reason for it.

> **"An overburdened, over-stretched executive is the best executive, because he or she doesn't have the time to meddle, to deal in trivia, to bother people."**
> *Jack Welch*

Middle Managers and the Linkage between IT and the Business

Linkage is a major problem for any IT leader. This is often because many companies still fail to recognise that the most senior IT leader must be a fully paid up member of the top executive team to be effective. He or she is often buried in the management structure of other functions, such as Finance or heaven forbid, maybe even some kind of Shared Services function. This means that the linkage between the rest of the IT organisation and the business will also occur at correspondingly lower levels in the hierarchy. The whole question of the management of IT, unlike other disciplines, seems to have a curious optionality about it. No CEO in their right mind would leave their Finance Director buried several layers down in another function. However, they seem to think it is quite acceptable for this to happen to their IT leader. Some even believe that IT can be led by someone with no experience whatsoever in the discipline. There is also a curious penchant for relatively junior managers with a hobby interest in IT to end up as main points of engagement between business units and the IT function. People seem to end up in these positions irrespective of their seniority, their role or more importantly, their degree of common sense.

Figure 1.4 shows a notional organisation by level. The CEO sits astride the top of the chart, with the real workers at the bottom. The main area of responsibility of each role is identified, together with the types of things that these individuals will be worrying about in normal day-to-day business. The main interactions are represented by the thickness of the arrows.

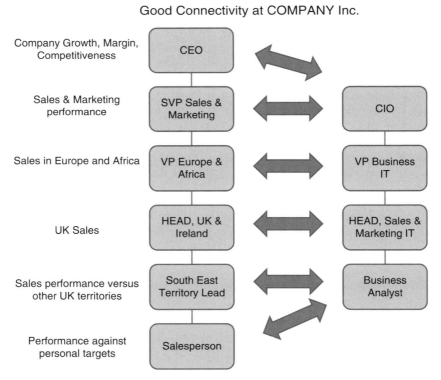

Figure 1.4 A Well-Connected IT Organisation

In this example, the linkage is established at the top level. In other words, the IT leader is a bona fide member of the executive team. They have a direct reporting relationship with the CEO and the status to match. When the IT leader is seen as a proper member of the management team, it is much easier to generate an agenda where IT is an important enabler for the strategic plans of the company. The thickness of the arrows in the diagram above is very similar, indicating consistent interactions between the IT function and all levels of the organisation. Discussions between the CIO and the SVP of Sales for example, will all be about meaningful topics, such as how they can work together to improve global Sales and Marketing performance.

The second case, shown in Figure 1.5, is unfortunately much more common in our industry. The major links between the business units and the IT function are established at much lower levels in the hierarchy. In this model, the IT leader can also become completely detached from the main business leadership. This is a much more dangerous operating model. It often results

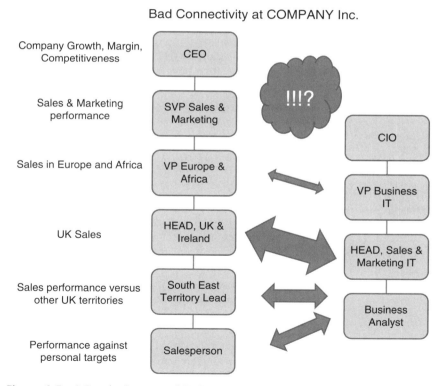

Figure 1.5 A Poorly Connected IT Organisation

in demands for large-scale tactical engagements which in turn spawn large numbers of small-scale projects. In this example, the leader of the Sales organisation does not interact with his IT counterpart, or anyone else in the IT function for that matter. Most of the exchanges are occurring between the UK Sales department and their own local IT support unit. It should come as no surprise, therefore, that any attempts to implement a sales automation system will almost certainly end up as a tactical, UK-centric system focused on capturing and analysing data at a country level. Nobody is talking about improving overall Sales and Marketing performance across the enterprise.

The relative lack of interaction between the IT leader and his business counterpart is also very dangerous in other ways. It may for example, encourage the IT organisation to take on a more inward-looking emphasis. This might lead to a progressive lack of alignment and an increasing risk of dislocation from the leadership of the organisation.

To avoid such problems, it is essential that any IT leader achieves good quality interactions with the leaders in the business. He or she should operate an IT division that is well integrated at all levels. Without this, it will not be possible (or at least intensely difficult) to develop any kind of strategic agenda—at least one that will make any large and positive impact on the company. This is bad for IT but even worse for the company. Thoughtfully conceived, well-designed and skilfully executed IT projects enabling process change can automate and change the core business processes themselves to create enormous advantage to the corporation. But you do have to be the right person who is—critically—in the right place in the organisation.

The View from the Top of the Tree

IT leaders often fret about how they should support the company's leaders. Many believe these lofty folk are the most vexatious group to satisfy. Clearly, such interactions will be easier if the IT leader is a full and active member of the management team. Nonetheless the needs of the leadership are often very different to the rest of the user community and the wise IT leader should tread very carefully.

In terms of company leadership candidates, organisations are usually only interested in promoting those with experience, ability and a track record. It therefore takes quite a while for the ambitious Young Turks to climb to the top of the tree. This means that many company leaders today are Old Turks and have a degree of computer literacy that would probably cause a bunch of 16-year-olds to guffaw in disbelief into their social media networks. This is not the time to make ageist comments about baby boomers, but many of your leaders will be handicapped as far as modern technology is concerned. Most grew their careers in times when Information Technology played a much more peripheral role in industry than it does today. Many will favour traditional paper-based methods of communication control, often leaving email and other electronic wonders to their much younger assistants. I recall the first email I received from a CEO I worked for some years back. It simply said (in capital letters):

"PLEASE COME AND SEE ME NOW"

I scrambled straight up to his office expecting to get fired. Instead, the meeting was convivial. Our leader wanted to follow up on a piece of strategy work we had been discussing the previous week. When I asked the Boss why he shouted at me with his email, he just looked at me blankly. He thought I'd be pleased that I was chosen to be the recipient of his very first email.

For every electronic dinosaur, there are of course plenty of fast trackers who are interested in IT. They may also be great exponents of that wonderful concept—"a little knowledge is dangerous". The cleverest IT leaders have developed clever ways to please these folk. The steady provision of coloured glass beads, trinkets and other worthless bits of shiny technological metal works well. Trinkets, in this sense, cover all the latest and greatest pieces of new technology, many of which will be named after inappropriate fruits. Many companies are still unfortunately under-represented by female leaders. This means that when great executives from different companies get together at meetings, conferences or symposia, a "boys with their toys" situation can often develop in the breaks between the punch-ups. Everyone will be comparing their "tech" with the innocent yet passionate enthusiasm of primary school kids swapping Pokémon cards in the school playground. You may have put in the best ERP solution in the world, but if one of your Senior VPs hasn't received his 64 gigabyte diamond geezer super-smartphone running the strawberry cheesecake muffin operating system on the very first day it is released, then you could find yourself being very unjustly turned into jam very quickly indeed.

> **"Leaders are visionaries with a poorly developed sense of fear**
> **and no concept of the odds against them."**
> *Robert Jarvik*

So, it's likely that you will find an astonishing variation in computer literacy amongst your leadership. This might also be tricky to spot at least initially, because the illiterates will almost certainly be experts at concealing this from you. Hiding ignorance is a skill that will have been essential for one who has ascended quite so far in the organisation. One of the ways that concerned IT leaders deal with this issue is to build an Executive Support team. These are composed of people who can pander to every wit and whim of the company's leaders. If you carefully hand-pick your staff, then you can match up your support staff's temperament and skill to each leader. Those leaders that are particularly illiterate can be sympathetically assisted. Assigning a trusted, patient and discreet member of staff who speaks beautiful English rather than dot-net-talk works well. Those bosses that are techno-geeks can of course be regularly fed the latest techno-babble and 4th generation shiny things by your resident geeks. I learned the value of Executive support very early on in my IT career. One leader in a company where I worked had a penchant for smashing his fist onto his mouse when he became particularly upset about things. At one stage he was crunching his way through mice at a rate of more than one per week. However, an unusually empathic member of the support team, armed with a liberal supply of spare electronic rodents, transformed the whole relationship between this business unit and the IT function. A couple of hundred dollars' worth of mice helped build trust. From this platform we found we could implement quite dramatic change through technological innovation in medicine discovery. This isn't the kind of example that you find in any textbook, but it worked a treat for us. I for one would never have thought that meek and gentle people could achieve such a powerful outcome with just a few plastic animals. Executive support isn't a particularly egalitarian concept, but let's not be too pure about this—after all you want to extend your shelf life, rather than ascend to an ethereal spiritual plane of IT enlightenment. All that stuff can come later when you get into the thorny subject of delivering projects.

Assuming you are able to get some kind of engagement with your leadership, then it's never a bad idea to play your strategic cards early on. The implementation of a highly aligned IT strategy shortly after you work out which way is up is crucially important to long-term success. Just doing it is probably even more important than getting the strategy right. Any alternatives involve laps and Gods. Strategy Schizophrenia is something you do not want to catch (which is why we talk about it in another chapter). If you are not successful in engaging the leadership, then life will initially be difficult, then intolerable, before finally becoming impossible. Each horror-story anecdote about a project screw-up or a lengthy service outage will steadily chip away at the sandy foundations of your support. Eventually, you will look down and discover, like any good cartoon character, that there is no longer any corporate ground underneath you. After a couple of futile seconds while you thrash your legs and try to defy gravity, the audience laughs and then down you go.

Bored Boards

Company Boards in most countries, are highly populated by non-executive directors. These folk do not directly intervene in the detailed day-to-day decision making that goes on. However, the non-execs are the nominated representatives of the shareholders (who after all, own your company). They have a responsibility to hold the executive management accountable for their actions. The detailed function of company boards differs slightly between countries and different companies sometimes have different bylaws. The smallest Boards can contain only three or four people, but some companies have extended the representation to over thirty individuals. In my experience, Boards in the US tend to be smaller affairs than their European counterparts. Often, only the CEO and CFO attend the meeting as executive representatives, while the rest of the places are occupied by non-executive members. It is generally considered good practice in corporate governance for the non-executives to outnumber executive members of the Board. In the UK, Boards are often larger with key business representatives joining the executive representation. In Europe, members of the workers' councils also attend Board meetings.

In the normal business of a Board meeting, the non-executives will generally be concerned about the application of company strategy. They also worry about the risks the executives are taking together with the general performance of the company. In the US, the Board also needs to conform to the requirements of the Sarbanes-Oxley Act of 2002 (Soxlaw, 2002). The eleven sections of the Act cover a range of additional corporate Board responsibilities. Most of these are directed towards higher levels of oversight and corporate control so that the accuracy and reliability of corporate disclosures is improved.

IT leaders occasionally are called in to explain themselves to Boards, particularly when major strategies have been developed. My own presentations to main Boards have largely centred on strategy, controls, risks, business outcomes and the money we are planning to spend. I was also aware that my personal credibility was being assessed. Talking a good game is one thing, but Boards will be looking hard to satisfy themselves that the person in front of them can deliver.

All of these questions are entirely reasonable. Good Boards always provide good support to the executive team. However, the micro-level needs of computer users and middle managers will conflict drastically with the macro-level objectives your Board members will expect you to be pursuing. We will examine the mechanics of the Board relationship later, when we discuss strategies and budgets.

The Relationship Conundrum

Having examined some of the conflicting attributes of your major stakeholders, we now come to the tricky problem of choosing what sort of relationship you are going to have with each of them. There are a surprising range of options, varying from what could be considered to be fairly autocratic approaches on the one hand, to simpering, subservient whipping-dog wimps on the other. There are any number of variations in between these two extremes. Here are three of the most common that I've seen in operation.

The Henry VIII Method

This approach towards dealing with your user community fits fairly and squarely into what Good King Henry would have suggested to his son. It comes about when you have a powerful central organisation that believes it has the best interests of the community at heart. As with all good dictatorships it doesn't take long before the corrupting effect of absolute power takes its inevitable grip. What started out as firm, but essentially well-meaning leadership rarely stays that way. In short, this ends up as a full-blown cold-war Soviet operating model (only without any vodka). You might not be shooting people who try to make a break for it over the Berlin Wall, but the best exponents of this method can certainly create Soviet Gulag-level unpleasantness for their intransigent users.

> **"Smith & Wesson—the original point and click interface."**
> *Anon.*

This "one size fits none" approach generally hasn't got very much going for it in the good times. However, it can work well in the bad times if your company is in dire straits and needs firm and decisive action. Here, autocratic authority, which disregards the snivelling and whining from the unbelievers, can accomplish quite large strides. It's possible that these strides might even be in the right direction. However, the absence of any burning platforms, damsels in distress and towering infernos in most organisations generally makes this approach a non-starter for most. There are some geographies where a higher level of "higher-level" control is accepted as a cultural norm. Here the successful implementation of Henry's centrally planned "I will do what I want" model is easier and it allows much ground to be covered. If you want to build a new motorway for example, it is much easier and cheaper to put any protesters in jail than let them star in a public enquiry at your expense for the next ten years.

The Customer/Supplier Model

The use of the customer/supplier model in the IT world is widespread and would probably be considered by many to be the "de facto" operating model for all good IT organisations. This is a great shame because it is probably the dumbest, stupidest and least effective of any of the engagement models you could ever hope to find. Many people who consider themselves to be "customer orientated" will disagree, but this is not about ideology. There are sound, structural reasons why customer/supplier does not work inside large corporate companies.

Figure 1.6 shows how the customer/supplier model is constructed inside large companies. In essence, your IT department becomes a sole supplier and your user becomes the customer. This is very attractive to the user community because they can have great fun being customers. It's a good life. They get to order you around a lot and spend a lot of time moaning about how their "needs" are not being satisfied.

There are two problems with this.

First, once the more vociferous users see themselves cast in the role of customers, it's not very long before they start to live the adage that "the customer is always right". This potentially creates huge problems for any IT leader. It is possible that each and every self-styled "customer" might be completely aligned with the company strategy *and* they have the best interests of the organisation at heart. However, if this is not the case (which occurs 100% of the time), then the "customers" will, consciously or unconsciously, push their own parochial interests. In some cases, they will even get that rare and wonderful chance to further their own personal agendas. When large budgets are involved, you can be sure that you are sowing the seeds that may lead to a disaster of biblical proportions. We're talking real plague of frogs stuff here. Any chance of delivering a coherent strategy will evaporate. Instead you will be subjected to a World War I-scale artillery barrage of small-scale demands, each entirely independent of one another. You may even find that two projects in your portfolio are pursuing two mutually conflicting objectives.

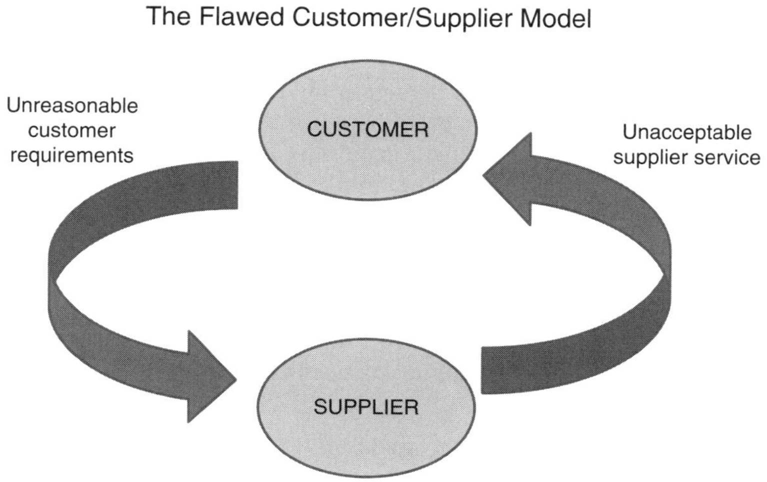

The Flawed Customer/Supplier Model

Figure 1.6   The Much-used but Fundamentally Flawed IT Operating Model

In such a scenario, development costs will escalate. But this will be nothing compared to the monstrous increases in operational costs you will suffer once this menagerie of systems "go live" and start to wreak their havoc. Dr Frankenstein only created one monster; your team might just be turning out hundreds each year. Just to put icing on this particularly gruesome cake, when your rampaging monsters crawl out of the lab and do all the usual things that rampaging monsters do, your customers will swiftly and effortlessly metamorphose into the role of an innocent and badly wronged victim. Many of them will love this. You know what's coming next. Someone is to blame for the mayhem. It can't be the customer of course, because the customer is always right.

The second problem with the internal customer/supplier model is more fundamental and deeply structural in nature. To be effective, the customer and his supplier cannot and must not exist together in a vacuum. There is a crucial and necessary third component that most people conveniently forget when they are implementing such models in large organisations. For the customer/supplier model to work you *must* have a *working market* in the picture as well. The whole concept of being a customer is that you can choose the product you want. If you are locked into buying from a sole-source, in-house supplier, then your freedom to choose from the market is denied you. This can lead to the "hostile buyer–captive supplier" end-game. All it takes is a few project failures and even the meekest people are transformed into red-faced, ranting monsters. They will think that the IT function is comprised of a bunch of really stupid people whose sole goal in life is to spread untold misery over them and their kin. The customer's prerogative to take their business elsewhere is denied them so there isn't much they can do about it. So they vent (or sometimes even resort to physical violence towards people or nearby peripheral devices). On the "supplier" side, the situation is even worse. Without the benefit of a market, the supplier cannot easily refuse to supply his customer because there are no alternative customers available to him or her. There are no safeguards to protect the supplier from the bad behaviour of the customer. The IT bar-owner cannot throw the drunks out of his or her establishment in this model.

When the market is working properly from the supplier's perspective, the supplier will see an ocean of customers, or what is often referred to as the "addressable market" (see Figure 1.7). He or she will not be able to service every single customer in his addressable market, but he will wish to develop relationships with as many customers as possible in order to secure as many orders as possible.

> **"Nothing is perfect. Life is messy. Relationships are complex.**
> **Outcomes are uncertain. People are irrational."**
> *Hugh Mackay*

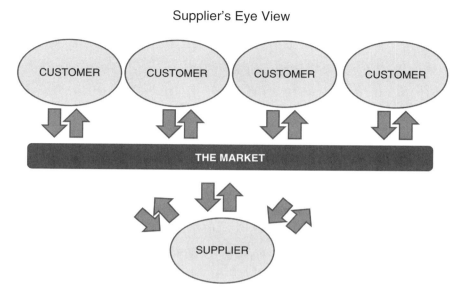

Figure 1.7   How a Supplier Should See Things

When the market is working from the customer's perspective (Figure 1.8), the customer similarly will see many suppliers who could possibly provide goods or services for him. He or she may be less concerned about the addressable supplier base. Although in some specialist areas, they may well choose to develop relationships with a number of key suppliers, particularly where expertise is rare. The customer may help them by investing time, money or expertise in order to provide security of supply (and keep the supplier interested). Alternatively, he or she may choose to enter into long-term contracts. Few sensible customers however, enter into "exclusive" arrangements with suppliers, except for short periods of time. They prefer to exert the customer prerogative through either active means (changing suppliers) or implied means (threat to change when there are alternatives available). It would be very unwise to enter into an exclusive arrangement with a captive supplier because none of these market forces would then be able to operate.

Teamwork!

The team model is quite different to the previous two approaches. For those using the team approach, the only customers in their world are those people in the market place who buy the company's products and services. In this model, every individual in the company is simply seen as a member of your team. It

Customer's Eye View

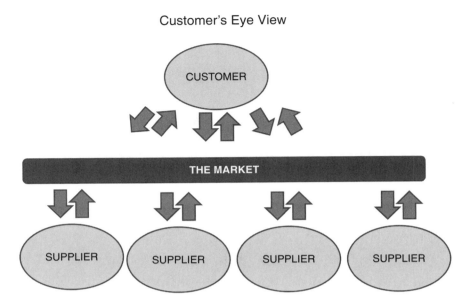

Figure 1.8 How a Customer Should See Things

is practised by at least one employee-owned retail chain I know and it works very well. The philosophy of the approach is based on the premise that human beings naturally and unavoidably group themselves into tribes. This means that they can get on with the essential job of throwing rocks at another nearby tribe. The team approach attempts to recalibrate everyone's tribal orientation away from small groups or departments within the company (who are notoriously prone to internecine warfare) towards the concept of the whole company as the single tribe. The intention is to reduce the level of internal game-playing and promote an outward-looking focus. It has a lot going for it, but on the downside it is extremely difficult to make it work. It requires a large number of people to behave in a very mature fashion. This is tricky for corporate creatures. Shameless empire building, testosterone-fuelled concepts of "winning" and the pursuance of personal agendas are formidable obstacles that need to be overcome.

> **"It is not the employer who pays the wages. Employers only handle the money. It is the customer who pays the wages."**
> *Henry Ford*

The team model is perhaps unsurprisingly best seen in organisations that cannot operate unless they play as a team. The game of soccer (football) is a good example. Soccer is a game where you try to kick a round ball into the goal of the opposition. The team that scores the most goals wins the game.

In soccer, teams generally organise themselves into two units—attack and defence. The attacking players try to keep the game in the opposition's half of the field and they are therefore the people that score most of the goals. The defending players protect the team's goal and they also try to dominate the middle area of the field. The pundits will tell you that midfield domination provides a platform from which the team can launch attacking moves. This general formula works well, but it has to have a level of fluidity because threatening situations can develop in a matter of a seconds. When the team are attacking their opposition's goal for example, a large number of players (including defenders) may be committed into the forward area of the field. Should possession be lost, the opposition may quickly counter-attack in order to exploit your team's weakened defensive position. When this happens, any team member that is able to get into a defensive position does so, irrespective of whether they are an attacker or a defender. If your team is subject to a particularly heavy onslaught from the opposition, large numbers of attacking players may take up defensive positions for protracted periods.

In an industrial landscape, the attacking players could be represented as the sales team. Winning sales is like scoring goals. Support staff such as those in Information Technology usually form part of the defence. In this model, the job of the IT team is to create a supportive environment from which attacks (or sales campaigns) can be launched. This will provide a platform for the business to achieve its goals.

The team model is attractive as a concept, but it is difficult to execute well. Tribal influences are extremely hard to break down. Many people feel an overwhelming desire to propagate the concept of pecking order, particularly when they think they are near the top of it. Those working at the front of the organisation often see themselves as "more important" than those in "back office" functions. The reality of course, is that everyone in the team is important, even if the glamour of goal-scoring is asymmetrically distributed. The IT may be "back-office", but its problems can cause untold damage to a company. In the UK for example, recent major industrial catastrophes in sectors as diverse as confectionary, supermarkets and stationery retailers have been traced back to computer problems. At least one major corporate I know of lost its independence and recently succumbed to a hostile take-over. This was due at least in part to some major IT failings, though as always there were other issues as well. In such situations, the attacking players can score as many goals as they like, but when millions of goals are going in at the other end it renders all efforts utterly futile.

So in summary, some of the main models for user relationships are the Henry VIII, customer/supplier or the team approaches. All have their advocates. On balance, I have generally found that the team approach has worked best for me, unless the company's very existence is in question. Only in dire circumstances would I recommend that you don the Royal robes of office and let your executioner know that he can expect to see a spouse or two on his "to-do" list. If for some reason, you decide to play the market-free, customer/supplier game, then you will need lots of patience and a good relationship with a head-hunter. From the starting gun, my guess is that you will do well to last more than two years in the job. Which leads us neatly on to dead-heroes.

Could I Have Something Impossible Please?

Human beings, in general, are creatures whose glasses are half-full. We are usually cheerful, sociable, optimistic folk and we have a natural tendency to expect things to get better in the future. The key word here is "expect". Should our expectations be allowed to run ahead of what it is possible for us to obtain, then grave dissatisfaction quickly sets in and we cease to be happy bunnies.

There is also another important human characteristic that IT leaders need to be aware of. This is best described by the term "taking things for granted". For example, most of us would happily accept that someone has managed to achieve the spectacular micro-molecular achievement of placing a zillion transistors on a chip and making it do useful things. "That's cool" would be most people's response, oblivious of the Herculean efforts required to reach this goal. If this technological advance allows us to watch television on our wristwatches, then we will be happy—at least for a while. However, it won't take long before the "taking things for granted" ratchet will wind on. Questions such as, "When are we going to have high-definition television on our watches?" or "Can you project the images directly onto our retinas or into our brains?" are likely to be our next utterances. As our needs are satisfied, then our expectations inevitably ratchet onwards and upwards, oblivious to the effect this might have on those who are trying to satisfy us or indeed to the laws of physics, chemistry, biology or common sense. These two effects—where people want to be satisfied but where the satisfaction criteria become progressively more challenging—are a real headache for any IT leader or indeed anyone else who is in the business of making things or selling services.

The Dead-Hero Zone

To address the conundrum, we have to look to the field of "expectation management". In this exciting area of people management, there are two important markers we need to understand:

- The first of these is a bar which defines the expectation level of the audience. The higher the bar is set, the higher the achievement that is required to meet that expectation.

- The second marker represents the maximum capability level of the individual or organisation that is trying to meet that expectation. The higher your capability level, the better you are at what you are doing and therefore the better chance you have of meeting any expectation placed upon you.

Expectation management is all about how the expectation bar and the capability level relate to one another within the context of an axis of achievement. A scenario where high expectations are matched by low capability is not a good place to start from.

If the bar is set high and the capability level of an individual, a product or a service ever falls below the expectation level of the audience, then we know that failure is assured. The bigger the gap between the capability level and the expectation bar, the bigger the sense of frustration felt by the recipient. Figure 1.9 shows such a circumstance. In this example, every outcome will still be regarded as abject failure even if the provider delivers a new personal best for the task at hand. This is because the expectation level of the audience can never be reached, at least by this person or by their organisation. I have to thank a former boss of mine for a wonderful term that explains the gulf between the high expectation bar and the low capability line. He coined the term "dead-hero zone" or DHZ for short. It really is quite pointless trying to participate in this scenario if things have been set up in this way. It is a maze with no exit. Even if

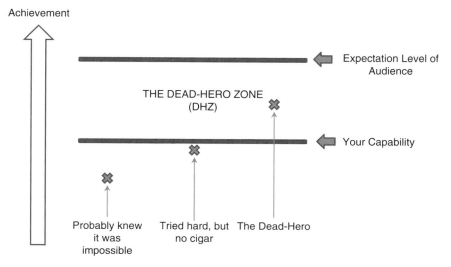

Figure 1.9 Heroic Failure and How to Accomplish it

you bust a gut you will still fail. The only outcome that you can expect is to end the day as a dead-hero with a busted gut. Sadly, many IT organisations fall foul of this scenario and their world is littered with the corpses of innocent but very dead-heroes. Each did their very best work only to find that their reward was a bullet with their name on it and some unpleasant intestinal rupturing.

Magicians, Circuses, and Keeping Something in the Tank

However, it does not follow that every interaction where you attempt to service the ever-increasing demands of your adoring public needs to end up a full blown dead-hero experience. There are people out there who have been incredibly successful at delighting their audiences for centuries. We can learn a lot from them. Take the role of a successful illusionist or a magician for example. As we take our seats, we know that he or she is going to try to perform some tricks that are intended to confound us. Our expectations are set very high. However, the cunning magician, through great skill, coupled with some snazzy sleight of hand and possibly the odd diversionary tactic, will effortlessly lead us up the garden path and delight us with the "magical" outcome. The magician's capability is even higher than our elevated expectations, which is probably why he or she is called a magician. To achieve this feat the magician will have to know a great deal about people, specifically about how we think and react to situations, not to mention the mental assumptions we make when we watch things happening. These attributes are what our HR colleagues would doubtless call "soft skills". He or she will also be prepared to spend hours and hours honing some fine and unusual dextrous prestidigitation which will be outside the experience of a normal audience. The circus profession uses very similar methods to delight their punters. Performers in the Ring carry out acts which most people would think are nearly impossible to achieve. I derived some insight into their methods some years ago, when I enrolled on a circus skills course at a local night school. Surely everyone wants to run away to the circus at some point in their lives, especially if like me, they were a beleaguered project manager struggling to deliver yet another flaky database system?

I learned a great deal from my disturbingly quirky, but nonetheless sympathetic, tutor. After ten weeks of study and probably about twenty hours of practice, I became a passable juggler. I even managed to impress the owner of one Central London juggling shop. Having slipped out of my corporate office one lunch-time to buy some clubs, he looked me up and down and said "Great costume mate! Not seen anyone perform in the Ring in a grey suit and designer specs before. Is that a silk tie?"

Some weeks later I was offered some weekend work as an apprentice juggling clown. I was set to become Alberto Grissini, the younger member of the

---

[1]Giocolieri mediocri is the Italian for "mediocre jugglers". It sounds a lot better in Italian.

famous Grissini Brothers—the notorious "giocolieri mediocri"[1] of Harlow, Essex. Alas it was not to be. Both my juggling partner and I "bottled out" of this not-so-lucrative opportunity and sadly no further offers were ever forthcoming. Alberto and Enrico Grissini would never tread the boards. The only time the breadsticks[2] would appear again would be when we next visited our local Italian restaurant. Still, the skills we learned stood us in good stead for life ahead. My juggling partner went on to become a highly successful CIO in both the oil and telecoms industries as well as a rather nifty plate-spinner. Even today, when too much red wine is flowing at dinner parties, I can still fling the old clubs around to "delight and impress" my house guests. There are however, different levels to this game of capability acquisition. My attempts to master the unicycle in the night-school gym were not quite so successful. I have the dental bills to prove it.

The simple lesson that I learned at the circus night school was that the whole premise in the industry is to keep your capability level above the expectation levels of the audience, by fair means of skill, the occasional sleight of hand and above all lots and lots of practice. It should be no different in the IT world. Vulgar sleight of hand of course is frowned on in polite corporate society, but there is no reason why we cannot build a rare skill with which we can delight our audiences.

Figure 1.10 shows what happens when the expectation bar is kept below the capability line. A new area is opened up that has none of the unpleasantness

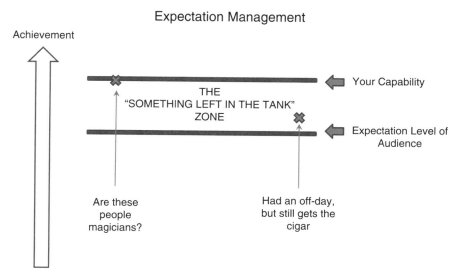

Figure 1.10   Expectation Management—Keeping a Little Bit in the Tank

---

[2]"Grissini" is the Italian name for "breadstick". These tasty snacks are believed to have originated in Turin.

of the dead-hero zone. It is something that is a lot more positive. It is a contingency zone, or to give it a better name "the something left in the tank" zone.

All this leads to the obvious question as to how you can keep your capability levels above the expectation levels of your much-loved user community and any other stakeholders. The following box gives some clues, but to get the full low-down, we must move on to the succeeding chapters. Here we will examine methods for dealing with trials and challenges which might inhibit your ability to demonstrate high capability. We might also find areas where some potential capability shortfalls can be shored up. I can't promise that you'll be able to spin plates on your chin whilst juggling clubs on a unicycle—you'll need to go to night school for that—but we'll nevertheless do our best to keep you alive in planet corporate.

EXPECTATION MANAGEMENT PRIMER

1. Never promise anything unless you are at least 100% certain you can deliver it.
2. Make sure that you've left something "in the tank" so that your promise can still be delivered even if you run into difficulties.
3. If you can't promise the earth, then promise a few pieces of dirt. Break the task up into smaller pieces until you are certain that you can deliver on one or more of the bits.

CHAPTER 2

Pathogenic Projects

"You may dispense with the pleasantries Commander,
I am here to put you back on schedule."

(Darth Vader)

Projects really are quite splendid things. Everybody loves them. Everybody wants one. Everybody wants to work on one. When new ones come along, the grey and drab world that IT people inhabit is suddenly transformed into a wondrous playground of excitement and opportunity. And as for size, in corporate life there's just one simple rule when it comes to projects—the bigger the better. You would be hard pressed to find any IT professional who wouldn't give their right arm to be involved in a really gargantuan project of epic proportions. Even Christmas[1] has to work hard to match the joyous spirit in the office. Each new venture creates a sense of great occasion and it isn't long before grand words such as "Strategic Project" (which translates more accurately as "it is important and it is mine") are bandied about the office. You may even hear of "Flagship Projects" which for some strange reason never have anything to do with flags or indeed ships. However, the ultimate goal in the IT project firmament is achieved after a clutch of tenuously related projects (or perhaps one ill-defined megalith), have ascended heavenwards and metamorphosed into what is known as an "initiative". "Initiatives" represent IT project nirvana. An "initiative" is a corporate battering ram with the power of a Royal Train. All the signals will be green. Indeed if for some reason you are unfortunate enough not to be working on one of these "initiatives", you may as well be living under a rock on a distant moon of Mars. Nobody will give a hoot about your work, indeed the only hoots you will hear are those telling you to get out of the way ...

As a result, embittered software support teams who rarely get to play in these exciting games of chance will congregate by a coffee machine, darkly muttering about how unfair life has become. Grumpily they will bolster their

---

[1]Or Passover, Eid, Diwali or Wesak, depending on your faith.

flagging self-esteem by reassuring one another that their work—of course—is really the most important thing in the company. If only people could understand this simple fact they reason, then the world would be a fairer place. While the journeymen will wallow in self-pity, the brightest of the unloved will set to work. They will be the ones who identify cunning ways of becoming involved. It won't be long before the details of various dubious "project liaison" roles are fleshed out and submitted to the project director. The smartest of the un-anointed may just end up giving themselves at least a sniff of a chance of sampling a few crumbs from the table of project plenty.

So, wherever you may be working, nothing can beat the sense of quivering anticipation and elation when a real Godzilla, monster-truck, megalith of a project proposal triumphantly reaches the end of its glacial journey through the constipated digestive system of the company's financial approval system. As it flops out in front of the cheering throng, mugs and T-shirts are ordered while potential team members step upon one another's heads as they scramble for the privilege of being included in this great new adventure. The lucky owner of the project budget—for a while at least—will be seen as a minor deity in the eyes of his or her colleagues. And the followers will worship him or her with adoration in the hope of securing that all-important place on the team. Without prompting, new team members will spontaneously compete to design a logo for the project. This logo will almost certainly include a globe and a toe-curling strapline such as "Widening Horizons in Advanced People Management" (which is probably better described as "another expensive human resources database that probably won't ever get finished").

But while IT projects undoubtedly have the seductive qualities of a Hollywood starlet and the gravitational attraction of a black hole, for the IT leader they are dangerous—very dangerous indeed. Many can become pathogenic. Pathogenic is a great and (in my view) well-underused medical term which means "causing or capable of disease" (Merriam Webster, 2013). And we're not talking about just any old disease here. A really good pathogenic project can easily maim or even kill the careers of all those it infects. It can even cause famine and strife across the whole enterprise. Indeed, it is not unknown for a "Black Death" IT project to take out a whole company and destroy the jobs of everyone who works there. This of course, often won't be of any concern to the IT leaders. They will almost certainly have been the "patient zeros" amongst the first wave of fatal casualties. Their badly mangled careers would have been unceremoniously collected in a rickety old cart and dumped in a festering pit far from the city. Grateful survivors will frantically shovel over the corpses with copious amounts of lime, before burying the miscreants as deeply as possible, hopefully to be forgotten forever. But all such attempts at disinfecting the situation are ultimately futile. Project failures have stubbornly persisted throughout human history and will doubtless persist as long as there are people around who want to get stuff done and there are other people who are dumb enough to try to do it for them.

IT Projects are Harder than Climbing Everest

To understand the challenges of IT projects, let us delve briefly into the grey-bearded world of IT research. Be reassured that we are not the only concerned souls. People in ivory towers and dreaming spires have been worrying about this problem for many years. A really useful piece of work on this topic was published in England way back in 2004. The respected UK Chartered Institute for IT, also known as the British Computer Society (BCS) carried out an academic study of project failure. The BCS in terms of greybeard quotient can be regarded as "very grey indeed", and indeed I should declare an interest in that it counts me and the rapidly ever-receding greyness to which I cling, as one of its proud fellows. Drs John McManus and Trevor Wood-Harper, from the society, found to their dismay that only *one in eight* information technology projects can be considered truly successful. Success in this regard was defined as the essential goals of meeting the original time, cost and quality requirements criteria. However, they make no comment as to whether any business benefits were ultimately achieved, so we have no idea of the full and unabridged horror of the business outcomes—or probably more accurately the lack of them.

> **"The operation was a success, but the patients died."**
> *(Higgins, 1994)*

In short, many of what the learned pair might call "successful projects" by these criteria may not have even resulted in anything useful being delivered at all. For in my experience, the measurement of business benefits after IT projects are completed rarely ever happens. Everyone is usually so traumatised and exhausted by the experience that they climb out of their fetid, muddy trenches, call a truce, shake hands before everyone declares victory and move on. Years later, incoming leaders will find themselves perplexed and frustrated by what appear to be an array of "net-negative" systems (i.e. they do more harm than good) together with an unhealthy collection of festering dog's breakfasts[2] that the previous incumbents have thoughtfully left for them. Nobody should be surprised. This has happened in every organisation where I've worked. Even prestigious, high profile companies with plump, well-funded IT organisations have a large and extensive collection of grubby

---

[2]Dog's Breakfast – British slang, used since the 1930s which means "complete mess".

skeletons in the closet. In fact, because such units are so well-funded, it is often the biggest companies who can boast the most frightening, smelliest messes in their odorous cupboards. This is otherwise known as the "systems portfolio".

In their work, McManus and Harper analysed a wide range of projects. Totting up what must have been an increasingly depressing set of numbers showing a plethora of disasters and disappointments, they estimated that the cost of IT project failure across the European Union was about €142 billion in that year (Wood-Harper, 2008). This is truly stunning. €142 billion for example, is about the same size as the Greek banks' liability to all other nations in the Eurozone in 2012 (Macro-Business, 2012). I'm sure that few if any of the great observers who pontificated on the financial travails of the late noughties would have put "not starting doomed IT projects" at the top of their list as a sure-fire method of saving western economies from the dual horrors of a broken banking system and unassailable public debt. But it's certainly one to think about—particularly if you are the leader of a Eurozone country who has an imminent election in prospect.

> **"We don't have any IT project failures around here; we just have some really expensive successes."**
> *Anonymous IT leader, Pharmaceutical Industry, UK, 1999*

And there is plenty more corroborating evidence that this is happening all around the world. Nobody is immune. Perhaps the sixteenth-century English reformer John Bradford made the most incisive observation on this phenomenon. While imprisoned in the Tower of London, he watched a group of fellow prisoners being led to their death. "There but for the grace of God go I", was his observation. In IT terms this loosely translates into "I'm not laughing because any one of my projects could easily go supernova tomorrow." When everything has turned lemon-shaped, complete and utter contrition and humility is probably all you will have left in your toolbox of project methodologies that stands any chance of working.

Back to the plot, the Standish Chaos Reports, US National Institute of Standards and Technology and the European Services Strategy Unit all report woeful success rates in IT projects. Even the most optimistic reports you are likely to find on the web suggests that barely one third of IT projects get remotely close to doing what they were supposed to do. One particularly interesting study was undertaken by Oxford University (Sauer & Cuthbertson, 2003). These researchers discovered that only around 16% of projects they examined were "successful" while 10% had been "abandoned". The remaining 74% they describe with beautiful English understatement as "challenged". There are lots of ways that projects can be "challenged", but in my experience they generally fall into two major categories. Some of the projects will be in the "we are completely out of control but we daren't admit it" grouping, while the remainder make up the altogether more whimsically appealing "we are completely out of control, but we are blissfully ignorant about it" category.

Which brings us neatly to Mount Everest.

Let me now transport you to the wild and barren borderlands of China, Nepal and India, where the majestic peaks of the Himalayas thrust themselves nearly six miles heavenward through the bitter-cold azure skies. Let us also examine the intrepid exploits of those hardy souls who have attempted to climb to the near 9 km (more than 29,000 feet) summit of Mount Everest. The statistics here are rather different to those that we've found for IT projects. But surely conquering Mount Everest must be tougher than implementing a run-of-the-mill software accounting package in a sleepy corporate company in the Midwest of the USA or the Midlands of England?

Not so it appears. The statistics really are quite alarming.

Between the initial and celebrated first conquest of Everest by Hillary and Tenzing in 1953 and the end of 2010, there have been 5,104 successful ascents to the summit of this iconic peak; 3,142 individuals have made it to the top of the world, suggesting that quite a few of them got the bug and have unaccountably made a hobby of it. Since 1922, when good records began, there have been 219 fatalities, a rate of 4.3 deaths for every 100 successful summit ascents. After analysing the data, Discovery Channel writer Hannah Harris has estimated that about *one in four climbers* succeeds in making it to the summit, and (perhaps more importantly for them) getting safely back down again (Harris, 2012). This seems to be a fairly consistent success rate over the years. AdventureStats.com report that 10,094 attempts were made up to 2006 of which 2,972 (or 29.44%) were successful (AdventureStats.com/ Explorersweb.com, 2013).

So, putting this data together with our Oxford University research, we have a score of ...

Everest mountaineers 25–29%—IT project teams 16%

... and we have to gracefully declare that our IT project teams have been soundly beaten.

Maybe the Everest conquistadors have a special something our IT project managers do not possess? What characteristics do the climbers enjoy which makes them so successful? Does the possession of brightly-coloured ropes, a few carabiners, a cagoule, a thermos flask and a scraggy beard confer super-human powers upon an individual? Probably not is the merciful answer. More likely is that their planning skills have almost certainly been raised to levels rarely seen in sleepy offices peppered with warm cubes, expensive coffee machines and too much email. Why would this be?

A short examination gives us some clues. For the climbers, the terrifying prospect of slipping off the sheer wall of ice of Everest's notorious Lhotse Face (which rises a full two miles from its base), only to clatter to a horrible limb-crunching death on the sharp and pointy glacial rocks below, possibly adds a bit of an incentive. Then of course there are the temperatures of minus 40F. This in itself would be bad enough, but once you add the abyssal levels of barometric pressure, floating in at a featherweight 346 millibars (or 10.2 inches of mercury) at the summit, any shortfall in planning will result in even more severe shortfalls in breath. These oxygen levels are less than a third of those that fill our lungs at sea-level. Such a low partial pressure of oxygen in the atmosphere will reduce your blood-oxygen saturation to less than 85% (which believe me, will set off every alarm in a hospital Emergency Room). Indeed if you are not extremely fit as well as being well organised, then you can look forward to collapsing through exhaustion simply as a result of having to breathe the 90 times a minute required to stay alive. Olympian levels of panting are required. This is not a time to forget that oxygen bottle, particularly if you don't have any medals in your trophy cabinet. Alternatively, might it just be that an Everest ascent project will cost about $100,000 of your own money (Harris, 2012)? Whether it is death or destitution, both are probably great motivators for any budding project planner.

"I have not conquered Everest, it has merely tolerated me."
Peter Habeler

So, having established that the protégés of Sir Edmund Hillary and Tenzing Norgay are rather better at doing their job than those of us in the IT industry, together with some overwhelming evidence that tells us that our project difficulties are a global phenomenon, where do we go next? Was it always this way and are there any things we can do to stop the creeping pathogenesis ruining our day and our careers? What happened in the past? Did anyone ever get it right?

Not Everyone Gets to be a Pharaoh

In the beginning, there was a time when projects were easy—at least if you were a Pharaoh. With an unlimited supply of slave labour and an almost infinite amount of gold, ably assisted by the not insignificant advantage of absolute power, you could do pretty much anything you wanted. And so they did! The construction of the Great Pyramid of Giza at Cheops in Egypt was a real belter of a project that was launched sometime around 2560 BC (or nearly 5,000 years ago). It is thought that the construction took between ten and twenty years, which is considerably less than it will take to build one high-speed railway line or a new runway at an airport in the UK in the twenty-first century (Financial Times, 2012). At 481 feet high, the pyramid was the largest man-made structure in the world, an accolade which it staggeringly maintained for more than 3,800 years. It is estimated that 5.5 million tons of limestone, 8,000 tons of granite (all imported from Aswan) and half a million tons of mortar were used in the construction of this iconic structure. And as you'd expect from an omnipotent leader who clearly decided that it was high time that the words "vanity-project" were inserted into the Egyptian dictionary, this pyramid wasn't just thrown together. Oh no, the accuracy of the pyramid's workmanship is such that the four sides of the base have an average error of only 58 millimetres in length (Romer, 2007). And what's more the project team managed to achieve this breath-taking rate of precision more than 4,000 years before the victors of the French Revolution even invented the millimetre.

The pyramid imperiously guarded its "tallest building in the world" record until 1311AD, when in the city of Lincoln in Merrie Olde England, 'ye greatefte and beftest' spire-makers in the land gathered themselves together and started mixing mortar. Struggling against the distractions of the day, which included the Black Death and an invasion by Scottish King Robert-the-Bruce, they manfully managed to project the pointy bit of their new cathedral just a little bit higher than the pyramid—albeit by a mere 44 feet. But it was not to last. In 1549, a storm knocked down their spire, while the pyramid of Giza remains unmolested to the present day (Lincoln-Cathedral, 2013) (Hartshorn, 2011). Obviously building a sphinx to guard your magnum opus was a smart thing to include in the project plan.

Pharaoh Khufu, who commissioned the pyramid project, was clearly wise as well as being fantastically rich and infinitely powerful (an appealing job description if ever there was one). Legend has it that he entrusted his Vizier—the equally smart Heminu or Hemon—to carry out the project management to deliver this wonderful tomb (River, 2013). Other than driving what are thought to be thousands of peasants and slaves to death with what might be best described as a "sporty" project schedule, Hemon introduced some working practices that would certainly raise a few eyebrows today. For example, if you had the good fortune to be the slave or a servant of the Pharaoh, then the accepted protocol of the day was you were going to get buried with your boss when he died. You do not need to be much of a student of Ancient Egyptian psychology to guess that the staff and project team all took an unnatural interest in both the health and the welfare of their employer. It's amazing the things you could do in the days before Human Resources departments. Today project managers enjoy no such budgetary, financial or employment policy freedoms. Indeed, omnipotence is one of the things they disappointingly missed out when they invented democracy. This, together with the absence of an unlimited supply of cheap labour, means that project management is a much harder discipline in today's world. We need, it seems, to take a great deal of care before we place the cornerstones of any modern pyramids in place.

So where do we start?

Don't Start Anything You Can't Finish

"Don't start anything you can't finish" were wise words my father once said to me when I was knee-high to a grasshopper. I can't be sure that he ever actually said such a thing, but he ought to have and more importantly, I should have listened.

Most people in corporate life also obviously didn't listen to their fathers; otherwise we wouldn't see such a rotten set of IT project performance statistics across the industry. If the Pharaoh Khufu and master project manager Grand Vizier Hemon were around today, then they would doubtless throw back their heads and laugh raucously like Bond villains before they dispatched the majority of today's project managers into oblivion. Apparently, one of the preferred methods of correctional punishment in ancient times was to bind the offender in a closed sack and then toss them into the Nile. This practice was dubbed "poena cullei" by the Romans who were also enthusiastic proponents. In fact they liked it so much that they later "enhanced" the process by introducing an assortment of animals (such as the ever-popular snake) into the sack before tying it up. Picture if you will a myriad of bulging sacks all bobbing down the river with various strains of "it wasn't my fault" or "it will be fixed in the next version" together with the odd "ouch" all floating across the desert. This is where your project management team would probably end up if Hemon and Khufu were around today.

So before you started your project, how many times have you asked yourself what is probably the most important question?

Why are we doing this?

And the rather excellent follow-up …

… and what benefits do we expect to get out of it?

This is a great pair of questions to start with. They are the very first vaccinations you will need to administer to protect yourself against contracting deadly pathogenesis from your team or stakeholders. They're the sort of questions your partner or spouse would ask you if you ever dared to talk about your work with them at home (which is not recommended). So, if you can't get a really good, compelling set of answers from your team or anyone else at this initial stage, or if there is an undue amount of arm-waving while unconvincing retorts are cobbled together, then your best course of action is to pack up your toys and head for home. Here is yet another project that should not be started. Perhaps, if you felt charitable, you could even use the money to start propping up some European banks?

Peaches are not the Only Fruit

However, if you are a soft and kind soul, then you might like to give your guys and girls a second chance. You should tell them to go away and have a good, long, hard think about these questions before you are prepared to entertain any further debate. Do not accept any fluff in response, either from the user community, any of the management or your staff. It is easy to spot a peach when it is spelt out to you.

HOW TO SPOT A PEACH

The ripest Peaches are simple, low-risk projects with modest project costs and clear outcomes, which are so beautifully executed that the thumping great benefits contained therein tumble out and blossom early after completion.

Such projects are every IT leader's dream. But if you haven't already worked it out, it's also easy to see the tell-tale signs of a lemon.

HOW TO SPOT A LEMON

The sourest Lemons are over-complex, high risk projects (or groups of interlinked projects) with enormous project costs which will probably never finish. They rarely deliver the platitudinous benefits that were boldly asserted in the proposal even if such benefits could be measured.

As the miscreants try to persuade you that their rancid, sour lemon is in fact a fat, juicy peach, they will probably shuffle from foot to foot, looking uncomfortable. They may even start mumbling unconvincing technicalities at you, whilst avoiding any meaningful eye contact. On such occasions, one or more of those irritating IT priests might be rolled out blinking into the light. These are the people whom you never understood; neither anything they have ever said, nor indeed why they were on the payroll. Such clerics may make religious signs and whisper guttural incantations in your direction. Beware; all the believers have almost certainly formed their judgements based on faith-based views, unencumbered by any facts, or at least those facts that don't support their prejudices. Your staff and stakeholders will put on their pointy hats, look pious and take a deep breath before belching a big blast of smelly old twaddle in your general direction. They might not even take a second breath before they roll out a battery of emotional howitzers, cunningly designed to leave you cowering in a foxhole begging for mercy while you reach for your signing pen.

Ungrouping Group-Think

Now is the time when you get to see the full madness of corporate group-think in action. These people WANT this project. They have waited for it. They have jumped through endless financial hoops to get the money approved. They have rewritten the proposal so many times that it has taken on the form of religious verse "And the Angels said: 'Behold, it is written that business benefits greater than thy wildest dreams shall be delivered unto thee, by the heavenly magic of a heavily customised SAP system.'" Your staff, your project managers, the user community, their managers and possibly even many of your senior colleagues have subconsciously assembled themselves into a posse. Even now, they are saddling up the horses. Barstools scatter like bowling pins as they burst out of the last-chance saloon and leap onto their mounts. This project is their birth-right and they intend to inherit it. There is a bounty on your head cowboy.

> **"I cannot always control what goes on outside. But I can always control what goes on inside."**
> *Wayne Dyer*

By now you might be thinking that you may have already gone mad. Desist and quietly reassure yourself. Remember, all you have asked these folks to do is to explain why they want to do the project and what they expect to get out of it. With growing awareness you realise that you are not the mad one. In fact, you are probably the only sane individual left on planet corporate. Sure it's lonely, but you have a role and a destiny to fulfil. Look inward and be strong. It is time to grab your leadership mouse, drag your cursor to the management menu and select …

>Options>GroupThink>Ungroup (see Figure 2.1).

Now is the time to take a deep breath and don't be swayed by the group-think that's bearing down on you like a wardrobe filled with the Emperor's New Clothes. At this stage your stakeholders and your staff will be bringing all their combined life-force and malevolent will to bear so that they can remove that very last obstacle to their fiendish and glorious plan (which is you if you hadn't already worked it out). Now is the time for fortitude. Now is the time to show your leadership qualities. You are a leader. You might be a prophet, a future King, or possibly even a descendent of the Grand Vizier himself. Your job is to lead these unfortunates to their promised land. You must not allow them to assemble themselves into

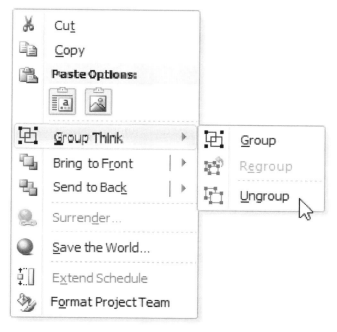

Figure 2.1   The "Ungrouping Group-Think" Wizard

legions of lemmings and sweep across the plain. This is because every single time hordes of little furry things are unleashed, they will helplessly stream over the cliff of harsh reality. From there they will plunge into the abyss of despair only to be finally dashed, thousands of feet below, upon the cruel rocks of abject project failure. The tangled wreckage of the project and its broken survivors will be washed out to sea. All that will remain will be puzzling fossil traces which will confound any future industrial palaeontologists. Put simply, it ends badly. As it turns out, it's not much different to failure in ancient Egypt. The team will end up in that same wet place as if they had worked for the Pharaoh—except without the sacks and all that bobbing about in the river of course. The messes it seems, all just get washed out to sea in the end.

Now is the time to show them what you are made of. Leonardo knew all this. He wasn't just a three-trick pony that painted chapels and invented parachutes and helicopters you know.

> **"It is easier to resist at the beginning than at the end."**
> *Leonardo da Vinci*

Mugging by PowerPoint

If the "we must have it" mantra and the particularly catchy "if you're not on the road-roller then you are part of the road" assertions fail, then the rainbow coalition will regroup and prepare their third and final phase of attack. This usually takes the form of the well-tried, corporate complexity trick. This method relies on hunting for the smallest chink of doubt you may have on the subject and then exploiting it until it has grown to a whole gallery of show caves. It usually takes the form of "you don't understand—what we are dealing with here is much more complicated than you think". Increasingly sophisticated versions of the complexity argument are usually launched in carefully prepared waves. Some will take the deadly form of voluminous and highly complex PowerPoint presentations. These are slick affairs, where the delicate beauty of animated builds and detailed pictures are lovingly crafted—possibly over weeks—into an incomprehensible and unsatisfying glossy presentation of doom which Satan himself would be proud of. You'll find that the slide deck which fills up your entire mailbox is both very deep, profound and frighteningly extensive. Most of all it will be utterly incomprehensible. Much of the text will be of a font size so small as to be unreadable by mortal eyes and anything you can read will be riddled with buzzwords and lofty assertions, designed to swell the heart and turn the soul. The authors may have produced world-class drivel, but as far as they are concerned, they have struggled down from the heights of Mount Sinai clutching sacred "tablets of stone" that will change history. The rather harsher reality is more often a bunch of deluded middle managers strolling past the coffee machine waving a memory stick.

All these things are tell-tale signs that your staff are trying to mug you.

So, at this stage the muggers will be brandishing their PowerPoint weaponry and they will be demanding your money (or at least your signature). You must now decide whether you are happy to allow yourself to be mugged or whether you are going to be a "have-a-go" hero.

"Everybody has a plan until they get punched in the face."
Mike Tyson

Choosing the former course is easy for you. Capitulation is their goal. Just sign on the dotted line and sit back. All you have to do now is to wait for the disaster to happen. It might take weeks or months, but unless you have the good fortune to have a messiah or a miracle worker in the team the outcome is all pretty inevitable in my experience. Shortly after the fireball, when the post-mortems audits have curiously made everything your fault, you will probably get to find out which termination method is favoured by your employer.

However, if you choose the tougher course, now is the time for you to narrow your eyes and take another deep breath. You must carefully disarm these rogues. Do not waver nor succumb to the quasi-intellectual clutter they are attempting to peddle. If the pitch makes no sense to you, then this is categorically their fault not yours. You are not stupid. Even if you think you might be stupid you don't have to admit it to them. After all, you are an IT leader and they are not.

Communication is the responsibility of those who send, not those who receive. So this is the perfect opportunity to play your "Get out of jail free" card, also known in IT leadership circles as the "I'm not dumb" play. It goes something like this …

> *I've been in the industry 25 years and this all looks like rubbish to me. Tell me in plain English what you are trying to do and why?*

This can work well. Sensing deep defences, consternation may set in. The besiegers become the besieged. Panic quickly spreads through the ranks. The "I'm not dumb" Sicilian defence can sometimes even flip the metaphorical safety catch onto their fully-cocked PowerPoint deck, rendering it harmless. When the priests of presentation are disarmed in this way, the tide can turn and the initiative will start flowing back towards you. You now have the glimmer of a chance as uncertainty fills their minds. Use it wisely.

Back to the Himalayas

Now is the time for you to get the team to explain everything to you in simple language. You'll quickly learn whether you've got a communication problem or a common sense deficiency. You can of course, work in some dramatic effect at this stage. A good dollop of emotion never goes amiss. But you would be advised to be careful. You should not abuse your power. The confused faces before you are your people and your stakeholders and even though they may not like what you are saying, you are still their leader (remember dignity, company values and all that). As they start listening, you must now start the process of education. With the sound of wind chimes in the background and the gentle whiff of incense drifting through your office, gather your robes, pick up your (wooden) staff and smile wisely and benevolently at the assembled throng. You must take on the role of a guide, leading the disciples on a journey to enlightenment. It's time to go back to the Himalayas.

As you sit cross-legged with your team and your stakeholders, perched serenely on the terraces of Shangri-La, the sound of gentle birdsong will drift across the valley. The majestic peaks of Everest and K2 are sharply etched as they stroke the cobalt blue skies. Equilibrium and harmony are now complete "Why did we not ask these questions before teacher?" they will murmur. "It matters not", you reply benignly as enlightenment and common sense take their benevolent hold. Then under your breath—barely audible—you will mutter quietly to yourself. "OK, so it looks like we've got a project that makes sense. Now we have to work out if we can damn well deliver it."

This all might seem pretty simple stuff, but you should not underestimate how far you've got. Some humungous projects running into hundreds of millions and even billions of dollars in both the private and public sectors never got this far in their thinking. Instead they ended up wasting eye-watering amounts of money shoring up what can only be described as "Emperor's New Clothes" projects. In such projects, corporate group-think meant that hundreds of people were rabidly insisting that they were staring at a brilliant-white, modern incarnation as beautiful as the Taj Mahal, while instead they were actually peering into a fetid, pitch-black hole next to which there was a nasty looking goblin holding a sign that said "Shovel very large amounts of money in here—you will never see any of it again". Such megaprojects are only a good thing if you are a partner in a consultancy who is brought in shortly after the client has just begun to realise just how awful things have become. You at least, have avoided that ignominy and can pass to the next level.

And so you now know what you are doing and why you are doing it. It is time to progress to the next step of the quest. Project Management itself!

Stalinist Project Management

Some years ago, I had the good fortune to meet someone who was probably the best project manager in the world. This man was to "risk management" what Usain Bolt is to "running rather quickly". The project manager also had a ruthless purposefulness which, to my mind at least, rivalled that of the late Soviet leader, Joseph Stalin. Our man however, was not a mass-murderer and his social skills were much better than his Georgian role model. The master project manager once offered some words of wisdom about projects that I for one had never heard before.

Projects only fail for two reasons. Either it's because they simply can't be done (at least with the technology and skills available in the world today), or else it's because you let them fail.

Undo-able Projects

Before we travel too far down this train of thought, as with all good rules, there have to be a few exceptions. So let's get them out of the way first. All three of my top three "The Best Ever Projects in History – Ever", are exceptions to this fundamental rule and indeed they are on the list for that very reason. With the Giza Cheops pyramid construction project coming in at a solid number three, we must add the wonderful and inspirational US NASA moon program at number two before finally conferring the number one "best-ever" project crown on the Stonehenge temple project in England.

Sadly no IT projects make it up into the top three and in fact it would be doubtful whether any would even make it into the top million, at least on any list of mine. Anyhow, each of these three special projects, in my opinion, carries the same unique characteristic. None of these projects should have been possible at the stage in human history when each of them was attempted. The skills and the technology to do it simply didn't exist (to quote our master project manager). But somehow someone managed it. Maybe humanity does have something going for it after all? Successfully putting not just one, but twelve men on the moon (and bringing them all back safely to the Earth) armed with little more than thin 1960s ties, a few slide-rules, some radios that beeped a lot, tin foil, and an enormous tube stuffed with a disturbingly large volume of caustic combustible nastiness was indeed a magnificent achievement. And as for the Stonehenge project team, just how they managed to transport hundreds of tons of spectacularly large stones from quarries from Preseli, Wales (over 150 miles away) to the Stonehenge site in Southern England is utterly incomprehensible—especially given the fact that the (always-useful) wheel probably didn't roll into Britain until nearly a thousand years later (Fortuna, 2013). Some authors suggest that supernatural powers were employed on the project, while others less charitably believe that the stones were already on the site, having been conveniently moved by a convenient glacier—which has of course long since melted conveniently leaving no trace. However, perhaps there is a different explanation. Given that much of Stonehenge went up around 2,500 BC, could it be that the Egyptian Giza vanity-project team, flushed with success from their pyramid program, was approached by a bunch of scruffy, stone-age, animal-skin clad Englishmen who said "Hey guys, that's neat! Do you do temples as well?" In any event, these three projects to me at least, represent the high-water mark of historic achievement in project delivery, even if there were only two project teams at work.

Stalin's Special Question

Getting back to the plot, if we assume that the overwhelming majority of the squillions of projects dotted about the IT firmament are not on the "undoable by humanity" list, then the question we need to ask ourselves is "how do we prevent them going wrong?" As our master project manager would say "If they are do-able then we're not going to let them fail."

> **"I believe in one thing only, the power of human will."**
> *Joseph Stalin*

But before we despair about how all this can be achieved, be reassured that there are strategies we can employ. For these we must look to the former Soviet Union.

Once upon a time, there was a leader with an unusually strong, steely will. We know this because Joseph, sensing that the name "Ioseb Besarionis dze Jughashvili" (or more correctly "Иосиф Виссарио́нович Джугашви́ли") wasn't going to cut it as the snappy, fearsome label of a tyrannical leader. Not mucking around with platitudes was something of a trademark of this young Bolshevik and so, in 1912, he simply started calling himself "steel", or more correctly the Russian form we know today as "Stalin". In terms of a description it was perfect. Everyone knew what they were getting—a powerful, towering, unassailable, case-hardened leader. It worked a treat and terrified an entire population as well as half the world. This is an emotion that turns out to have been entirely appropriate, given his later genocidal actions (Naimark, 2011). Even today, most people do not realise that Stalin was only 5"4" (160cm) in height. Images of him simply don't convey his small stature. There is a reason for this of course. Some say that any portrait painters who Stalin felt were not depicting him as what he described as "right", (by which he probably meant "height") found that their artistic careers were cut short by a firing squad (Bell, 2006). Clearly here was a learned man who was skilled in the subtle project management methods originally honed by Pharaohs and Viziers more than two millennia ago, ably enhanced of course by a dose of "little man" syndrome of truly epic proportions.

So, if our friend Joseph Stalin were alive today, how would he approach the problem? We can only guess, but since we are guessing, let's guess it like this.

Imagine, if you will, the cream of the Soviet project management team all hastily assembled in the sumptuous beauty of the Grand Kremlin Palace in Moscow. The nervous chatter of anticipation is abruptly quenched to a sudden hush as a surprisingly short, stocky man, sporting a fearsomely bushy moustache, a rather severe Soviet uniform, and a military cap to die for, strides purposefully onto the stage. He fixes his audience with a steely gaze and opens his mouth to speak …

> **Stalin: (to an assembled throng of project managers): "So, comrades. Is each and every one of you satisfied with your plans, your estimates and your progress of your projects? Can you guarantee me that each of these fine projects will be delivered on time, to budget and to the required quality. Can you also promise me that every single one of the wonderful business benefits we require will not only be realized, but we will get them when you said we will get them?"**

PMs: (after a pause): "We all are, General Secretary!"

Stalin: "That is good to know. Thank you for your promises and your commitment. So, from now on, we can be sure that anyone who fails in any of these respects must be an enemy of the Soviet Union. Should any of you therefore fall short in any regard, you will be taken to a dacha outside Moscow and will be shot in the back of the head. One last question. Are you still happy about your plans my friends?"

PMs: (after another pause and with rising panic) "Um"

The first time I saw this technique used, I was astounded at the outcome. With an assembled management team of a very large and complex project, their IT leader posed Joseph Stalin's question to the team. Present was the Project Director, together with several of his senior project managers. This was one of the company's largest adventures; it was burning through nearly £30m ($48m) of funding a year. The project was not only set to transform our company's core processes when it was completed, but it was going to wipe a third of a billion (yes, billion) dollars off the development costs of each new product. In short, it was big potatoes.

The Project Director was forthright. "We are in GREAT shape" he confidently asserted with just the nuance of a whiff of a hint of smugness. He smiled and surveyed his team imperiously. The rest of the project management team nodded and beamed confidently back at him. Yet more smiles were exchanged. The tension began to evaporate. Perhaps this ad-hoc review that their awkward boss had inconveniently scheduled was going to be easy-peasy after all?

Pausing for dramatic effect, much like an ageing thespian savouring a rare (and disappointingly short) Hollywood cameo role, the IT leader then advanced Stalin's second question (the one about guns and dachas), with the suggestion that being fired at (at least in the job sense) was now on offer. The Project Director furrowed his brow and looked stern. "Absolutely!" he retorted with a snort, "we are completely on track." Glancing at each of his managers in turn he added, "We are all confident, aren't we?" At this point, one of the project managers in the team started to look slightly uncomfortable. Maybe it was a slight change in the pallor of his cheeks. The untrained eye would have missed it. Shortly afterwards, a single bead of sweat materialised on his temple, glistening harshly under the cold artificial light in the arctic atmosphere of the meeting room. Then, slowly, yet purposefully, the droplet swelled and commenced its glacial journey through the canyons of his cheek. Gravity lazily exerted its authority and the bead of betrayal slowly increased in velocity. As the remaining colour drained from his cheeks, others began a gentle "buttock-shuffling" movement as gathering discomfort took hold in the room. An elephantine pregnant pause ensued. No-one took a single breath (which is a pretty spectacular achievement given the gestation period of the typical pachyderm). Eventually, after like what seemed an age, the weak but honest project manager cracked. He morosely stared at his shoes and reluctantly mumbled an "excuse me". The silence was deafening. He continued, "Actually, if we have a chance to re-plan, I'd like to extend the schedule for these sets of tasks." He made a few vague flourishes at an incomprehensible Gantt chart covered in pencil marks whilst continuing to stare pointedly at the floor. A further pause ensued, encompassing the gestation period of another large mammal. It was punctuated only by a curious gurgling noise as the blood pressure of the Project Director started rising with the primeval force of an Icelandic geyser.

The Project Director's face turned red, then purple and then a rather unpleasant hue that you won't find on any colour chart. Several people started looking towards the door fearing that some kind of Monty Pythonesque biological explosion was imminent. "What?!" he bellowed. Jumping around like a jack-rabbit, his utterances quickly became incomprehensible. But swiftly things became worse. With the hairline crack in the dam now firmly established, the water began to well and surge and before long the crack had quickly yawned into a chasm that the RAF's "Dambuster" squadron would have been proud of. Several other project managers, sensing they were not the furthest souls over the line of shame, saw their chance to atone. Each in turn, expressed their concerns and before long every single project manager started requesting more time and a bit more money for the toughest areas of their project landscape. All of course were "special cases". Only the word "contingency" could be discerned amongst the rising babble. The Project Director sat down heavily, his eyes rolling in circles as wide as the orbit of a geostationary satellite. The disgraced team scurried off to re-plan. In the absence of anything stronger, coffee was poured for the incredulous and somewhat spectacularly crestfallen Project Director. Mercifully he had not blown a blood vessel nor suffered a stroke. It took the poor chap a full half-hour to comprehend the horrible reality that he had committed his life and reputation to a plan that none of his trusted generals believed in. The fact that he was carrying monumental levels of undeclared risk which was not present on any risk register also troubled him greatly. And this is not the only time it has happened. In fact, it happens every time—*every single time*. Any idiot who thinks that their risk register has them adequately covered should know that even a cycling holiday into the core of the sun protected only by a roll of aluminium foil and a bottle of factor ten sun-cream will be safer than starting an adventure like this. In my experience, long before you formally start anything called "a project", undeclared risk creeps in. There is a moral to this story. It's simple. If you can persuade your people that the work they are doing is as hard and as dangerous as climbing Mount Everest, with all the unpleasant consequences and danger that mucking about with this mighty peak can bring, then you will always get different and more conservative answers at project reviews. Otherwise, all you are doing is sending your project managers to Las Vegas with someone else's money—yours!

So now you have a plan and more importantly it's a plan that you can believe in—that's good. But how long is this all really going to take?

Being Nostradamus

In 1555, in Saint-Rémy-de-Provence in France, a man called Michel de Nostradame, better known to us as Nostradamus, wrote a book entitled *The Prophesies* (Nostradamus, 1555). The book is a collection of four-line verses, known as "quatrains" (another great underused word). Michel's quatrains were grouped into nine sets of one hundred verses and one set of forty-two verses. Many people believe that these verses contain predictions of what has happened since the book was written, together with explanations of what will happen out centuries into in the future. From the Great Fire of London to the detonation of the first nuclear bomb and even to the death of Princess Diana, supporters claim that all these events were accurately predicted in a book completed nearly half a millennium ago. For an author that hasn't written anything for the last four hundred years, Nostradamus's book still sells extraordinarily well all over the world. There are two things you can take from this. Either he is indeed a wonderful prophet (which inconveniently raises the question as to why we don't do anything to stop the bad stuff that he says is going to happen), or else nobody is good at working out what's going to happen in the future. In hopeless inadequacy, they hang on the words of those who claim they have the special gift. Here's an easy one for you to decode.

> **Where all is good, the Sun all beneficial and the Moon**
> **Is abundant, its ruin approaches:**
>
> **From the sky it advances to change your fortune.**
>
> **In the same state as the seventh rock.**
> *Nostradamus, The Prophecies, Century V, V32*

Nope, me neither, unless it means a meteorite the size of Uranus is about to fall on my garden.

I fall into the category of inadequacy and unfortunately so does every single project manager I've ever met. I've not come across anyone who can accurately predict what will happen in the future in their project, even if he or she is brandishing a Gantt chart that looks like the wiring diagram of the Space Shuttle.

So just how long is this all going to take?

**"The bearing of a child takes nine months, no matter how
many women are assigned."**
Frederick P. Brooks Jr.

If we cast aside the obvious handicap that none of us can claim to be a sixteenth-century French chemist who has effortlessly kept his book of predictions in the bestseller lists for five hundred years, then we probably have two other obstacles to overcome when we come to estimate how long our projects are going to take.

First of all, we are all mostly human. Even the least human people you could wish to meet (who can incidentally often be found in the bowels of data centres or in queues outside night clubs) are at least humanoid, even if they have a zombie-like complexion and red eyes. One of the great attributes of our species is the single thing that sets us aside from all the other animals in the world. *We can lie and they can't* (or at least that's what they said).

What's even better is that we can lie to ourselves and not even know that we are doing it. If ever there was a perfect recipe for utopia, then surely this has to be it. Who needs reality when you can enjoy unlimited levels of self-delusion instead? But let me take a controversial step further and advance the thesis that this is the trait that manifests itself in what we know as the inbuilt optimism of the human race. Even post the 2008 financial crash, all of us harbour hopes about the future and for our children's future, even though we all know that our banks don't have any money in them, that our governments have unsustainable levels of debt and industrial productivity improvement was something that seemed to go away about a decade ago. Consequently, it follows that we as creatures must be programmed by evolution to play down the negatives and overemphasise the positives. If you don't believe me, then tell me when you ever saw an IT project come in early! Optimism is a fantastic way of storing up undeclared risk in your projects.

The second obstacle is more subtle. Despite the phenomenal capability of the human brain, it still struggles hard to keep up with Mother Nature's complex reality. We, as humans, therefore compensate by making lots of approximations and assumptions about what is going on around us. But this handy property has an interesting side-effect. It means that we can easily persuade ourselves to believe things without needing to see the specific data to confirm that belief. This was probably a really whizzy thing in the days when we were being chased all over the savannah by sabre-toothed tigers. Running away before thinking and analysing things was definitely "best practice" in the Stone Age, at least before bows and arrows and semi-automatic assault rifles came along.

In the world of modern project management however, too much faith and optimism usually leads to unmitigated disasters. Many people cling to the belief that their plan is still on track even when all the data you could ever wish to analyse point steadfastly the other way. The very best project managers therefore have to be pessimists. Words such as "half-full" or "good chance" don't appear in these peoples' dictionaries. This can make them very miserable people. They are always looking for the things that could go wrong. These are people you try to avoid at parties. You know them. They sip fruit cocktails adorned by little umbrellas as they lurk in the corner pretending not to be on their own. Being cornered in social conversation by a project manager is bad, nearly as bad in fact as being engaged in small-talk by a Six-Sigma Master Black Belt.

Once we accept that we believe we can't predict the future, that we habitually lie to ourselves and that we are over-optimistic as a species, you might think that it's a wonder how we ever managed to estimate anything. But we did and we still do. And here's how.

My Piece of String is Skewed

"How long is a piece of string?" is a much used idiom which people love to quote when they don't know how long things are going to take. But to be fair to them, estimating the length of tasks is a really difficult thing to do. We persistently get it wrong and we persistently underestimate how long it takes to do things. I submit that our inbuilt human qualities of faith and optimism conspire to generate an outcome that will cause much amusement and incredulity amongst the scoffing audit team that is ultimately called in to explain to the boss why your latest magnum opus became another entry on that ever-expanding list of pathogenic project failures.

But it is not hopeless. We can estimate some things accurately— particularly when we practice.

Let me give you an example.

When you travel to the office in the morning, you generally know how long it is going to take you to get there. You also know that you may suffer some hold-ups, particularly if you are travelling in the rush-hour. Given that you travel to work so frequently, perhaps it isn't a surprise that you can make a reasonable guess how long it will take today. But there are days when you will get it wrong. A shunt on the freeway or a problem with a set of points on a railway might mess things up. In England, you might even fall foul of the wrong type of snow, which will probably mean that your train won't pull into the station until at least a week on Thursday.

In short, you are pretty good at estimating how long it will take you to travel to work and you know roughly how variable the journey time might be. You occasionally will get caught out, but because you make this estimation every day, you are now probably quite good at it.

So you know it's going to take you about an hour to get to work with normal traffic flow; that it could take little as fifty minutes if the traffic is light and maybe as much as a couple of hours on a really bad day. But now that you are safely in the office and have cleared those tiresome emails, why do you throw all this hard-earned estimating expertise into the bin? For some reason, most of us cheerfully accept single man-day estimates as a completely accurate prediction, despite the fact that neither you, nor the estimator, nor the person who is going to do the task has ever done this piece of work before?

It seems crazy, but this is the normal "modus operandi" in the IT projects industry. We do it all the time. Many people still use much-loved and hopelessly inaccurate Stone Age estimating techniques. There are two particularly popular methods.

ANCIENT ESTIMATING TECHNIQUES

The FITW (or finger-in-the-wind) technique is very common. Here the estimator licks their index finger and waiting for the attention of the project team, slowly raises it into the air. After a few seconds of teeth-sucking and narrowing of eyes, an accurate estimate then somehow immediately appears in the estimator's head, causing them to cry out to the assembled throng.

The other much-loved IT estimating methodology, known as WOTC, is even more ethereal and curiously spiritual. When asked for an estimate, the estimator has to look up to the heavens, close their eyes and pray. Lo, it is written that when they re-open their eyes, they will be rewarded. All they need to do is to read out the number because it is quite plainly written on the ceiling above them. (WOTC).

Things Can Go Badly Wrong, but They Rarely Go Badly Right

Going back to your hour-long rush-hour trip to work, if it doesn't go as you planned, you might possibly arrive an hour late, but you certainly won't arrive an hour early. The reason for this is because the mysterious and magical world of statistics is now casting some of its nefarious necromancy upon your life. In scientific terms, the statisticians will tell you the probabilities for this type of task are statistically skewed. Indulge them. This has nothing to do with kebabs.

What the statistical necromancers will say to you is that you aren't going to shave many minutes off your normal journey time, even by jumping red lights. But if something goes badly wrong, then you could be in for a very long trip indeed. This is what's called "positive skew" which is also known as "a skew to the right". Things go badly wrong, but sadly, they rarely ever go badly right in the world of IT projects or indeed when it comes to rush-hour journeys to work.

> **"There are two kinds of people in the world, those who believe there are two kinds of people in the world and those who don't."**
> *Robert Benchley's Law of Distinction*

Figure 2.2 shows such a skew. The top of the curve gives you the most likely time you will arrive (one hour) and the area under the curve up to a given time point tells you the probability. In short, this tells you what you already know. You're pretty likely to arrive in around an hour, but there's a small chance is could be much, much longer. So what?

The reason for showing this graph is to illustrate one monstrously terrible feature that has blighted the lives of millions of IT people and other project managers over millennia. It is, on the face of it, a rather innocuous observation but as innocuous goes, this one is monumentally innocuous. Here it is.

The gradient of the curve on the right of the mean is much shallower than the curve on the left.

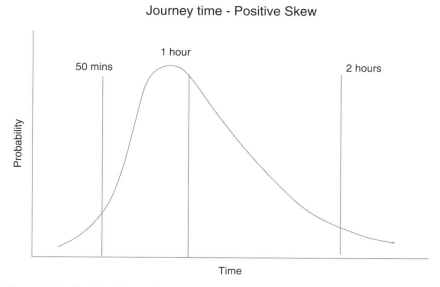

Figure 2.2 shows a graph titled "Journey time - Positive Skew" with the y-axis labelled "Probability" and x-axis labelled "Time", marked with vertical lines at "50 mins", "1 hour", and "2 hours".

Figure 2.2 The Positively Skewed Distribution Curve

"So what?" you may say again. But take careful note. It is this curious statistical property that is almost single-handedly responsible for the spectacular and stupendously costly over-runs that happen in difficult projects. The deceptively shallow incline means that there is a small but nonetheless real possibility that you may never complete that journey to work or indeed ever finish that project no matter how much money you throw at it. The curve could go asymptotic, which means it never hits the zero mark on the probability axis. And one thing you really don't want is a touch of the asymptotes. They are right up there in the Premier League of pathogenic nasties. Perhaps more practically, this graph predicts that one day in the future, the wrong type of snow will indeed show up and you might end up starving to death in a railway carriage.

> **"The first 90 per cent of the code accounts for the first**
> **90 per cent of the development time … The remaining**
> **10 per cent of the code accounts for the other 90 per cent**
> **of the development time."**
> *Tom Cargill*

It also rather neatly explains the phenomenon known as "the software is 90% complete" paradox. The completion statistics your team have calculated may indeed be true and the fellowship of the ring may well be within a tantalising 10% of their goal. But what also may be true is that to haul this project over the finishing line requires both an infinite amount of energy and an infinite amount of time. "Infinite" is never a good word to hear in the field of project management. It could just be that you have a genuine black-death (or perhaps more accurately a "black hole") project on your hands. If so, then your only hope is to try and stop it and then run away before it sucks you and the rest of your company into oblivion. The lime-filled pit beckons.

Inoculating against Skew—Percentile Therapy

If we can persist with the journey to work for a few more minutes, there is one other thing we can learn from the positive skew graph. Figure 2.3 reproduces the skewed probability curve, but this time some percentiles are added. Percentiles are really useful things. They are more useful than a Gantt chart and nearly as useful as a coffee machine.

The 50-minute journey approximates to the 5th percentile. That means that there is a 5% chance that the journey to work will be 50 minutes or less. On the other hand, the 95th percentile predicts that there is a 95% chance that your journey will take less than two hours.

This delicate, beautiful and rather simple graph confers great power on its owner. Perhaps we're not talking about dominating Middle Earth with the

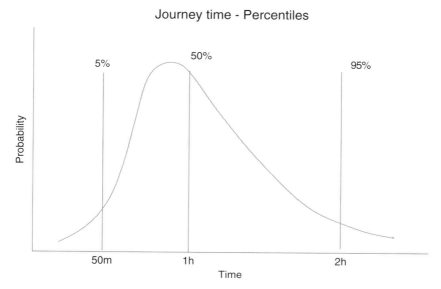

Figure 2.3   Percentiles and Probability: How to Guesstimate Accurately

ring of Mordor, but now you at least have the information you need to decide when you should leave home if you have an important meeting to attend first thing (Tolkein, 1954).

We could delve further into a deep and meaningful treatise on project management with percentiles at this point, but as a leader, you can skip all this. Provided that your teams are doing percentile estimations of each task in a plan, then you can get a picture of what is happening in your projects. In my experience, the fifth percentile roughly equates to "best-case", the fiftieth percentile to "expected" and the ninety-fifth percentile is a good surrogate for "worst case".

Figure 2.4 shows how this useful probability trick can be used. For Activity 2 of this traditional IT project plan, there are four tasks. Each has been estimated with the three point percentile technique. From this, you can now deduce that this activity is really unlikely to ever end up being shorter than 18 man days, but that if it turns out to be longer than 30 man days, then you are going to be really unlucky indeed. So armed with this information, when you are summoned to the Grand Kremlin Palace for that encounter with the bloke with the bushy moustache, which estimate are you going to choose to give him?

Don't agonise for too long, there is a cunning little trick to help you choose the right answer

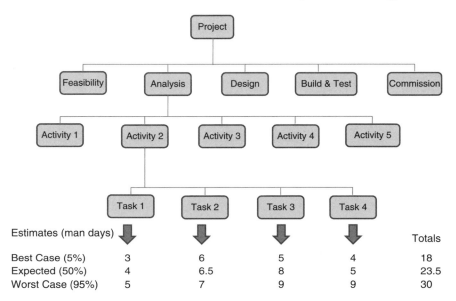

Figure 2.4 Work Breakdown Structures

What Happens in Projects Stays in Projects

Being disingenuous is generally a bad thing, but in the context of project management it has a useful and necessary place. Project planning is a messy business and you don't want the whole world seeing the unpleasant machinations that whir away beneath the surface. A German statesman rather nicely summed it up well over a century ago.

> **"Laws are like sausages. It's better not to see them being made."**
> *Otto von Bismarck (1815–1898)*

The disingenuousness in this context is to create two plans. One is known as the "private plan" and the other is known as a "public plan". Your private plan, involving all sorts of unsavoury machinations, if you've not already worked it out, stays in the project team room. This twin-plan technique is widely used in the construction industry, but for some reason it is much less prevalent in the IT world. If you've ever puzzled about that rather smug sign next to a new bypass which broadly proclaims that the project that's just finished was completed six months ahead of schedule, then here is how they do it.

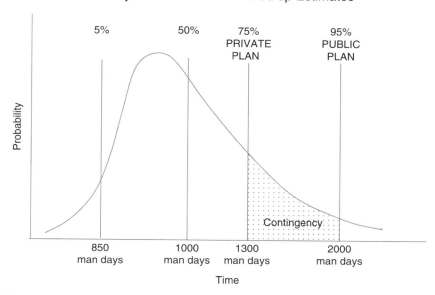

Figure 2.5 How to Create Private and Public Plan Estimates

Figure 2.5 shows that positively skewed probability curve once again. This time the rolled-up man-day estimates for the full project are included. This is the graph you need to be looking at with your senior project managers before you plunge into any meeting with Comrade Stalin (or any other stakeholders for that matter). The master project manager descendent of the Vizier that I mentioned earlier in this chapter was quite magnificent at doing this. He taught me that we publish a public plan which shows completion after 2,000 man days, while the team works to the more aggressive 75th percentile project plan of 1,300 man days. Not only does the private plan contain contingency, but since it was based on task estimates, you now even know where which tasks are most likely to use up your contingency.

As the team progressed through the plan, the master project manager would track what was actually happening and refine his estimates. He even started building a database which ascribed estimating accuracy to his team members as the actuals came in. He knew which team members habitually underestimated the length of their tasks and by how much. Truth and reconciliation were never so easy. For the advanced practitioners, the shapes of the task curves held even more information, particularly when the shapes didn't show up with the usual positive skew (see Figure 2.6).

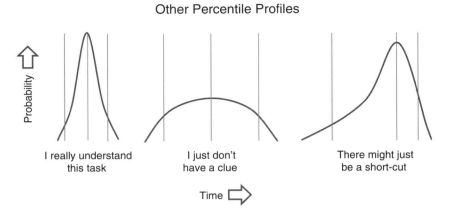

Figure 2.6   Probing the Mysteries of Distribution Curve Shapes

The Gates of Wrath

When it comes to talking about gates within the context of IT, most people immediately think of Microsoft Bill. However, in project management terms, the most important gates are those that have no windows in them. For even if you know why you are doing the project, and if you clearly understand the benefits that will accrue, then this is not enough. Even if you believe your estimates, understand the uncertainties and have good probability distributions on the entire work breakdown structure, then this is not enough. Even if you have good people on the project and if they are not only competent, but somewhat fearful of the Stalinist consequences if the project fails, this is still not enough. Because even with all these elements in place major projects still spectacularly fail. And what's more they fail with relentless regularity in ugly ways. Nobody wants a life of relentless ugliness, so one further and essential handful of pixie dust is necessary before you should embark on any major project enterprise. There is no grand name for it. It is known simply as "the gated process".

> **"Gandalf: You cannot pass! I am a servant of the Secret Fire,
> wielder of the Flame of Anor. The dark fire will not avail you,
> Flame of Udun! Go back to the shadow. You shall not pass!"**
> *Tolkein, The Fellowship of the Ring (1954)*

Each of my previous employers in sectors as diverse as oil, pharmaceutical and engineering businesses were critically dependent on exceptional project management to deliver their lofty goals. Whether it is the discovery and exploitation of billions of barrels of oil at the edge of geological understanding or earth-shattering research at the edge of genetics and biology to rid the world of malaria or AIDS or even the creation of spectacularly fuel efficient and reliable jet engines at the edge of physics, none of these companies could exist without superb project capability. Developing an oilfield, a medicine or a jet engine will each run into billions of dollars. In the project world, these are the big boys. However, in 1970 one of these companies didn't quite get it right and suffered what later became known as one of the mothers of all project failures. Back in the late sixties, the engineering company Rolls-Royce was attempting to create an entirely new jet engine with an innovative internal architecture completely unlike any of its competitors. It was called the RB211. The company believed that it had a superior design and that all the elements of success were in place. However, as the project neared completion, it became increasingly clear to everyone that all was not well. The project team found to their horror that they had created a monster that was not only devouring its way through all the company's money but all the cash of its lenders as well. There has been much written about it, but insiders reckon that in the last couple of years of the project, the costs more than doubled against the estimates and that the production costs had risen to a point where they had exceeded the sale price of the product. The company filed for bankruptcy and was subsequently nationalised by the British government. The receivers were called in on 4 February 1971. The company remained in public ownership until 1987, when it was privatised by Margaret Thatcher's administration.

In the years that followed the bankruptcy, the engineers in the company slowly recovered from the trauma of the RB211 project. They eventually made their innovative creation work, recovered some cost control and even managed to sell an impressive number of these ground-breaking engines to airlines all over the world. Even today, there are thousands of these Rolls-Royce turbines still in service powering nearly 1,000 aircraft (Rolls-Royce plc, 2013). However, the spectre of project disaster continued to loom darkly in everyone's minds. The company recognised that it would always be dependent on large, complex projects, where the technology being created not only needed to be engineered at extreme levels of excellence, but also needed to perform at incredible levels of safety and reliability. So they decided that drastic action had to be taken to ensure that no more major projects would fail. Some of the smartest people devoted themselves to devising a revised set of processes together with what turned out to be a massive cultural change program. This led to the creation of what is known as the "Derwent process" (named after an early successful Rolls-Royce engine project). The process is still used today and very few changes have been made in the decades that have passed (Figure 2.7). Derwent projects in themselves are not revolutionary. Many IT practitioners will recognise the process as bearing marked similarities to something they

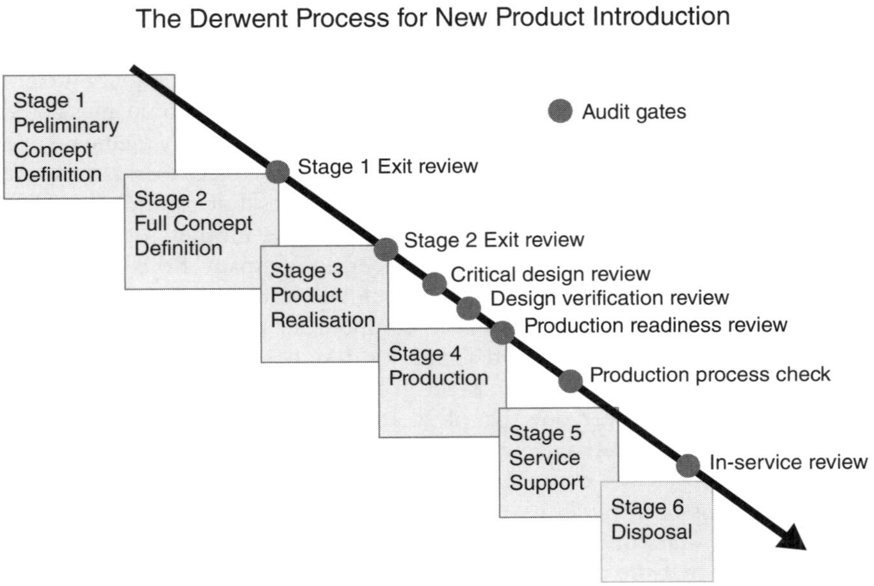

The Derwent Process for New Product Introduction

Figure 2.7   The Rolls-Royce "Derwent" Gated Process

Source: Reproduced by permission of Rolls Royce Plc. All rights reserved.

might describe as the discredited old fashioned "waterfall" process. Indeed, they may scoff at it or even dismiss it, preferring to think about more modern, fashionable fads. But they would be foolish to do so. Why? Because this method has a track record and it works. And like other perfectly designed things, such as the shark, it will also not need to change very much for the next 400 million years. In project management, a successful track record is everything, whether it's in the processes or the people (and preferably both).

The magic pixie dust that helps the Derwent process leap off the runway and soar into the blue skies, outperforming anything else I have ever seen in the project management world, is a simple piece of engineering logic. The boffins at Rolls-Royce worked out that it wasn't just about tools and process. Attitude was as important. Sure, you need good tools, but it's more about how you use your tools and the mind-set with which you approach the job. Given that most of the folk at this company were engineers, it must have been a truly seismic shock for them to realise that these "human factors" were so important. Near extinction is a great way of focussing the mind.

"Art imitates nature and necessity is the mother of invention."
Franck (1658)

It goes something like this. Consider the paintbrush. It is a simple, even humble tool. But it is nonetheless pretty important if you want to get some painting done. However, what you do with that tool and what you get out of it depends on who you are, how you are trained and, critically, the environment you are working in and the attitudes you hold. When I am handed a paintbrush for example, the outcome is always very disappointing. However, when professional decorators use that very same tool to paint the walls of my house the results are much more pleasing. However, should you ever give a paint brush to Michelangelo or Leonardo da Vinci, then what eventually gets up there on the walls or the ceiling of your chapel will blow your socks off (as well as increasing the value of your house beyond your wildest dreams).

The critical difference between this approach and many other project management methods is down to execution. Rolls-Royce introduced obsessive professionalism and a kind of attitudinal dogma that means that it is *simply not possible to move onto the next stage of the project until a clear set of gate criteria are met*. These criteria confirm that the previous stage was completed satisfactorily in all regards. If any single one of these the gate criteria is not met, then the project is halted. No "fudging" of any data is tolerated. The project is stopped dead—as dead as a dodo or a Monty Python Norwegian Blue parrot. In industry, lots of people talk about stopping projects, but this company actually does it. And in the past it has done it a lot.

This cold, unrelenting ruthlessness would doubtless warm the cockles of Joseph Stalin's heart. Today, project managers in Rolls-Royce take extraordinary precautions to make sure that all the gate criteria are met long before any independent gate review is carried out. For should there be a gate review failure, suppliers are sent home and the project team quickly become pariahs. I recall an episode some years ago when deteriorating project statistics suggested that gate criteria may not have been applied with sufficient force. The entire IT project portfolio was halted for more than two months. When the IT suppliers discovered they were losing more than $20m of revenue each month, it did not take them very long before they became converted to the religion of gated processes.

As we've already suggested, it costs about a billion dollars to bring an innovative jet engine to the market place. In the last decade or so, Rolls-Royce has successfully delivered more than half a dozen of these projects successfully from inception through to completion, beating off competitors ten times its size. This is not to mention the nuclear reactors and a wide range of industrial and marine engines which came along as well. These successes helped the company increase its share price eighteen-fold between 2003 and 2013. A moderate £10,000 investment in the company in 2003 would be worth £180,000 (ca. $290,000) today. That would be enough to buy yourself a brand new Rolls-Royce motor car.

One final interesting property is that the Derwent process considers the full lifecycle of the project. Note that Stage 6 includes the orderly shut-down of the whole program and everything else associated with it (including all remaining extant product out in the field). When did you last see an IT project or product roadmap that used the *real* meaning of the word "lifecycle"? Many I have seen over the years do not consider any activities beyond that desperate first release date and the frantic bug-fixing that followed. Presumably they thought that this was the point when the world ended—which it sometimes did, at least for them.

Looking Up from the Pit

Improbable as it sounds, the learnings we have extracted from a bunch of thrill-seeking Everest mountaineers, Pharaoh Khufu, Grand Vizier Hemon, Nostradamus, Comrade Stalin, Otto von Bismarck, not to mention Leonardo da Vinci, the Stonehenge architects and of course Mike Tyson, should hopefully have injected sufficient antigens into your capability to ward off the worst of the project management ailments. Hopefully the oppressive and creeping horror of pathogenesis can be ameliorated, inoculated against or driven off into the undergrowth. The fruit-picking lesson has hopefully also shown you that you need optimal orchards of peaches, not ghastly groves of lemons. And finally, that enlightenment should triumph over enthusiasm and that gates are good. Understanding why you are doing the project, knowing what benefits it will bring and whether you have a set of plans and estimates that will—with high probability—carry you triumphantly to that goal are all essential ingredients. And the control with all its gates must be ruthless. All this advice (which sounds disappointingly trite as it is summarised) must be followed to the letter. An iron will, great process and ruthless control can carry the day comrade, with or without a moustache.

But as with all nasty ailments, even an unpleasant course of vaccinations in good practice does not guarantee you immunity. Nature is far too devious for that. So, if by chance you have followed all the good advice of all these wise people, yet you still find yourself staring unblinkingly up from the deep rotting abyss of project failure with the squeak of cartwheels and the throaty strains of "bring out your dead" ringing out around you, then you can at least reassure yourself—before that first shovel of lime is cast—that there was only a 5% chance that you were not going to stay the course.

CHAPTER **3**

Seriously Shaky Software

"We dream of it, then we try to write it – and all hell breaks loose."

(Scott Rosenberd)

You might be familiar with the term "the devil is in the details", a phrase often attributed to the catchily named German-born architect, Ludwig Mies van der Rohe (1886–1969). While details are almost certainly important to people who like detail, the statement unfortunately cannot be true. This is because as every code developer knows, the devil isn't in the detail. He has made his home in software, the digital incarnation of hell. And the stuff he gets up to in there is completely without mercy. Indeed, if you do not apply superhuman levels of professional care, then software will quickly turn sour and then begin to fester. From there it doesn't take much more before things begin to degenerate into a full-blown septic-shock horror nightmare after which the prognosis for the patient is pretty bleak.

How do we know this? Well, to be fair, the evidence is purely circumstantial—which is pretty much the way things go when it comes to deities, even fallen ones. But let's see how it all stacks up.

First of all, if we take a look around the IT world, we can see that hardware, in stark contrast to software, works really well. To be honest, you'd be hard pressed to find any evil-ness at all in the pure world of plastic and silicon. The degree of advanced, atomic-level engineering that has to be achieved in order to make a computer work never fails to impress me. Whether it is the mysteries of how you interleave memory (or whatever it is they interleave) or the monumental task of squeezing zillions of transistors onto a pin-head, all of it to me at least, is pretty spectacular stuff.

"It's hardware that makes a machine fast. It's software that makes a fast machine slow."
Craig Bruce

When I was a data centre manager, I used to enjoy my daily walks through the labyrinthine, twisty little passage-ways of the machine room. Towering cream and grey boxes festooned with important-looking LEDs gently twinkled like the jewels in a Caribbean pirate's treasure chest. Meanwhile, the closely packed racks of servers each labelled with incomprehensible algorithmic node names soothingly hummed as they wafted insistent blasts of warm, dry air into my path. How can you not marvel at such beauty and the awesome processing power locked within these edifices of enlightenment? Glancing back into the cathedral before attempting to remember the exit code, I briefly think of the hundred and twenty thousand or so people whose working lives depend on this modern museum of marvellous machination. With a pang of concern, I resolve to descend to the basement to check the diesel generators next.

Hardware is surely as delicate and as innocent as the people that work with it. Boffin-brained hardware engineers even address the mundane aspects of their job with beauty and perhaps even a nuance of sartorial elegance. Brain-the-size-of-a-planet processors, nestling gently on a wafer-thin silicon substrate, are delicately cooled by exotic fins and fans as the electronic mind relentlessly grinds its multi-threaded way to its inevitable computational solution. In short, the creation of computer hardware (with the possible exception of printers, which I believe have some kind of vendetta of hate against me) is a magnificent achievement for which the human race (or at least the people in California and China who actually do all this clever stuff) should be justly proud. And what's more hardware rarely goes wrong.

When it comes to software however, things are very, very different indeed. Software is quite vicious and dangerous and it doesn't even look nice (at least when someone bothers to print it out). I dislike software even more than broccoli or visiting the dentist (Herald Tribune, 2012).

> **"I do not like broccoli. And I haven't liked it since I was a little kid and my mother made me eat it. And I'm President of the United States and I'm not going to eat any more broccoli."**
> *George H.W. Bush*

Steve McConnell, in his influential book, *Code Complete* (McConnell, 1993), reckons that industry average performance for writing software results in 15–50 errors per thousand lines of computer code (or 15–50 KLOCs in techno-babble). Not many mistakes you might think, but if the pilots and air-traffic controllers at Atlanta Hartsfield airport in the US put in a similar performance on Monday morning, then we could expect to see a "Breaking News" story every nine or so minutes. In fact, around 47,509 of the million or so aircraft movements (Hartsfield-Jackson Airport, 2014), in 2010 would end really badly. At London Heathrow, the situation would be only marginally better with 22,740 flights each year making a mess of the London suburbs, three times an hour, every hour. The only respite the poor residents would get would be when the wind changed direction (which would be bad news for tourists in Central London). Most Englishmen would agree that showering parks and streets with pieces of aluminium, titanium, suitcase fragments, and lashings of aviation fuel is just not cricket. True, it would certainly make plane-spotting a completely different type of spectator sport, but I'm sure everyone would get bored quite quickly and anyway, the airlines would run out of aircraft in short order. FAA statistics for 2011 tell us that there were only 7,185 US-based commercial aircraft flying in the country that year, which means that if the air traffic controllers and pilots in Georgia performed as badly as the average code writer, then they could crunch their way through the entire US aviation fleet in a little over six weeks. But long before that of course, every man and his dog would have decided that a five-day, 3,000 mile drive across the country followed by a week and a half on a ship would be by far the best way to travel from the West Coast to Europe. And we might even get the chance to see another Golden Age of the Railways. It's interesting to think that if Air Traffic Controllers did their jobs as badly as programmers, then one of the outcomes might be to see an exponential rise in the number of train-spotters around the world.

"You land a million planes safely, then you have one little mid-air and you never hear the end of it ..."
Air Traffic Controller, New York TRACON, Westbury Long Island
(Opening quotation in the 1999 movie "Pushing Tin")

So on balance I submit that hardware works and software generally doesn't. This leads us to the unsettling but nonetheless logically sound conclusion that software must be harder than hardware. And the problems just don't get any better. There is no shortage of software ghosts in the machine just to make sure that those glitches keep on coming. It's easy to believe that the diabolical one has a hand in "helping things along" in the world of software. If you are dedicated to the science of tormenting as many people as often and as much as possible, what could be better than messing around with a new baggage-handling system in a brand-new airport terminal? Seriously Shaky Software is just such a perfect answer.

Software Just Doesn't Wo..

Damn. It's hung again ...You move your mouse around the screen but nothing responds as you click. You click again, again ... and again. In the moments that follow, you will have clicked enough clicks to encode an entire MAYDAY message in Morse code together with next week's shopping list. Still nothing happens, except perhaps to your blood pressure. You eye the big button marked "OFF" on the side of your computer. In your heart you know what comes next, but you still kid yourself that there must be another pathway towards salvation. You will probably continue clicking your increasingly sweaty mouse with a machine-gun like intensity, interspersed with violent but futile random thumping of the keys on your keyboard. Then, assuming the software doesn't magically come to life and start executing several hundred commands you did not want it to execute (which will doubtless include the deletion of your work), you will have to reluctantly concede that you have had enough. You will probably then move onto making menacing threats towards the manufacturers of your equipment, the designers, Bill Gates, Steve Jobs, the nice man in the shop that sold the computer to you, together with anyone else who could possibly be implicated in this monstrous thing called computing. Eventually, you will reach the inevitable end-game position for which there is only one option—complete and unconditional surrender. As the image of an hourglass embosses itself onto your retina, the grim spectre of the hard reboot beckons. In a curious mixture of anger and despair that only software can invoke, you reluctantly reach for the side of the computer. Your mind desperately clutches for the straws of yet another hopeless hope. Somehow, surely, the purification and cleansing ritual of toggling the ON/OFF switch will magically drive the demons out of the computer and make the world a safe and happy place to live in once again? You press that button and wait. A muffled bleep heralding your reboot eventually breaks your sad and lonely silence. Congratulations, you have just sacrificed an electronic goat. Everything will now be fine until it goes wrong again. Which will be in about two hours' time.

This is of course, the joy of software. Every PC user in the world must have enjoyed the experience of a BSOD—or blue screen of death, just as every tablet user surely has been unceremoniously dumped out of the application they were using into the electronic gutter of the operating system. Many of us in the industry think it really shouldn't be this way. Hardware itself certainly isn't like this. Electronic components typically boast stupendous reliability levels. 20,000 hour mean-time-between-failure rates or more are not uncommon. The thought of a piece of software achieving similar reliability levels would be laughable (except of course that it isn't funny). But even these hardware reliability levels are conservative. Each and every piece of equipment I have ever owned or managed has beaten this target by at least a factor of three.

But software is different. Barely a couple of hours pass before that gut-wrenching feeling that everything has stopped happening again, and you are left wondering just how much time has elapsed since you last saved your critical files. "Save" incidentally, is a great word to describe this process. Many users, prompted by a nagging feeling of dread, periodically click the little floppy-disk icon at the top of the word processor menu. It is their lifeboat of hope. As I click this icon, I often reflect on how the plucky floppy disk icon has managed to survive in a world where the humble and rarely-dependable floppy disk itself has long since been swept away by the predatory ravages of the hard drive and its wicked, virus-laden portable accomplice we know as the memory stick. As the icon blinks, I now imagine my precious files clambering over the deck before gratefully flopping into the hard disk lifeboat. Then they dramatically lower themselves into the cold Atlantic water, while cruel gales drunkenly swing the lifeboat around, before it eventually splashes into the dark waters of the boiling ocean. Moments later, the noise of splintering metal announces the arrival of an iceberg. Bobbing about in the briny while they await rescue, your files will inflate their lifejackets, blow their whistles, fire off their flares and break out the emergency rations. They know that they are safe and that soon all will be well. Software liners are not unsinkable. Many users will feel the urge to repeat this process every few minutes. For some it might even become a nervous affectation causing you to twitch involuntarily each time you click "save".

Only when it's clear that the precious cargo is safely written to the lifeboat that is your hard drive can you breathe a sigh of relief. But if you are a responsible user, there is one further action to you must complete. Once the sun has set, your overnight backups should swing into action. In the wee small hours of the morning, while the owls hoot and the bats bat about, your computer should chatter into life. Steadily and safely, the crown jewels of knowledge should be backed up incrementally onto a hard drive that you have cunningly attached to a router in a far-away land or at least another building. Now you have insured yourself in case the devil brings some genuine fire and brimstone with him on his next visit. Unless of course, the backup software has failed.

Assuming you can successfully tuck your files away on the hard drive; let us return for a moment into research done on software coding quality. According to the experts, it seems that even "industry-standard" major-vendor applications are thought to contain 10–20 KLOCs. Researchers Cobb and Mills (Cobb, 1990) reckoned that "Cleanroom development" methods could keep the defects down to 3 KLOCs during in-house testing and perhaps as little as 0.1 KLOCs for released code. High levels of achievement are rare. Only the Space Shuttle software team is thought to have actually managed the ultimate zenith of accomplishment in this area. These space-age heroes were reportedly able to spawn half a million lines of code without fault, aided only by formal development methods, peer reviews and statistical testing, supported by a process known technically as "being extremely careful".

> **"If you think your management doesn't know what it's doing**
> **or that your organisation turns out low-quality software crap**
> **that embarrasses you, then leave."**
> *Edward Yourdon*

A short analysis of learned papers on the subject of software failures is surprisingly unilluminating. Indian Professor Pankaj Jalote's 2005 study for example, identified twenty-nine major categories of failure (Jalote, 2005), each of which broke down further into a plethora of failure classes. From buffer overflows to useless flows and from arithmetic exceptions to leaking memory, the ways in which programmers can screw up seems almost endless. West Virginian researchers Hammill and Goševa-Popstojanova found even more bad news. They debunked the widely held myth that many problems occur early in the software development lifecycle. No, their evidence suggested that problems could happen at any time. A case of "if it can go wrong it will go wrong" (Hammill & Goševa-Popstojanova, 2009). Moreover, from analysing real world case studies, they found that large complex systems were disproportionally difficult to fix and that, intriguingly, multiple minor problems in the code often conspire to gang up on you with the express intention of ruining your weekend.

> **"I have always wished for my computer to be as easy to use as my telephone; my wish has come true because I can no longer figure out how to use my telephone."**
> **Bjarne Stroustrup**

After an abortive attempt at a "computing for scientists" course as a seventies undergraduate, my own proper first brush with the forces of darkness was as an overconfident postgraduate. It was a truly terrifying experience. In the early eighties life was supposed to be simple. It was a time when most of us were reluctantly throwing out our flared jeans as we tried to come to terms with a post-disco society. While the cool strains of Fleetwood Mac and early Genesis drifted around my student flat (along with equally-liked, but studently-uncool Abba and Carpenters anthems), I struggled with the first proper rudiments of programming. Having failed to handle the multi-dimensional modelling I needed to do for my postgraduate research via the traditional media of brain, coffee, paper, pencil, sleep deprivation and rock music, I was drawn to the seductive charms of the University Mainframe. "Perhaps a computer could do it" was my innocent and not unreasonable thought. Little did I know that this was going to lead me to a place where I would stare into the face of hell itself. On warm summer days in a beautiful Welsh university in a pretty seaside town, picture a happy band of graduate students each filling in space-age looking coding sheets. Before long, these carefully crafted forms were deposited into boxes outside the mighty computer room. Beyond keypad secured doors, a mysterious group of magicians and druids performed their strange machinations upon this paperwork. The secret card-punching rituals they enacted were as noisy as a group of swarthy fishermen beating raw squid on a sun-baked Mediterranean quayside. And it was not a swift process. Hours passed before the fruits of their travails were completed. Eventually a neat pack of cards approximating the dimensions of a house-brick would appear in my pigeonhole in the Computer Centre. More days passed while I made the inevitable numerous corrections armed with a similarly frighteningly and noisy machine that resembled a steam-powered pneumatic drill filled with rusty spanners. The thrilling moment when I could submit the program so that it could be "run" drew ever closer. It was entirely possible that the software I was trying to write would have been hand-coded, prepared, and corrected, finally to be sent to the computer in less than three days.

Unfortunately for me, three days didn't take long to become three months. For inside the computer was a dark oppressive sentinel known to us simply as "The Compiler". For the younger generation, "The Compiler" might sound like a reality game-show host for some kind of TV dating programme about wild boys who spend too much time in the gym and even wilder girls who have too many pairs of shoes (and eyelashes measured in centimetres). But it was much worse than that. "The Compiler" was real, he was dark and he was truly terrifying. In fact, many of us worked out pretty quickly that this monster could only be one of Satan's demons. Thanks to him, my software was destined for festering oblivion. On the face of it, "The Compiler" presented himself as an entirely reasonable and innocent program that turned 3rd generation language programs—such as the ever-friendly FORTRAN—into mysterious machine code the computer could understand. However, this dark spirit had no shred of kindness in its electronic heart. Fortunately, I was too young and naïve to realise the full might, majesty and horrible darkness of the forces that I was messing with. I was not writing a computer program. No, it appears I was trying to make a pact with the Devil himself (or at least one of his most trusted lieutenants). As a graduate student I had some academic status, a car and position (and even a girlfriend) out in the mortal world. But in the virtual world, I was naked, in way over my head, playing out of my league with only bitter torment and world-class demons for company. The fruits of my clumsy programming efforts barely warranted the faintest glimmer of attention from the ghost in the machine. My program ran through the computer as if it had been turbocharged by a powerful laxative. Within milliseconds "The Compiler" had cast its judgement and my feeble efforts were swept aside with contempt. Game Over.

The stacks of punched cards, lovingly prepared over many hours, rarely made it past this sentinel. If by chance, any did manage the unmanageable, the program certainly didn't do anything I had intended. The mocking yet pitiful smile of the computer operator still haunts me today. On arrival at the entrance to the temple of the mainframe, my pigeonhole would be strangely empty. As I looked around quizzically, a bearded computer operator, who bore a disturbing resemblance to the lead male character in Dr Alex Comfort's famous book of the time, would suddenly appear (fully clothed I'm relieved to say), his arms filled with an improbable volume of what we knew as "output". The bearded one would look at it, wince and then theatrically unload the large fans of lined paper into my arms with a groan. Each of these fans of failure would inevitably be covered in gobbledygook, mercifully terminated by a short message at the end that said.

```
XXXXXXXXXXXXXXXXXX OPERATOR KILLED JOB XXXXXXXXXXXXXXXXXX
```

Which actually meant…

```
        XXXXXXXXXXXX YOU ARE A MORON XXXXXXXXXXXX
        XXXXXXXXXXXX STOP WASTING OUR PAPER XXXXXXXXXXXX
```

And it never got any better. It left me with no illusions whatsoever that writing software could ever be "easy". And it wasn't.

> **"FORTRAN is about as user-friendly as a kick in the groin."**
> *Anon.*

Several decades later, life in the industry is still just as tough. The technology might be different, but the patterns of horror just seem to repeat themselves again and again. Without fail, each fresh batch of greenhorn newbies, convinced that "this time it will be different", will eagerly cut their code with mustard-like keenness. Alas each batch lasts no longer than a bunch of hapless AK47-toting extras in the jungle of a Rambo movie before they too succumb to a grisly end in a hail of software lead. If you are a software writer, then you may as well be wearing a red shirt on Captain Kirk's Enterprise. You are doomed from the moment you step onto the transporter pad (Wilson, 2013).

Is the writing of software beyond the wit of mere mortals? If so, why might this be? What's so special about software that causes all these problems? And why is hardware so reliable in comparison?

Being Immune to Tangerines

One of the biggest problems with software is the fact that it is fundamentally intangible. You can't hold it, touch it, see it, taste it or hear it. You can sometimes smell it, but only when it's really gone off. Some people question whether software even exists, instead suggesting that it might just be the figment of someone else's tortured imagination. Buying software, whether it is a packaged "solution" (which of course doesn't solve anything) or a bespoke application (which does tend to put a spoke in things) is quite different. It's not like buying apples. That is much easier.

In the non-virtual world, if you suddenly have a craving for a juicy apple then life is pretty simple. When you wander over to a nearby market stall and try to buy a kilo or a pound of apples, you know exactly what you are going to get. You can even choose specific apples by using a technique known as "pointing at them" (you don't even have to click). It's a nice simple transaction. All you need is some cash and a brown paper bag to carry away your booty and you're all set. If only software were as easy as this.

In the virtual world if an analyst sits down with a "user" or "customer" to flesh out a set of requirements for a new system, the only thing you can be sure of is that the two parties are thinking of completely different things. My own view is that it's the level of abstraction (or intangerine-ness) with software that creates many of these problems. As the analysts sit with their customers, I have learned that no amount of beautifully drawn circles, boxes and arrows or indeed any cunningly crafted reports generated by wonderful new advanced methodologies is ever going to cut it. All you have at the end of the exercise is a set of beautifully drawn circles, boxes and arrows and a bored user. Since telepathy hasn't yet been invented, I fear the analyst may always be doomed.

"Intangible—to be immune to tangerines."
Urban Dictionary definition

Every activity that I can think of which bears any similarity to software creation has a degree of tangibility that allows some kind of connection to be made between the provider and the customer. And what's more, in almost all other similar activities, there are rules that the customer both understands and accepts that they must observe. Take architecture for example. On the face of it, there would appear to be a strong citrus whiff of intangibility about it. An architect is going to help you design your dream home. This must be a tall order surely? But even the dumbest customer knows that if they want an exterior door on an upper floor, then they are going to get a set of steps down to the ground whether they like it or not. The architect, together with the regulatory authorities, further constrain the customer by mandating how high a doorway must be and even defining what type of roofing material must be used. Not so in software. A software architect gives no such guidance and certainly doesn't get involved with mandates or even womandates for that matter. Planning permission is not required before anyone starts writing computer programs (which is probably a shame). This means that you can have anything you want; howsoever you want it, no matter what you are smoking. You start with a completely blank sheet of paper and incredibly, it just seems to get blanker as you move on. This flexibility, of course, is a perfect recipe for disaster and is a big reason why software ends up being so shaky and flaky. The image in the mind's eye of the customer simply bears no resemblance whatsoever in any shape or form to that perceived by the analyst or software architect. The customer has a dream and all the analyst or software writer has to offer in return is an expensive and time-consuming nightmare that will hang around like a bad smell in an elevator for the rest of time (or at least until someone has a few more millions to throw away). And that's even before the good old law of unintended consequences has got its hands on your convoluted software "solution". Dr Frankenstein's creations have a nasty habit of doing unpleasant things to both cast members and the rest of the world that you neither expect nor want.

> **"If builders built buildings the way programmers wrote**
> **programs, then the first woodpecker that came along**
> **would destroy civilization."**
> *Gerald Weinberg*

There would seem to be very few remedies to the citrus problem. Many would implore you not to do it. Software is so dangerous that the wise IT practitioner should not attempt to write it unless they absolutely have to. And even then it is best to write the minimum amount of code that you can get away with and make absolutely sure that it packs the fullest possible punch in terms of benefit. There is simply no way you can get away from the tangerine immunity problem. Care, professionalism and rigour are weak defences in this game, but they are the only ones you have.

The Unfortunate Side-Effect of Moore's Law

The next major problem with software relates to that iconic and unassailable IT mantra we know as Moore's Law. Gordon Moore, a revered founder of the Intel Corporation, is one of the much-loved fathers of our industry. Gordon of course is not the problem, but his law has much to answer for. Moore's Law has some horrible consequences that have blighted the whole industry pretty much from the point he delved into Pandora's world of integrated circuits and discovered it.

In 1965, Mr Moore came up with an interesting concept. He postulated that the number of transistors that can be inexpensively placed in an integrated circuit will double about every two years. The die was cast. Since that day Moore's Law has accurately forecasted what have turned out to be spectacular, consistent hardware improvements from 1958 to the present day. There have of course been times when technology has been a bit ahead and also times where it has fallen behind the prediction, but on balance it has been remarkably consistent. It's certainly been more consistent than anything else you are likely to find in the world of IT.

MOORE'S LAW

In 1965, Gordon Moore suggested that the number of transistors on a chip could double in size approximately every two years. He thought that "With unit cost falling as the number of components per circuit rises, by 1975 economics may dictate squeezing as many as 65,000 components on a single silicon chip". The concept "Moore's Law" was coined in 1970 by Caltech Professor Carver Mead and it has quickly found its way into technical language. Moore's predictions have proved uncannily accurate. His initial prediction looked forward ten years to 1975, but the pace of improvement in computational power has surprisingly kept pace to the present day and looks to continue for a fair while yet.

The problem the law creates interestingly is nothing to do with software "per se". It's to do with our industry's attitude towards software within the context of Moore's Law. Of course, we all know that hardware is improving so quickly that we accept that we are going to have to upgrade our personal computers and our servers at some stage. Two years after buying our laptop there is kit on the market that is twice as fast and once four years have elapsed, the speed of the new boxes has doubled again. By now our old computers are groaning and we all are happy to agree that it is time to go and buy another one, particularly if the new hardware stacked up on the shelves in front of us is a nice colour and is going to be double-double fast. To be honest, I think most of us are probably OK with this. It is what accountants call "writing the asset off over four years". The Men in Grey Suits, struggling to balance the finances, would prefer it if you could stretch things out to five years, but four years is OK and some corporations even replace their IT equipment on a three year cycle. So, if you spent, say, forty thousand dollars to buy a server farm to run your email service and you decide to upgrade it after four years, then the depreciated hardware costs even out at ten thousand dollars a year over the period. A snip.

For some inexplicable reason however, the people who write software have got it into their heads that software needs to follow the similar release cycle times as hardware. There is no reason for this whatsoever. It is completely and utterly inexcusable and people who do this kind of thing should hang their heads in shame and flog themselves in penance with any nearby computer leads. This is because software doesn't follow Moore's Law in terms of speed—it follows it in terms of size.

Typically, a major release (also known as a "complete rewrite") of large, commercially successful software packages happens once every two years.

Most vendors also introduce an annual "major-point" upgrade or even a six-monthly "minor-point" upgrade. This, on the face of it, all seems pretty innocuous, but because software is so complex and because systems are layered, the scope for problems is enormous. As Hammill and Goševa-Popstojanova found, the more complex the system, the more impossible it is to fix. What's worse is that as a result of these decisions, software releases now follow calendar-driven schedules rather than needs-driven events. The tail is firmly wagging the dog and the side-effects are horrendous. It drives some behaviours that are as interesting as they are alarming.

It Will be Fixed in the Next Release

I'm sure that you've heard this one a few times. It refers to the response you get when you report a bug or problem in a piece of software or a software package. When you make the call to the vendor or software writer, the person on the end of the phone will politely listen to you, write down what you said and then ask you to hold for a moment. After they have taken a sip of their coffee, tweeted some profound thoughts to their followers and checked their social media picture wall, they will then un-hold your call and utter the healing incantation: "I've just checked with engineering—it will be fixed in the next release." This is spectacularly successful as a strategy to make your customer go away and I reckon that it must be used hundreds if not thousands of times every single day. The "fixed in the next release" play is designed to convey the sense that the writer knows about the problem (which they probably don't), that they have produced a fix for it (which they probably haven't) and that this beautifully engineered fix will triumphantly be rolled out in a few months' time (which it probably won't, and certainly not triumphantly). The more likely scenario is that the software writer simply hasn't got time to deal with your problem because they have too many problems of their own. With the software release deadlines coming in thick and fast, the very last thing that the development team needs is to waste precious time tracking down what to them is an obscure singleton problem. Surely, they will think, they've sold loads of this software to willing punters, so it's got to be working right? It must be a "user" problem. Besides, they are now already so far behind the aggressive and unrealistic development schedules imposed upon them that they are already starting to drastically prune back the testing phase of that next release. And of course we know where that goes (right back to the top of this paragraph if you hadn't already worked it out). So if you are hoping for an early diagnosis of your problem, a well-researched fix, followed by a full set of regression tests before a patched version appears in a timely fashion, then you are dreaming hopelessly. In the ten thousand or so days I've worked in the industry, I reckon this happy outcome has happened just the once. I remember the day well. The moon was blue, the pigs were cleared to taxi to the runway and the politicians were agreeing budgets and healthcare proposals with one another. More normally, when the next release comes, we all know what happens. The bug will almost certainly still be there. If the problem has by some miracle gone away, it isn't because it is fixed. It's because it has usually been replaced by another problem. When it comes to a straight fist fight between quality and Father Time, we all know how it goes in the software industry. The old guy gets to win every time.

Upgrade or You Will be Banished Naked to a World of Loneliness and Isolation

Having succumbed to the unfortunate side-effect of Moore's Law, software vendors are only now beginning to realise the full implication of the manic code-fest they are engaging in. With their programmers being overloaded with impossible schedules and an army of competitors snapping at their heels in the "who's got the most functionality" competition, they now have to work very hard indeed to keep their financial margins in positive territory. This means that they don't have the time, energy or indeed the inclination to provide support to earlier versions of their software. So they've come up with an ingenious plan to deal with what could have been a thorny problem of quality support.

They don't.

Instead, most employ a cunning but effective strategy. It's a technique that's been around for a long time. It has been successfully used by despotic dictators and bad-boy barons for centuries and perhaps even millennia. It's called "blackmail". In short, many vendors "remove support" from their previous products at some arbitrary point in time. Each "upgrade" obviously costs the customer money, so the future revenue stream is now secured. And of course, as a customer you get the advantage of new features you hadn't asked for. But most of all, this strategy gives the vendors a blessed opportunity to make their lives bearable once again and they can get back to the important job of adding yet more features.

> **"How can you tell when a software vendor is lying to you?
> You can see his lips moving."**
> *Anon.*

So, as your friendly vendor is holding the metaphoric gun to your head, you could be brave and choose to take the hard-ball route. You say to them "go ahead and shoot, punk". In response they will simply re-holster their magnum and tell you that you are now on your own. You can be sure that any problems from now on will simply be blamed on "unsupported software". The prospect of running mission-critical software that is "unsupported" gets many IT leaders jittery, but that's nothing compared to how frightened CEOs will become when the vendor leaks this little titbit in their direction. Despite the fact that the software is now working fine and will probably continue to do so (provided nobody mucks about with anything), you are now in hostile, uncharted territory. Your vendor will explain that an "unsupported" environment is much like a trek across the sea-ice at the North Pole. You might think that everything is OK as you trudge your lonely way through the pack-ice with your sled and your tent trailing behind you. But the vendor will remind you that there's always the chance of a large crevasse opening up which will plunge you and your huskies into the cold, black ocean beneath. You might also be told that you could also wake up one morning to find yourself on a piece of ice that has detached from the main flow with only a polar bear for company. The answer is always the same. You are on your own and it is dangerous out there. If only you had upgraded, you'd be safely tucked up in base camp with all the other customers and the vendor would be patrolling the secured perimeter with a large polar bear rifle. They will take care of you. Just send money.

When the vendors are freed from the shackles of supporting all their old stuff, people who write software can often get carried away. The serried ranks of programmers who had spent months and possibly years slogging away at the previous version of the software are now so bored that they want to do something different and altogether whizzier. So they often do. This is all great fun until a customer wants to install the new version. I use "want" here rather than the more contentious, but probably more accurate, "blackmailed into". There will indeed be some early technology-mad adopters who want the newest version (known to the old lags as "cannon fodder" or "newbies"). These bright souls will of course be rewarded for their optimism with a spectacularly horrendous and expensive upgrade process. To software vendors, early adopters are seen in the same light as canaries in a coal mine—very useful, but ultimately expendable. That is the reward you get for loving technology. It's all very Darwinian, so be careful. As the early adopters try to adopt, nothing will probably work first time. Dependencies and interfaces with other software systems will now turn into labour-intensive exercises of pyramid-building proportions underpinned by stratospheric levels of unbudgeted costs. The IT leader is now firmly nailed between the proverbial "rock and a hard place" by their soft parts. Don't upgrade and be damned to an unsupported future running away from polar bears, or else you'll spend your entire development budget for months or even years just getting yourself back to where you were yesterday. These are the two unpalatable choices for the IT leader in these difficult times.

This business model of what an old boss of mine once called the "breaking-up-the-road-behind-you" approach seems pretty unique to the software industry. In other industries, support is offered for much longer periods of time. One of my previous employers cheerfully supported every product they had made pretty much since Queen Victoria was alive. If for example, you ever needed a spare part for a World War II aircraft engine, then they would be happy to provide it—even though the alloys for the part may no longer be available. Why? Because this company had taken a simple decision that blackmailing customers was bad for business. If this idea ever catches on you might be able to look forward to the day when your software vendor isn't standing behind you, with their arm around your throat and that magnum barrel pressed against your temple, throatily telling you to "be sensible".

Finally on this topic, there is a handy and useful method where you can gauge the level of greedy bad behaviour in your chosen software vendor. The best way to do this is to measure the time between the date you purchased your software and the date when the vendor's salesman tells you that this software is now too old and you need to upgrade. The shortest period I ever experienced was eight weeks before the sales team made the "you are running outdated software" play. After spending nearly a year of twenty people's lives and a million dollars on the previous upgrade, it is extremely fortunate for the salesman that assault, battery, ritual human sacrifice, disembowelment and setting fire to human remains on company property are all illegal in this country.

Belchware not Bloatware

We are all familiar with the curse of bloatware (Smith, 2010). But did you know that one of the industry's other great grandees warned us about it as far back as 1995?

> **"Software is getting slower more rapidly than hardware becomes faster."**
> *Niklaus Wirth*

Professor Niklaus Wirth certainly knows a thing or two about software. He was the architect of a number of programming languages, not least of which was the wonderful creation we oldies know as Pascal. At the time it was released in the early seventies, Pascal was regarded as a quantum leap, at least by the few who weren't high on recreational substances at the time. It was logical and friendly. For many, Pascal was the cavalry that rode over the horizon to save everyone from being endlessly kicked in the groin by the monster that is FORTRAN. You even got to write Pascal code in lower case without SHOUTING.

In his scientific paper "A Plea for Lean Software" (Wirth, 1995), the good professor bemoans what he calls "fat software" or what we would today call "bloatware". If things were bad when he complained about it, they are certainly a lot worse now. Wirth tells us that a text editor could have been written into eight thousand bytes of storage in the early seventies, but by 1995, he points out that program editors demanded more than one hundred times as much space and a lot more processing power. Heaven only knows where the word processors of today have got up to—probably whatever comes after a terror-byte (which is probably a shock-and-awe-byte). Wirth continues with what many would regard as the seminal statement on bloatware which, given that it was made twenty years ago, is right up there with Nostradamus in terms predicting the future of the software world.

> **"A primary cause of complexity is that software vendors
> uncritically adopt almost any feature that users want.
> Any incompatibility with the original system concept is
> either ignored or passes unrecognised, which renders the
> design more complicated and its use more cumbersome.
> When a system's power is measured by the number of its
> features, quantity becomes more important than quality.
> Every new release must offer additional features, even if
> some don't add functionality."**
> *Niklaus Wirth*

Certainly, any current word processing software doesn't work very well on a five-year-old computer. The software we try to use today is clearly much larger in size than its previous incarnations. It consumes an unimaginable amount of computing power and last and by no means least of course it contains an amazing array of fantastic features, the purpose of which will completely mystify any normal person. Even teenagers might not know what some features do. Wirth's warning is compounded by the tangerine immunity problem mentioned earlier. What programmers routinely do today when they produce new versions of their software would be a bit like modern-day architects grafting an ugly huge concrete extension half-way up the Giza Pyramid in Egypt. That would look abominable and we would of course hate it—which is why it will never happen. Unfortunately, the very intangibility of software hides similar crimes like this from us, allowing horrible messes to be created in splendid virtual isolation inside the safety of the machine.

Other authors have coined similar phrases to explain bloatware. Indeed, David May, a respected English professor of computing recently pointed out what we now know as the unfortunate side-effect of Moore's Law (Eadline, 2011).

> **"Software efficiency halves every 18 months,
> compensating Moore's Law."**
> *David May*

If only such a thing as "belchware" existed. If it did we could apply it to the rows of obese and wobbly software packages that make up today's systems portfolio. Imagine if you will, our fizzy belchware solution being carefully applied to the offending package of bloated software. As the medicine does its work, there will be a pause of some minutes after which your bloatware will let out a gargantuan burp. As the pressure is released, all the unnecessary code and unwanted features will spill out from the software in an explosion of giblets, leaving a lean, mean computer program and a large warehouse full of wriggling spaghetti.

Wouldn't it be wonderful if this could ever happen? Your software would look like one of those airbrushed, smiling people in an "after" picture from a dubious weight-loss programme. But sadly, it's far too much to hope for. Bloatware is a fact of life in today's IT world. The only defence to bloatware is to be extremely vigilant so that you can spot it early and avoid it—both in the stuff you write and the stuff you buy. If you have no alternative options, then sadly the only thing you can do is to go buy some grit, because you are going to need it for your teeth.

Perhaps the Irish writer and poet Oscar Wilde should have the final word on this subject. It's true that computers and software hadn't been invented until half a century after his death, but his quote just seems to sum things up so nicely:

> **"I welcome this opportunity of pricking the bloated bladder of lies with the poniard of truth."**
> *Oscar Wilde*

Patched, Leaking and Lost in a Maze

With intangibility and the unfortunate side-effect of Moore's law all conspiring to trip up our programmers, you might think things cannot get any worse, at least as far as software is concerned. But you'd be wrong. Not content with driving ourselves towards unrealistic schedules with ever-more complex code, the next major problem we in the IT industry must negotiate is that most dreaded source of software misery—the patch.

Patches are clever pieces of software (if such an adjective could ever be used), that can make changes to executable images of other computer programs. They are traditionally used to correct problems. They generally come in three sizes.

- The "hot-fix" is usually a binary image that is used to correct a bug in the original program. It is also widely used to close security loopholes shortly after a virus-writer has found yet another way to hijack someone's sloppily written software.

- The "patch" is the generic term which can include hot-fixes. Although a typical patch is generally a little larger in size than a hot-fix, it is still relatively minor compared to the number of lines of code in the original program. A patch can either make one or more alterations to the executable or in some cases completely replace it if the original program isn't very large (fat chance!).
- When programmers have a real mess on their hands and they need to plug a whole plethora of leaks, lest the good ship "software" sink beneath the waves, then we move into exciting new territory. Comprehensive patching and even complete re-writes are firmly in the realm of what we know as the "service pack". "Service-pack" is another of those great sounding names. It conjures up pleasant images of lots of good things, each expertly packaged and lovingly dispatched so that they will deliver improved service to you, the dear customer. It's a shame life isn't like this. If your vendor tells you that a service pack is imminent, the two things you can be sure of are that first, they aren't going to fix any more problems for you in the meantime and second that the software you are currently running is so full of holes that a major overhaul is coming along before the whole thing collapses in a heap. And the third thing is that the service pack probably won't work either.

As with our previous software issues, patches themselves are not intrinsically to blame for the problems we encounter. It is, sadly, the undisciplined way that we use them that causes the misery.

We all know for example that some PC operating system vendors provide monthly updates to their systems. Typically, these come in batches of about half a dozen at a time. However, the number of patches "out there" would surprise you. Once upon a time I discovered that a major supplier of Unix Operating system software, which populated thousands of the servers in our data centre, was issuing between seven hundred and twelve hundred patches for the operating system each year. This works out at more than two patches each day. Somewhere, there must be satanic mill-like warehouses on dreary industrial estates in unfashionable cities where row upon row of red-eyed worker-bees are endlessly crunching out patchy machine code at frightening rates. My contact cheerfully admitted that around three hundred of the patches issued so far that year were correcting problems that the first thousand had introduced. It also became clear that it was highly unlikely that any two customers were running the same patch configuration on their systems. This came as a rather nasty shock as some of the applications we were running were pretty mission-critical and people's lives rather depended on them working properly. Once the first patch has been installed on your clean-build server, then you begin your journey into the maze. You are no longer running the code paths that you had tested prior to the software's release. A couple of thousand patches later and you have no idea where you are. Regression testing is extremely challenging and to all intents and purposes you are now lost in a colossal maze of twisty little passages, all alike. This circumstance at least explained the behaviour of the vendor's technical team. When things went wrong, they would send us a "hot-fix" with instructions to "give this a whirl and tell us what happens". Now we knew that we were probably not running the same code paths as any other customer, we were truly on our own. It's just as well that we had the full backup and support of the vendor, for what it was worth. Is that a polar bear over there?

The Wobbly Stack

If we thought all these difficulties were bad, imagine how much worse they would be if we multiplied them many times. Software is layered and it is complicated. Figure 3.1 shows just how many pieces of software lie between the user and the computers. It depicts an architecture typical of a multi-national company's distributed implementation of a mission-critical application such as a materials resource planning system (MRP). The (usually heavily customised) application software sits atop a database, copies of which are then distributed on servers across the enterprise.

Starting at the top, we first have to surmount the computer that sits on the end-user's desk. Many companies do not "lock-down" their PCs, so the level of bizarre amateur surgery that users can get up to can be pretty awesome. Then we move onto the IT department's efforts. Few people can resist customising packaged software, so there is a usually a layer of bespoke code before we get to the application instance proper, which of course has a database running inside it. Then we finally get to the PC's operating system software. After this, network traffic is often encoded and distributed via hub and router software across a Local Area Network (LAN). This traffic will arrive at a local server which itself will probably have its own bespoke layer of software, before we get to the application and database instances and finally the server operating system. If multiple locations or countries are included in the implementation, then this sequence may be repeated several times across the Wide Area Network (WAN). Each will add another layer of router software, bespoke remote application software together with the application and database instances and finally the remote server's operating system.

All in all, this particular architecture requires the system to navigate across at least sixteen discrete pieces of software. Each of these has to be working

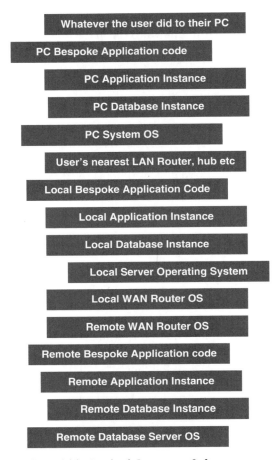

Figure 3.1 A Simple Wobbly Stack of Corporate Software

properly, not only for themselves, but also for each other. The fragility this causes gives the stack its essential characteristic—wobbliness. And while most IT leaders will be aware of the layers and the complexity, many are surprised at how precarious it looks when you put it all together. It won't surprise you to learn that this wobbliness is a major factor that helps the creation of Seriously Shaky Software (though it is far from the only reason).

The example above might look complicated, but it is in fact grossly simplified. Other applications that need an interface with this system have not been included for example. Some corporates have hundreds of Wobbly Stacks, all linked together.

In the physics of the real world, things get stronger when you link them together. Unfortunately in the virtual world of shaky software the reverse is true. For every single piece of every linked Wobbly Stack has to be working properly; otherwise you will get something you will not expect and you can be assured that it won't be pleasant.

So when it comes to robustness, it seems that the only thing you can say about the Wobbly Stack is that "it isn't". If we assume that the software authors have succumbed to the unfortunate side-effect of Moore's Law, then we can expect to see each of the layers in the stack requiring a major upgrade every two years, punctuated by a minor change about once a year or so. Even if we forget about the endless patching the operating system is enduring, a two year replacement cycle for each component will mean that this stack will only be stable on average for six and a half weeks before something within it changes. We get here by dividing the number of components into the cycle time. If however, you are vigilant enough (which in this case means dumb enough) to be upgrading all your software on an annual basis, then your Wobbly Stack isn't just wobbly—it is seriously wobbly. For after a mere twenty-two days and eighteen hours have passed, something in the tower will have been changed. And it is highly likely that all will not be well. This problem might quickly become obvious (which is a blessing). However, it may take weeks before the dark truth becomes clear and you have to assess just how much garbage has come out of your system since the upgrade. It may take even longer to assess the damage it may have caused. The smarter players of this game of course will immediately roll back the most recent change, abort the upgrade and pop a valium before wiping their brows and taking stock of the situation. But in the real world it's surprising how few IT organisations take a fully disciplined and controlled approach to managing software. Some even choose to upgrade a whole portfolio of different software all at the same time. In a towering stack of software, this creates a particularly entertaining game of torment. Here you have to determine whether it is one component causing the problem, more than one, or the most challenging of the lot—whether several components are interacting in an unexpected fashion. The latter is a great way of racking up astronomical overtime bills amongst your technical staff. It is possible to group major upgrades together, but there are two important precursors. You have to choose safe software and you have to complete a great deal of component testing and regression testing work prior to the day of actual upgrade. We will look at this "landing slot" concept later in this chapter.

Despite these pitfalls, many seem content to plough ahead with a mantra of "we must keep moving forward". In reality, there is no sense of "forward" at all with this strategy. All that happens is that they get lost yet again in another twisty maze of little passages. And you are unlikely to get much joy when you call the vendors. We've already talked about the types of responses they will give you in the previous section. And when problems such as these occur in massively distributed corporate systems (which unfortunately covers almost everything that large corporates do), it is going to be spectacularly difficult, time-consuming and very costly to even diagnose the fault, let alone fix it. Vendors are faced with the awful choice of trying to get to the bottom of the problem, or else haemorrhaging huge amounts of money and effort while their businesses quietly go bankrupt. Few dare risk it. Most opt for the other option. This is best described as a bizarre game of "pass the parcel" with a large ticking, black ball labelled "BOMB". It is of course "the other guy's fault". The client can only marvel at the speed at which the ball is frantically tossed to and from the clutches of your valued software suppliers all up and down the wibbly-wobbly stack. Each vendor earnestly hoping that they won't be holding the bomb when it goes "BANG!"

> **"Indeed, the woes of Software Engineering are not due to lack
> of tools, or proper management, but largely due to lack of
> sufficient technical competence."**
> *Niklaus Wirth*

So it's hardly any wonder that things go wrong all the time. Thanks to the fundamental intangibility of software and the problems it creates, the unfortunate side-effect of Moore's Law, indiscipline when programming and a raging torrent of patches and upgrades bedevilling complex distributed systems, it's a wonder that anything ever works at all. But sometimes it does and take heart, sensation can be found!

Stabilising Shakiness

By now, you may be reaching for the anti-depressants or a nearby samurai sword. But cover up your wrists and put that pill bottle back in the cabinet. Yes, the situation is bleak, but it is not yet time to commit hara-kiri (you can wait for the chapter on budgets for that). Software is problematic, but not impossible to deal with. It is merely challenging in a "let's put a man or woman on Mars" sense, requiring the levels of patience you would need to survive a six-week vacation with your in-laws without resorting to physical violence. In the aviation industry, test and ferry pilots will readily tell you that when they fly an unfamiliar aircraft, their working assumption is that the airplane is trying to kill them. This is a perfect attitude for the IT leader to take with respect to software. After all what you're attempting to do is indeed very testing and you are certainly a pilot, if not a canary. When you look at software imagine that you are performing low-level aerobatics at a large air-show in an unfamiliar experimental aircraft designed by someone whom you do not respect, which has been maintained by someone who you do not like very much. When you make that "buy" decision on a piece of software this is just what you are doing. As with the airplane, you should expect the software to do unexpected and nasty things to you. While the ride may be exhilarating, you will probably be wishing that someone else was doing it and you will certainly be glad when it is eventually over. It is exactly this frame of mind you need to have when you are thinking about software.

> **"Mix ignorance with arrogance at low altitude and the results are almost guaranteed to be spectacular."**
> *Bruce Landsberg, Executive Director of the Air Safety Foundation*
> *US Aircraft Owners & Pilots Association*

Safe Software

In the twenty-first century we live in a world where each year, the observance of zealous "health and safety" rules reaches ever more giddy new heights. In 2012 a council near London Gatwick airport for example, was even told to remove park benches because they are dangerous (The Argus newspaper, 2012). With all this in mind it is perhaps surprising that there are no "safe software" campaigns on the go across our industry.

Happily, high-integrity businesses such as those in the aerospace and nuclear industries teach us that it is possible to create safe software. As with the Space Shuttle mentioned earlier, aerospace control systems are most carefully written by people with very large foreheads who really know what they are doing. They usually write their routines using machine code on qualified hardware. Not a single layer of feature-rich-vendor-muddle or any unqualified pieces of software can be seen for miles. And these boffins do their job very well—as well as air traffic controllers in fact (which is why The Georgia International Conference Centre in Atlanta and Richmond Park in London are both very safe places to walk at least as far as falling aircraft debris is concerned). Indeed, if they did not write their code so beautifully, you would probably be reading this book from a transatlantic ferry with another four full days to go before you reach the long queue of ships waiting to traverse the Panama Canal. The reason for this perfection is probably due to the strong sense of professionalism of the boffins. They harbour a quiet determination that you are not going be turned into strawberry jam next time you go flying. They also have an obsessive devotion to the challenging subject of FMECAs, or failure mode, effects and criticality analysis to those of you who don't like acronyms (See-Larsson, 2010). A huge proportion of their code is devoted to checking and confirming that everything is working OK. FMECAs are much like the old cold war Soviet Commissars who used to watch over the grumpy military commanders, tirelessly scanning the craggy features of the unfortunate colonel for any sign of counter-revolutionary behaviour. Many believe that it clearly isn't cost-effective—or perhaps even possible—for this level of rigour to be injected into the voluminous volumes of today's shaky software. Unfortunately, it is likely that a period of several decades will have to pass before the software world arrives at the stellar quality levels we see in the aerospace and automotive industries.

So what should we do in the meantime?

If you have a strong constitution and a wicked sense of humour, you might wish to have a go at the "Safe Software Game". This involves waiting for the moment when a software salesman makes the tried, well used (and frankly inevitable) "your software is out of date" play. To play this game well you need to have a high degree of leverage (in the form of a big budget), which is essential for maximum enjoyment. The rules go like this.

The Safe Software Game

1. Your friendly software salesman shows up one day and tells you that you are "getting behind" and that you need to upgrade to the next version of his software (obviously for a deeply discounted rate). Alternatively they may tell you that you must immediately load a patch or even a service pack to your Wobbly Stack of software. The word "security" will almost certainly feature somewhere in their speech.

2. You ask the salesman if it safe to remain with the existing versions of the software.

3. If he or she replies "yes" (which almost never happens), then you ask him why he or she is wasting your time and you send them on their way. The game is now over. If on the other hand, he or she replies "no", then you simply ask them to send you an email to confirm this fact. Now you can move to the next level of the game and the fun starts. You even have the killer piece of email evidence if your much valued vendor subsequently tries to sue you.

4. So, if the answer was a "no", then you simply add the software to a "NOT SAFE" list. This list is then distributed to every company in your trade association. Just for that extra frisson of edginess, I once also sent it to all the software vendors I was currently using (which will include the competitors of the company in question). Software vendors in this context cover everyone, including hardware operating systems and router software suppliers. For the lawyers out there, remember I am holding a piece of paper from the vendor that says "my software isn't safe".

5. As with all good fireworks, having lit the blue touch paper, you now stand well back and wait to see what happens.

By now, your entire software vendor community and most of your staff and co-workers will have assumed that you have gone stark, raving mad. Obviously nobody in your organisation will mention it head-on, but when you talk to members of your team, you will notice that they always want to steer the conversation towards the subject of a check-up at the Occupational Health Department.

But there is a reason for this apparent madness. It is so challenging to run software successfully, that you simply can't afford to have your vendors yanking you around down code paths that nobody has tested. The only yanking you should do is to pull people out of the disastrous mind-set known as "keeping up to date". Continual upgrading, which puts your software into an ever-more unknown and almost certainly more unsafe state, is the absurd norm in the industry today. The "upgrade" question exposes a situation where people's goals are not aligned. You want a boring, stable, reliable set of systems that deliver business benefits. The vendors do not. They are unfortunately still struggling to out-do each other frantically fabricating fanciful features. This means a bewildering myriad of new stuff is added with each release, while their programming zombies are positively frothing at the mouth as they numbly cut even more code in response to the siren call of the unfortunate side-effect of Moore's law. Meanwhile the application grows ever more monstrous and everyone disappears deeper into the maze. And the key killer point here is that the risk associated with their Seriously Shaky Software remains firmly in your lap. I at least have never found a way to effect any meaningful risk transfer back towards any software vendors I have known.

> **"Yet, I am convinced that there is a need for high quality software, and the time will come when it will be recognized that it is worth investing effort in its development and in using a careful, structured approach based on safe, structured languages."**
> *Niklaus Wirth*

A good IT leader conditions the behaviour of those around them so that the IT organisation is not shovelling massive levels of risk into the company for no good reason. Handling software successfully requires a complete change in mind-set. Everyone in the chain has to take responsibility for their actions because you need every piece of software to be working properly all of the time. So having shocked everyone with the safe software game, you now have their attention. Here are some thoughts as to how you might want to reshape their behaviour within the context of "safe software".

Booking a Landing Slot at Heathrow

As you'd guess, you don't just turn up at London Heathrow or JFK in an airplane and expect to land when and where you want (unless perhaps you are a President or the King of an important country). In almost every jurisdiction that isn't engaged in a war with a neighbour, you have to file a flight plan prior to take-off if you cross international boundaries or want to land at a major airport. For large airports, when the plan is approved, you are allocated a landing slot. You may now start your engines and begin your journey.

When the time comes to upgrade your software, the smarter IT leaders follow the exact same principles. In a pharmaceutical company where I once worked, the policy the team operated was to install upgrades of any major software packages in August when most of the company was on vacation. Production was also scaled back at this time, meaning the business damage the IT team could inflict was much more limited. The team also reckoned that they could handle a minor upgrade slot in the spring, around the Easter public holidays. Performing upgrades when people aren't around is a great way to get things done quickly, easily and with a minimum of hassle—particularly when things go wrong (which they inevitably do). These two windows of time ended up being the best that they could find. IT professionals must expect to have to work out of hours for our users on occasion, so personal disruption is inevitable. Thanksgiving and Christmas are probably the worst times for scheduling major out-of-hours work, at least in westernised countries. March and August aren't anything like as disruptive and team members are usually happy to take their vacations after the work is completed, especially if you toss in some lieu days as a reward for their dedicated efforts.

The August upgrade window became known as the main "landing slot" of the year. It ran between the last week in July and the third week in August. Any upgrades or patching work needed to be completed more than five working days before the window closed so that regression testing could be fully completed.

Discussions with vendors and any in-house development teams then inevitably turned to the question of which patches and upgrades we were going to put into the August or March landing slots. The answer was always the same. The team would always put in the safest versions, and if they were all safe, then they put in the latest safe version. In other words they followed the (very sound) principle of not putting in the latest and greatest untested software. This meant that this organisation was always "behind the curve"—at least that was how the vendors and some of the developers would see it. The team was, however, adamant and could not be shifted from this position. They were looking at the situation on the basis that the code being installed had been proven to work, in comparison to code without provenance that probably didn't. Not a canary was in sight in their coal mine. Their safe software policy meant that methane was a rare commodity in their underground world. It is a rare skill to be able to write software that can withstand the fury that the user community can bring to bear.

Don't Try to Improve a Da Vinci, Unless You Are a Rembrandt

When the fifteenth-century polymath, painter, inventor, engineer, writer and all round clever dick Leonardo da Vinci (da Vinci, 2006) produced, the stuff he produced was really, really good. Anyone who can invent something as scary and out-of-the-box as a helicopter when the rest of the world is busy burning witches has to be regarded as something of a top guy (Pickering, 2013). Our intrepid Italian even dreamed up the rudiments of Plate Tectonics. So ahead of its time was this notion that the science of geology didn't catch up with Leonardo until the 1960s, nearly 600 years later (Read, 1975). So it's probably fair to say that most people would be horrified if they knew that you had whipped out your paint-box and started "improving" and "customising" that Mona Lisa painting you'd just purchased. I also don't think they would be that impressed if you showed up at the Sistine Chapel with a paint roller and a large tin of emulsion either.

It would of course, be too much to hope that every packaged software solution you ever buy will be right up there in the Da Vinci league, but software is extremely complex and the people who developed it probably thought a great deal about what they were doing at the time. Indeed, if we think about the development of a major commercial software package, I reckon that the people involved in it must have exchanged at least a million emails while they were writing the code. Meetings probably constituted a few hundred thousand more hours and it's likely that enough coffee was drunk during the development phase to fill the Pacific Ocean twice over and still have enough left over to reach the Moon. So, after you've installed your shiny new, zillion dollar package, if you whip out your painting set so you can immediately start mucking about with it, then you are probably making a big mistake (no matter how much fun you intend to have). But sadly in our industry, the urge to customise seems to be utterly irresistible. I can say without exaggeration that every IT professional I have ever met will admit to customising software at some time in their careers. Many will be compulsive customisers, chaining themselves to their computer for days and weeks on end like grizzled Las Vegas gamblers, each fixated on their favourite slot machine. All that is different is that software customisers don't tend to be offered complimentary cigarettes and alcohol when they are indulging their habit (at least in working hours). However, the method for treating both gambling and customising is the same. The unfortunate must either be weaned off their addiction humanely, or else be made to face an unpleasant dose of cold turkey.

When the people who originally designed the software package you just bought dreamed up their magnum opus, it probably didn't occur to them that the very first thing every corporate company would do was to start rewriting it. Software writers might be a bit naïve, but the designers not unreasonably thought they had made a product that met your needs.

It's amazing how the crazy world of software can delude everyone—customers, vendors, developers and the rest of us. It's diabolical in fact!

When you start fiddling with a package, you should be aware that you are no longer skiing on marked runs. You are now heading off-piste, where the snow is deep and the drops into the valley are even deeper. What's more you are very likely to start an avalanche.

The worst example of customisation (and perhaps the most criminal) I have ever seen was inflicted on a packaged HR "solution" some years ago. After a comprehensive and extensive product selection exercise, undertaken over many months, the chosen package was eventually purchased. After the celebrations were over, the development team, egged on by the user community, vigorously took their knife and fork to the software. In no time the package was carved up into something completely unrecognisable. The team even managed to alter the fundamental business logic at the core of the system. This customisation work was both time-consuming and expensive in the early stages, but only once the vendor upgraded their product did the full horror of the situation become apparent. The team had to perform the complete customisation exercise all over again.

For that very reason, there is a very simple rule about customisation that the experienced IT leader always follows. First, software customisation should not happen in your organisation at all without your explicit say-so. Failure to comply with this directive should be rewarded with the unpleasant attentions of the disciplinary squad of the HR department. Should anyone ever tell you that they need to customise packaged software, then you must ask them to write a full business case before it can be approved. Many people will simply go away at this point—which is a good answer. If the individuals do bother to do some work and they return to your office with such a document, then you should take a good look at the costs line. Now multiply it by a factor of five. This will give you a much closer idea of what this change will actually cost the corporation over the lifecycle of the system. If by some remote chance you still have a good positive business case despite these inflated costs, then you might reluctantly allow the team to proceed. Otherwise the proposal should be rejected. Beware however, for once you have sent the first disappointed team away, the unbelievers who really can't kick their addiction will be looking for nefarious ways of circumventing your authority. The most common wheeze is to redefine the meaning of words. If you are not careful, "customising" quickly becomes "configuring". So if you are ever getting confused, then make sure you know the definitions.

1. **Configuration—changes made within the package that will carry forward into the next upgrade without any further work.**
2. **Customisation—everything else.**

If you do decide to poke your ski pole out and step out onto the steep, rippled, snowy unmarked slopes of customisation, be warned! You have to be really good at it—world-class good in fact. Few of us can aspire to this level of competency. But it does happen. The Dutch artist Rembrandt Harmenszoon van Rijn for example was someone who was good enough to move Leonardo's ideas forward. Da Vinci pioneered a painting technique known as "chiaroscuro". This allows the painter to dramatically intensify actions or atmosphere through clever placement of illumination and muting. Fancying his chances, Rembrandt did decide to take out his paint box and push things along a bit. But he never mucked about with Da Vinci's paintings. Instead, the Dutch Master started from scratch with his own canvases, building on the teaching of the master while conducting his own experiments with shade and light (plenty of good lessons for the student here). The result was spectacularly wonderful art which took the representation of light and shadow to new levels. So, if you think you are as good as Rembrandt then feel free to go ahead and customise that customer relationship management (CRM) package.

Moving on from the Grand Masters, there are two good reasons why you should "customise only at your peril".

First, if we think for a moment about the immunity to tangerines problem and the absence of planning permission regulations in the software world, we know that we may well be driven to create something extremely complex that is highly customised to the whims of the user community. This is always expensive and rarely satisfactory.

Second, there are great examples of just how valuable "vanilla" systems can be to you. A short while ago, I was fortunate enough to be close to an operation which had the most spectacularly effective project management team. Cutting to the chase, these people were able to build a global supply chain based upon a single almost completely un-customised instance of a well-known German materials resources planning (MRP) package. It ended up being worth billions of dollars to the company. It is true that there were a few local barons (aka factory managers) who didn't want to play (and subsequently left for pastures new), but the benefits to the corporation from that one project were spectacular. The team was successful in persuading the leadership that they didn't need to go ahead and reinvent the wheel to try to produce something better than MRP-2. They knew they were not the best manufacturing company in the world. Their aim was to achieve a competitive edge through being innovative. For manufacturing, they just had to be devastatingly predictable and boringly effective. And who could wish for anything more devastating and boringly effective than German processes locked up in a software package whose full name needs to be written over three lines?

In summary, it's generally good advice not to muck about with your Da Vinci or your Rembrandt. Install your packages and enjoy them. If you want to get addicted to something, then a trip to Sin City, Nevada to do some gambling is a much better bet. As with software customisation, make sure you take plenty of money.

Bespoke Only When You're Bespoken to

The final question to think about with respect to software relates to the whole issue of in-house software, also known as bespoke programs. Any who have ever had to maintain bespoke systems will probably be having bad dreams where vast warehouses filled with spaghetti code burst open their doors spilling out wriggling monsters that will strangle them. Many people hate in-house systems, especially those who didn't originally write them. But despite this, bespoke code does have a vital place in the corporate company's armoury. But you must make sure that it is the right place. Nobody in their right mind would bespoke a Finance System or an HR package (except perhaps a large number of Fortune 500 and FTSE 100 companies who are now wishing they hadn't). Writing new code in such areas will demand a great deal of effort but in return there will be little or no gain—at least in terms of any meaningful business benefits. Instead, standard parts of the business need industry-standard packages. If such packages do not fit the needs, then the company's processes probably need to be changed to match. Over the last decade, packages have become much more useful, despite the plethora of unwanted features they may contain. Packages should be used wherever possible. Creating bespoke nightmare applications based on the incoherent ramblings of your business partners is not a good way to make money, let alone win friends and influence people.

So where should bespoke software be used?

Some of the more sophisticated IT leaders have had great success selectively using bespoke software in areas where they believe they can achieve genuine and real competitive advantage for the company. They also take care to keep the systems small, maintainable and free from clutter. This is because these applications are going to be expensive and extremely difficult to maintain over their lifetime, which is also the reason why they have to deliver some serious business punch.

"Always program as if the person who will be maintaining your program is a violent psychopath that knows where you live."
Martin Golding

Finding fertile areas to bespoke isn't as hard as it seems. The best place to look is in the areas that make a difference at the macro level in the company. This is not about keeping administrative middle managers who misguidedly think they are your "customers" happy. In the oil industry several decades ago, a team I was involved with was bespoking software in the exploration department, looking at analysis of seismic and borehole data to identify potential oil reservoirs. They needed to produce graphical vertical logs of boreholes really quickly. This meant that the hydrocarbon explorers could rapidly make sense of what was going on thousands of feet beneath the ground moments after the roustabouts on the oil rigs had heaved the cores from the boreholes they had drilled. This stuff is pretty old hat now, but it seemed exciting at the time. Finding that oilfield before the next guy was considered competitive advantage at the time. I suspect nothing has changed today.

In the pharmaceutical industry in the early nineties, a team was pioneering a new science which is now known as Bioinformatics. In simple terms, Bioinformatics represents all the computing behind the recent advances in genetics. I recall one example, where the whole gene sequence of a particularly nasty type of bacteria had been elucidated. Some fancy footwork with a bunch of bespoke software, together with some quickly thrown together databases determined that a mysterious part of the bacterium's sequence, that had been baffling the boffins, bore a striking resemblance to a piece of the human genome. This led the biologists to track down a specific enzyme via the biochemical pathways and proteins expressed by the gene … and bingo! They had found themselves a biological target to play with. Finding a medicine molecule to muck about with this enzyme would not be good news for the bacterium. At the time this success was celebrated as one of the first "in silico" targets (as opposed to "in vitro" (test-tube) or "in vivo"). Some cute biology had been done pretty much completely inside a computer without the need for a test tube or a culture in sight. This was a first and as with all firsts, there were no well-trodden solutions to help them on their way.

In Aerospace, there are obvious areas where bespoke software makes sense. Engineers, for example, will need to continually develop and improve their advanced stress algorithms and the mysterious computer codes which model the gas pathways through a jet engine. In recent decades, this diligence has yielded sustained benefits. The specific fuel consumption of the engines of the Boeing 787, for example, are more than 15% lower than the equivalent engines on the Boeing 767 (Boeing Corporation, 2013). That's an improvement in fuel burn of about 1% a year over the period. A typical airline consumes about a third of their total operating costs on fuel, so once again we are looking at an outcome where the benefits are being measured in billions.

The smartest and cutest example of bespoke software I have ever seen was also to be found in what started off as a dark corner at my previous employer in the Aerospace industry. Sadly, I was not the person who thought up the bright idea, though I really wish it had been me. Essentially, the parent company had implemented a game-changing model for maintenance. Rather than charging the customer the usual time and materials rates for scheduled maintenance and repairs, they instead charged a fixed subscription rate for every hour the aircraft was flying. This was a big bet on the product as it meant that the company would have to take a pretty substantial bath if the equipment turned out to be problematic when it was in service. The IT response was to smother the customer's equipment (an engine in this case) with sensors which collectively reported a massive stream of real-time data back to base while the aircraft was flying. A packaged database product from a well-respected vendor was used to capture the data, but all the clever analysis was done by bespoke systems. Not only could individual problems be identified, but trends could be analysed across the whole fleet and even across the entire customer base. This was pretty smart stuff as it allowed problem parts to be redesigned, it could predict certain types of failures, and it provided huge amounts of data to help diagnose rare faults. But someone in the team was bright enough to have taken things to a whole new level. They had worked out that the sensors, systems and processes were transferable into other business sectors. So today, this business unit operates as a subsidiary company in its own right, monitoring trains, planes and power stations. In effect, what was initially bespoke software had not only become a packaged solution in its own right, but it had advanced on to the next level where it became a full-blown service. This investment has paid for itself many times over, not only in the benefits it has given the company in its own products, but by the hundreds of millions of dollars in profits it has brought in as a trading company over the last few years.

All of this brings home to me the fact that, without care, you will always get Seriously Shaky Software. On the other hand, however, if you apply absolute diligence, brain-power, common sense and a bit of foresight, all mixed in with a large dose of discipline (or in short, superhuman levels of care and hygiene), software can be absolutely sensational. I certainly know which one I would choose.

CHAPTER 4

Obsessive Outsourcing Compulsion

"Do what you do best and outsource the rest."

(Tom Peters)

I f you ever start a debate about outsourcing with anyone in the IT industry, you will find it as inflammatory as a discussion about politics and religion, atop a petrol-soaked bonfire that has been liberally seeded with gas cylinders. Before long someone will show up with a match and it isn't hard to guess what happens next. After the explosion, soot-covered survivors will clamber through the wreckage of the office as earthquake and tsunami warnings are set off around the globe. Nearby supermarket shoppers will dodge between swaying, tottering shelves as cans of tinned milk and cat food rain down on them. Others in the vicinity will be frantically scanning the skies searching for a mushroom cloud. But those who have served their time in the IT industry will simply shrug their shoulders, sigh deeply and reflect quietly. There is more energy in a debate on outsourcing than there is in a kilogram of uranium.

The reason for all this passion is because outsourcing as a subject has more polarisation than a sunglasses factory. Vivid stories, exaggerated nightmare scenarios and dark suspicions of wrongdoing abound. Such tales are eagerly consumed in the halls, cubes and coffee stations of the hapless herds of prey, better known as the in-house IT department. For years, in-house IT organisations have quaked in fear at the prospect of being "out-sourced". And they have good reason to be frightened. In the nineties, huge swathes of loyal company servants were shovelled wholesale into the waiting jaws of the salivating outsourcing companies. Almost any "naughty" IT team that tripped over their shoelaces quickly found themselves dumped in the air-lock ready to be blasted into oblivion. If any lucky souls managed to cheat fate in the cruel vacuum of space, then their reward was to wake up next morning with a different company logo on the top of their payslips.

There is no doubt that outsourcing is a very emotive topic and making any sense of it will be something of a challenge to any IT leader. What makes it particularly difficult for those in search of beauty and truth is that outsourcing suffers from the persistent problem of "IT religion". Indeed, IT leaders in other companies will be unable to give you impartial advice because they will almost certainly have posted their allegiance to one particular church. Some will be fervent believers of the "better out than in" doctrine. These followers will be compulsively outsourcing every IT department they can find as quickly as they can. Meanwhile, those belonging to the Church of the Latter Day Employees will be making a career out of busily in-sourcing all the failing outsourced contracts. As with many aspects of IT, outsourcing can often be a case where some people dig holes while others fill them in.

Devotees of the outsourcing faith will talk of a nirvana state of milk and honey, where the IT costs are vanishingly small. Here smart professionals deliver exceptional services and the benign, expert outsourcer lovingly deploys only the highest level of skill to their craft. This of course will lead inevitably to stupendous value for money and deliriously happy computer users. Amen.

The Church Elders of the "employees only" creed will have quite a different view. They will see employees of the outsourcing company as dumb, insensitive zombies, who have absolutely no idea about IT and even less about your business. They will point out examples of where the malevolent outsourcer has fleeced clients for almost unimaginable amounts of money. Meanwhile projects spectacularly failed in showering cascades of sparks and IT services ground to a grinding halt. In their belief system, IT is decidedly feudal. It can only be serviced by loyal serfs, all honest and true to their masters. All must be willing to take on acts of self-sacrifice in order to go the extra mile for their dear leaders and their beloved company.

> **"The other part of outsourcing is this: it simply says where the work can be done outside better than it can be done inside, we should do it."**
> *Alphonso Jackson*

Nonetheless, despite the vast and serried ranks of unbelievers, outsourcing still has a siren call which repeatedly entices and seduces IT leaders all over the world. And once the outsourcing habit starts it often develops into a full-blown compulsion. People just can't help themselves and feel an irresistible need to purge the organisation of its in-house staff until none are left. I once took on the responsibility for an IT Division in a large multi-national corporate company where the level of outsourcing was impressively extensive. There were only four fully paid up IT professionals remaining in the entire central IT organisation. With the outsourcer able to field more than a thousand people, the scanty in-house team could only peep over the tops of the walls of the Alamo, gaze forlornly at their depleted ammunition boxes and contemplate a difficult morning ahead.

As far as outsourcing is concerned, we will usually get a violent, explosive debate, followed by an arbitrary religious decision. This will either lead us to a future of staid, in-house amateurism or a long-term contract of eternal despair. Sometimes you can get both.

Outsourcing is tough and it is not easy. But it has been around for a very long time.

Outsourcing an Empire

If we go back into the mists of time, we will find that outsourcing has been around since ancient days. One of the earliest contracts I could find may have been put together by the celebrated king, Alexander III of Macedon, better known as Alexander the Great. In little over a decade, this chap changed the whole nature of the ancient world as well as inventing an early form of outsourcing. He might even have precipitated the first recorded strike in history. Alex it seems had quite a few things going for him. In his short life he developed the concept of territory annexation to an art form and as a result quickly became history's biggest empire builder. Alex to be fair had a pretty good start in life. Not only was he the son of a powerful king, but he was taught by none other than the great Aristotle of Stagira himself. And if that wasn't good enough, his lessons took place in a classroom at the Temple of the Nymphs at Mieze (Livius, 2013). It's clear that Alex had a full and well-rounded education in all senses of the word.

Alex started his empire-building campaign in 334 BC, shortly after his father died. His Dad had already built up an experienced army with the intention of doing a bit of middle-eastern land-grabbing himself. So, with a ready-made team and body full of youthful testosterone (Goodall, 2005), Alex decided to get on with the job. After assassinating some irritating heirs who were competing for the throne and subjugating a few troublesome city-states who were kicking up a fuss, he prepared to embark on his first major adventure. Persian-controlled Asia Minor was the target (biography.com, 2013). Despite being outnumbered by Persian King Darius's armies, Alex and his happy band strutted their stuff and disassembled their opponent's army in quite short order. It turns out that this new general wasn't just an expert on philosophy and nymphs. He also had quite a flair for military campaigning. By 331 BC he had vanquished Alexandria and then went on to subdue what is now eastern Iran (327 BC). Stylishly pausing only to marry the daughter of his beaten enemy (the beautiful Rhoxana), the new King of Babylon, King of Asia and King of the Four Quarters of the World, went on to give the northern Indian armies of King Porus a good going over before striking for the Ganges.

It was only then that Alexander ran into problems. Our hero found that waging constant war can be a bit wearing on your army. Even loyal soldiers get fed up of repeatedly seeing their best friends scattered in small pieces on the battlefield. Eventually Alex's army decided that enough was enough. They downed tools and may well have invented what we know today as a strike. After strong words and much squatting around battlefield campfires, the troops were eventually able to persuade their boss to head back to Macedonia.

Despite this small employee relations setback, Alex knew his mission wasn't over. Now was the time to resort to cunning tactics, he reasoned. He therefore decided to try a bit of outsourcing, though perhaps strictly speaking in today's language it was technically a "service agreement". With what can only be described as inspired genius, Alex managed to persuade the vanquished Persians to join his army. Amazingly he was somehow able to quickly recruit tens of thousands of Persian soldiers. That's a pretty massive army for those ancient days. More than a millennium later, William the Conqueror barely needed 7,000 troops to subdue Saxon Britain in 1066 (British Battles, 2013). With such a huge number of trained soldiers at his disposal Alex quickly started planning his next grand exploit. Unlike William, he didn't even need to worry about too many troublesome amphibious landings. With his army in the bag, Alex then decided that it would be a great idea to command his leading managers to marry Persian princesses. Surely, he reasoned, matching hunky Macedonian warriors together with beautiful and wealthy, high-born Persian maidens would create a ruling class and cement his power as a unifying leader? So, it appears that Alex was not only au fait with the concept of using contract resources to fill skills and manpower gaps, but he also understood that long-term outsourcing with a single partner is in effect a marriage. Alex was so enthusiastic about his new service management organisation that he took on some of their working practices and dismissed many of the senior members of the existing in-house team.

As you'd expect, Alex's depleted followers were pretty miffed with all this upheaval. While there were no such things as water-coolers to moan around in those days, they did apparently spend a great deal of time bad-mouthing the new Persian managers. Ever the diplomat, Alex responded by setting up a meeting so he could entertain the Macedonian warriors' concerns. After listening carefully, he weighed up the points made before applying his now legendary skills of tact. Calling in the Persian military leaders, he immediately killed more than a dozen of them on the spot. This, he thought, would make his own boys a little happier. But it was not to be. The Thanksgiving Feast at Susa in Persia, intended as a vehicle for improving the relationship between Persians and Macedonians, was a bit of a flat night by all accounts (biography.com, 2013).

Alas, our outsourcing hero's exploits came to a sad and sweaty end in 323 BC. Having pretty much finished the "Let's build an empire to the east" project, he thought that having a go at the west would be fun. Unfortunately, Alex is believed to have contracted malaria at this time. While he was still contemplating the annexation of Carthage and an emerging upstart civilisation called Rome, he succumbed to the disease. Tunisia and Italy sadly still remained on his "to do" list when he died.

Speaking of Rome, a few hundred years later and probably oblivious of Alexander's exploits in this field, the Romans are thought to have also dipped their sandaled toes into the seductive waters of the River Outsource. (Hirschheim, Heinzl, & Dibbern, 2009). The Romans however, seemed not to be up for glamorous outsourcing. The service that they most routinely contracted out to private enterprise was that ever-popular job of tax collection. Doubtless, they would probably have contracted out traffic police as well if cars had been invented. Tax collection, at least for the bureaucrats we understand, was not a particularly popular occupation in the far-flung reaches of the empire. It's not a surprise that the clean-cut civil servants enjoying their civilised life in the sophisticated, sun-drenched capital of the empire were reluctant to spend their short lives hassling smelly, subjugated barbarians in distant, damp, cold corners of the empire for their hard-earned denarii.

How far outsourcing penetrated into Roman culture is difficult to judge. There are rumours that in the spirit of Alex the Great, some aspects of primary military defences may also have been outsourced at certain times. But in those days, when it was possible to enslave entire continents of people just to help you put your toga on in the morning, outsourcing had only a limited appeal. While Rome burned, I would like to think that Nero may have been fiddling around with the service level agreements of a poorly contracted-out city fire service. But alas, even this appears not to be the case. The mighty emperor might have been an unpleasant hedonist, but there are no records of any Neronic outsourcing exploits that I could find. According to the Roman historian Suetonius, Nero was a bit of a thespian and a pretty mean musician. No, it appears that the leader of the western world was so moved by the sight of the great fire in Rome in AD 64 that he dressed up in the garb of a cithara player. Then he climbed to the top of the city walls while reciting a now-lost epic poem concerning the destruction of Troy (MacNamee, 2012). Imagine how much happier he would have been if there had been a contract running with an ancient, but nevertheless world-class, service provider and a set of clear performance metrics?

While Alex and Nero obviously had some pretty big ancient world problems, they were at least spared some of the challenges of today. Running data centres, providing email services or the perennial difficulties of keeping a sales force that is dispersed across several continents in close electronic contact with their bases were not such big issues in ancient times. Controlling empires was so much easier in the days before electricity and social media. So, it is hardly surprising that once the IT industry really got going in the fifties, full-blown outsourcing burst into life fairly soon afterwards.

Perhaps the first modern milestone in IT outsourcing is marked by the creation of a company known as EDS (Electronic Data Systems). Ross Perot, who was to become a future US Presidential candidate, created this exciting new company. He went on to win his first landmark IT contract in 1962 (Kakabdase, 2002). Somewhat later, mainframe suppliers of the time also worked out that they could make good money servicing the softer world as well as selling "big iron". The full religious conversion of hardware providers (or re-invention as it is known in corporate-speak) to a "services" mentality only came a little later once fashions changed and their "big iron" suddenly started to look a little rusty. IBM was a prime exponent of this new movement. Big Blue was able to increase its services revenue from 10% of its turnover in 1991 to a staggering 40% in a little more than ten years (IBM, 2002).

Over the intervening decades, outsourcing has moved in and out of fashion with a clockwork-like regularity that even Big Ben would be hard pressed to match. But despite this, the industry has nonetheless managed to grow and expand. Early outsourcing contracts often came about when internal departments were overwhelmed by escalating complexity in the IT systems portfolio. Increasing volumes of in-house application development led to a festering, plague-ridden environment of complex, non-interoperating, un-maintainable, undocumented, shock, horror, nightmare legacy systems. Grateful in-house teams found that they could dump the tedious support of their old applications into the laps of willing outsourcers. This meant that they could get on with the things that they enjoyed and were good at—creating more projects that would lead to a festering, plague-ridden environment of complex, non-interoperating, un-maintainable, undocumented, shock, horror, nightmare legacy systems.

And so the market grew. It wasn't very long before others wanted a slice of the action. Big firms and sharp suits began to play in this exciting new game of chance. Accountancies who had already developed management consulting practices quickly found that some of their assignments could be used to create beach-heads to bring in new outsourcing business. All it needed was a second-hand data centre in Middle England or Utah or perhaps a rented office block. Add a few thousand graduates in a handy offshore location and you were off and away. Today, the industry is worth hundreds of billions of dollars. The world has flattened and it seems that every Tomás, Dick and Hari has become involved in outsourcing from places as diverse as Barcelona, Boston and Bangalore (Friedman, 2005).

Strains of Outsourcing Compulsion

If we assume that you are not a member of the "outsourcing deniers school" (which has nothing to do with stockings), then you are probably going to want to give this drug a try at least at some point in your career. There are two problems you need to be aware of.

First, once you start you often cannot stop. Outsourcing is an addictive substance. Like opium and email, you may be seduced by the euphoria and well-being associated with the joy of getting rid of bits of your organisation you do not like. But care is needed. Like all addictive substances outsourcing is dangerous. As with chemical addiction, you can easily overdose or become hooked. Eventually, you will start hearing voices and be drawn to rage, depression and possibly even schizophrenia. Madness swiftly follows. Certainly the serial outsourcing IT leaders I know seem to have a strange, glazed, faraway look in their eyes—and that's even before we start drinking.

The second problem is that doing outsourcing well is, like most things in our industry, unfortunately breathtakingly difficult. You need to take a lot of puff to be a successful IT leader. Few leaders attain the status of "grand masters" of the outsourcing art. Many manage quite well, but the majority fall into the category of "challenged". This could be a case of "I wish I'd done this differently", or perhaps more seriously, "I wish I'd never ever thought of doing this but I can't admit that to anyone". There are more ways to get outsourcing wrong than you can shake a stick at. Many of these difficulties will deserve your fullest attention. Outsourcing mistakes can be terminal. But to be fair, while some of these pitfalls can result in spectacular failures, most merely cause disappointment and long-term irritation. Outsourcing, for the many clients who do not manage it well, can end up being a bit like a persistent toothache. It is irritating and painful, but they do eventually get used to it in a miserable, grudging, kind of way.

There are some common types of outsourcing compulsion addiction we can look at. As with many events in our industry, the same old things just keep on appearing again and again. Entertaining examples are not hard to find. Each one of the group that follows is based on real experiences in real companies.

Despite the wide range of different unpleasant outcomes, the tale of outsourcing compulsion screw-ups begins in much the same way each time. It usually starts off with some kind of well-intentioned trigger intended to make the world a better place. However, despite initial optimism, the story played out badly and sadly it did not lead to the happy ending that everyone was hoping for. Difficult outsourcing journeys read like a good bestselling thriller. There's usually a twisting plot. It will include a flawed hero, plenty of villains (many of whom will claim to be on your side) and an impending disaster which, unlike the movies, often runs to a pleasingly explosive and satisfying terminal conclusion. In these stories, you might possibly find yourself cast as the hero, but more often you will probably be expected to play the part of the victim.

Madness with Metrics

My own personal favourite outsourcing "war-story" occurred some years back. The company in question was struggling to maintain its profitability shortly after a stock-market reversal. Firm leadership was required. The mantra constantly repeated by the senior management was that "cost walks on two legs". It therefore wasn't long before vigorous headcount controls came into play right across the company. A dispassionate internal project team was assembled to carry out an "activity analysis" exercise. This group of young, thrusting, head-office wannabees exuded all the charm of a communist cold war secret police unit. Helpless departments were ransacked faster than the Huns cleared out Rome. Some groups were even swept away completely without leaving a single trace of their existence. Joseph Stalin himself would have been hard pressed to keep up with these young guns as they set about their work.

But like any large organism, it wasn't long before the corporate animal started developing antibodies to the alien infection. The IT Director of the day was one of the first to cook up a scheme to save his job and some of his favourite managers. He worked out that if he outsourced most of his IT department, he could claim a massive headcount reduction in his function. Given that virtually all the company's IT was currently being provided through a vast array of in-house teams, an outsourcing deal of this size would move the dial on important company metrics. Once a couple of thousand employees had "gone", graphs such as "sales-per-employee" would look really good in those tables you find in the back of Company Annual Reports. The wheeze couldn't fail. Besides, nobody was counting any other costs, because cost as we know, walks on two legs.

The IT leader's inner circle of henchmen, together with those who were deemed important enough to escape the cull, enthusiastically jumped on this wonderful new bandwagon. The anointed would leave the besieged city, banners aflutter, in a convoy of salvation, while the honest citizens of the citadel of IT would be left to their fate. Invitations to tender were quickly cobbled together. Even the thought police from head office seemed impressed. In very short order, the deal was done and the glory duly accepted by the anointed heroes of the day. Articles in glossy corporate publications detailing the wonders of what had been achieved quickly followed. Other nervous leaders started to think about following suit.

Unsurprisingly for our heroes, the odd unexpected side-effect did cause a few jolts along the way. For example, there was a massive swathe of unbudgeted transition costs. They loomed juggernaut-like out of the fog before dumping themselves heavily on the company's balance sheet. It is also true that the total cost of IT alarmingly escalated in the first few years as control was lost, confusion reigned and panic spread. But these minor inconveniences were quietly forgotten. As often happens in our industry, everyone decided that now was a good time to declare victory and move on. I recall that someone even wrote a gushing case study in a respected journal citing this debacle as an example of "best practice". Headcount was reduced and services were "professionalised". And everyone all lived happily ever after (except that there was not much happiness nor much life about).

As a casual observer you might regard this little attempt at sleight of hand with incredulity or perhaps even amusement. Logic tells you that this was a really dumb thing to do without any clear terms of reference and the hopelessly abbreviated timescales this company attempted to adhere to. However, not only do dumb things happen in large companies but they happen much more frequently than you would think. In the scary world of corporate politics, the normal laws of physics and simple rules of common sense can often be suspended for very long periods of time. Once a powerful leader has decreed a religious stance, then the organisation must choose to bow down or else revolt and face the consequences of disobedience. Most people aren't revolutionaries. More usually, people will mindlessly obey, try to please or else leave the organisation. Corporate emperors often come off the shelves without any clothes, but it can take a very long time before anyone has the gumption to point this out. It might even have to wait until the (usually inevitable) assassination, after which the next emperor takes their place on the throne and begins his or her despotic reign. If you don't believe me, consider the concepts of "risk management" and "credit-ratings" in the banking industry between the years of 2000 and 2007. Anyhow, the moral of this story is to make sure you consider all the metrics in the KPI stack very carefully and to not lose sight of an all too rare commodity in the IT world—common sense.

Giving the Fox the Keys to the Chicken Coop …

One contract worthy of note was a remnant of one of the "mega-deals" from the 1990s that I mentioned earlier. Absolutely everything had been given away in those heady days of outsourcing opium. In this deal, anyone whose job title had the most tenuous link with IT found themselves either out on their ear or else rapidly transferred to the outsourcer (that old air-lock story again). The original intention of the leadership had been to pass the baton from a self-confessed, struggling in-house team to a "professional" IT outsourcing company. The plan was that the deal should result in lower costs and higher capability. In return, the outsourcer would receive a very long-term contract with exclusive rights to supply services. The client was very positive about his outsourcer at the outset and seemed content to hand a great deal of control to his bright, shiny, enthusiastic new partner. The leadership believed that everything could simply be overseen on the client side by little more than a manager and a secretary. IT can't be that hard to manage—surely? Some might say that this was a classic example of giving the fox the keys to the chicken coop, but it did have certain advantages. In the early years, this arrangement did a great job of dealing with the never-ending problem of never-ending user demand. It was very simple. IT costs were dumped on the department that asked for anything. So, every time those pesky users wanted a new project, the outsourcing company produced a young, smart "business development manager" in a shiny suit. He or she licked their pencil and produced a quote that had an uncomfortable number of zeros on it. People quickly thought again about living without that departmental database they believed they could not live without. There were of course, also "good" advantages. Service management was improved and the reliability of the computing estate benefited from genuine leveraged best practice. This outsourcer company was actually very good at running services. Some strict discipline around change control and a reduction in the amount of fiddling (without any sign of an emperor, a cithara or indeed a fire) meant that services stayed up and work got done.

> **"When you are skinning your customers, you should leave**
> **some skin on to grow again so that you can skin them again."**
> *Nikki Giovanni*

There were, however, also many downsides. Whilst having power is of course great fun, it does inevitably corrupt. So when you've got an exclusive contract with a dumb customer, it isn't long before some bright spark in the management ranks thinks that it is high time such advantages should be cashed in. In fact it's inevitable when the account team are given aggressive revenue growth and profit targets. In this example, operating costs eventually skyrocketed and frustration built up on each side. For the client, IT seemed to be spinning out of control with ever-increasing maintenance costs exacerbated by soaring budget demands from the user community. For the outsourcer, the situation was extremely complicated. There were multiple touch points where myriads of computer users made their demands. This meant that the outsourcer was doomed to implement many, many point solutions to the many, many point requests that were raining down upon them like cascading shards of pumice spewing from a violently erupting, unpronounceable Icelandic volcano. The user community, terrified by the prospect that large project costs would be dumped on their departmental budgets, responded by specifying increasingly smaller-scale systems in ever greater numbers. An ocean of infinite demand was being boiled a kettle at a time. The increasingly desperate client leadership eventually attempted to arrest increasing costs by capping the IT budget. However, operating costs continued to rise as the plethora of dis-coordinated small systems and incomplete projects proved cripplingly expensive to run. This trend meant that investment spending would be completely squeezed out in very short order. A catastrophic end-game was creeping closer with a sense of horrible inevitability. Alfred Hitchcock would have been proud of the pace of the plot. The moral of this story is that you have to be an intelligent customer to get the best out of your outsourcer. In this example, IT operating costs were spreading across the Serengeti like a plague of locusts, consuming everyone and everything in their path. Both parties wanted resolution but neither could see how they could get themselves out of it. Being an intelligent buyer is an essential ingredient for any antidote to problems like this. And as for "exclusive" IT arrangements, there is only one way to handle this concept when contracts are being created. Exclusive arrangements should simply be exclusively excluded from any negotiations, exclusively.

The Nineteenth Hole Contract

Global outsourcing is now big business. Now that the leaders of such organisations have become big fishes in the corporate ocean, it's almost certain that big fishes of the outsourcing companies will eventually bump into the big fishes in your company. I recall this happening some years ago to one very unfortunate large corporate. It was difficult for me to listen to the curiously compelling stories of friends who worked there without wincing and feeling the need to buy them consolatory drinks. The organisation in question was having extreme difficulty integrating two very different cultures after a tricky global merger. The story, as it was told to me by an insider, tells of how the CEO of the client company accidentally bumped into a big outsourcing cheese. They were playing a golf foursome one afternoon on a beautifully manicured course on the East Coast of the US. It was a lovely day. Cigars were lit, buggies were stocked with beer, the sun was shining and for once it wasn't too humid. The caddies even knew where the bunkers were. As the day drew on and the shadows lengthened, conversation eventually turned to work issues. "My IT is bugging me" was the trigger phrase that started it all off. The CEO was sick and tired of all the infighting between the newly merged IT functions he had inherited. As the CEO lined up for his final putt, the outsourcing big cheese lifted the flag, pulled his cigar out from his clenched teeth and said. "Let us sort it out. We are the best in the world at this IT stuff you know." It took little more than a couple of gin and tonics on the nineteenth hole before the outline of a deal was quickly shaped. "That'll teach them" were doubtless the parting thoughts of the CEO as he watched his golf bag being loaded into the corporate Mercedes.

> **"If you think your boss is stupid, remember: you wouldn't have a job if he was any smarter."**
> *John Got*

The chaos that ensued was highly entertaining, at least for anyone who was watching from the outside. I'm still not sure that everything has settled down today although more than a decade has passed. The key point here is that if an IT leader ever becomes detached from other members of the executive in any way, shape or form then they are running some serious health risks (Dislocated Stakeholders alert!). A loosely coupled IT leader is a fattened goat as far as those who promote outsourcing sacrifice are concerned. Any absence in connectedness is a very bad thing. It means that the CIO may not be involved in corporate decision making in any meaningful way. It isn't hard to see what that particular end-game looks like—irrelevance or expulsion are the two most common.

One of the great achievements of certain outsourcing companies is their ability to attain much higher levels of credibility than you yourself could ever wish for, despite their many and varied well-publicised disasters. The question you have to ask yourself is this: Is it because of stupendous marketing on their part or because of poor communication by you? But the moral here is simple. Show leadership, stay close to your leadership colleagues and make sure that your strategy is aligned with the company's goals. Take great care to make your colleagues understand what you are doing (especially the unpleasant stuff). If everything in your world can be changed by a few words on a golf course, then you obviously need to learn how to play golf.

> **"Only in his hometown and in his own house is a prophet without honour."**
> *The Bible, Matthew 13, 56:58 New International Version*

Dedicated Followers of Fashion

There was a time some years ago when outsourcing, at least in my corner of the world, was really considered trendy. The fashion pendulum was firmly welded to the "outsourcing is the greatest thing since sliced bread" side of the argument. The CIO at the time wanted to do some outsourcing because he thought it would be considered "fashionable" by the rest of the inhabitants of mahogany row. He told us that word from the home of thick carpets, tea-cups, doilies, finger buffets and executive-only washrooms was that "everyone is getting benefit from outsourcing" (though no data were forthcoming to support this lofty assertion). The inevitable logic was that his organisation should do it as well, lest they be "left behind". Knowing all the players, my suspicion was that he was being pushed into this by the CEO who'd almost certainly read a gushing article on outsourcing from an in-flight magazine. It's surprising how much company strategy comes from the sticky seat-back pockets of commuter airlines. Once again we were faced with that familiar old fight of corporate will versus logic and common sense. And we know who always wins that one, at least until the cold light of hard reality eventually gets its trousers on and kicks you in the butt.

So, within days, a specialist outsourcing assessment consultancy was duly hired and work began on constructing the PowerPoint presentation. To the astonishment of most of the senior IT management, the whole engagement was directed exclusively and entirely at collecting information which would be used solely to populate a pre-designed deck of PowerPoint slides.

"Fashions, after all, are only induced epidemics."
George Bernard Shaw

At first, many thought that this was a joke. Unfortunately, the joke was on them as they rapidly became slaves to the process, expending man-decades of effort in their organisations. Armies of people collected and analysed information so that bullet point 3 on Slide 24 could be completed to the consultant's satisfaction. What was even more disappointing was that the outcome had already been decided long before they even started the exercise. Initial discussions with the CIO and CEO had given the consultants enough clues as to what an "acceptable" answer would be. Everyone was being programmed to simply collect the evidence to support the view that something should be outsourced.

The work was duly completed, the presentation made and the decision was made to go on an outsourcing spree. It's a shame that nobody had considered in advance which services should be outsourced or even what the value proposition for such outsourcing should be. Still, everyone was happy and it had to make sense. There was even an eighty-four slide PowerPoint pack and a five million dollar consultancy bill to prove it.

The moral here for you as an IT leader is to make sure you aren't treating your organisation as if it were fashion accessory. And you certainly should not ever make anyone do useless, nugatory work. You'll lose credibility with your staff very quickly. You'll also end up with a particular outcome simply because everyone thinks that is what you want—irrespective of whether it makes sense or not. When everything does eventually blow up in your face (and it invariably will), you'll notice that everyone is looking the other way and that your best people have probably already left. After the event, you will be left as high and dry as an emperor's new clothing merchant.

Finance is not about Engineering Anything

Unfortunately, we cannot complete a discussion on the subject of outsourcing without facing up to the elephant in the room we know as financing. Many outsourcing deals have been put together entirely on the basis of financial engineering. The full horrors of this practice need to be understood, even in the hangover years since the 2008 financial crash. Things may not be as bad today as they were in the nineties or in the run-up to the crash, but history does have a funny habit of repeating itself. We must all therefore remain vigilant. Corporate amnesia is a very common ailment and no company is immune from this type of dementia.

In the course of normal business, revenue recognition should be a plain and simple affair. You should get to recognise your revenues when they are realised or realisable after they are earned. In simple terms, you put your notch on the scoreboard when cash is received, no matter when the goods or services were sold. However, if you are executing a contract over a very long period, life can be much harder. This is exacerbated if the outsourcing company is making up-front investments in the client's IT estate. It can be very punishing for the outsourcer after they have won the business. Even attractive new contracts can create massive dips in profitability in the early years. Boards, shareholders and the market don't like this. Rollercoaster financials and potentially hollow promises from executive management mean nothing to them. They much prefer steady and predictable growth in sales, improving profitability and increasing backlog. So when it comes to long-term contracts, booking profit around concepts such as "percentage of completion" has become popular with management.

> **"Business is not financial science, it's about trading, buying and selling. It's about creating a product or service so good that people will pay for it."**
> *Anita Roddick, Founder of the Bodyshop*

As with many things in life, financing complex contracts started with lots of good intentions and far too much optimism. Clients often look to outsourcing arrangements because it is hoped that they will make the costs of IT go down. Figure 4.1 shows the simple value proposition from the client perspective. Clients won't believe stories of massive savings in the out-years. They will want action now. As far as they are concerned, savings should flow before the ink has dried on their outsourcing contract.

Figure 4.1 shows the dilemma facing outsourcing companies. If an internal IT organisation can deliver services for a cost represented by the zero horizontal line, then the outsourcers will have to offer immediate savings in order to grab the client's attention. This will be a major problem. The poor

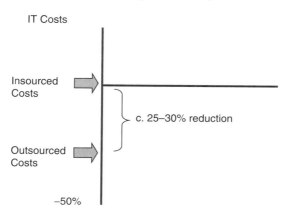

Figure 4.1   The Reason Why People Outsource

unfortunates, who have been parachuted in to work their magic, will have an insurmountable challenge in Year 1. Any outsourcing deal will require a certain element of transition costs. It will take a period of time for even the best team of superheroes to wring efficiencies out of client IT budgets. It doesn't matter how flabby the in-house team have become. If the outsourcing company already has a mature shared service model that they can bring to bear, it might be possible. Some standardised services might be put in place fairly promptly. But this is not easy. It would require most of the internal staff to be removed or retrained, leading to expensive severance costs and much grief in the employee relations arena. Indeed in many countries, employment laws seem to be designed explicitly to prevent such large-scale action being taken. Timescales can be often measured in geological periods. In some places you may be hard pressed to get anything done before humanity becomes extinct.

Just to make life even more difficult for our outsourcing heroes, their client's account will need to take its fair share of the corporate overhead of the outsourcing company itself. Finally, the accountants and senior managers at Outsourcing High Command will of course expect a profit to be made. So in short, while the finances of Year 1 of an outsourcing deal need to look stunning from the client's perspective, they will look terrible if you are one of the unfortunate heroes that must deliver on all these promises. The diagram from the outsourcer's perspective actually looks more like Figure 4.2.

To help what could seem like an impossible situation, the accountants often resort to various forms of financing to "spread the load" as they would describe it. Since the nineties, the whole science of financing, or to use the

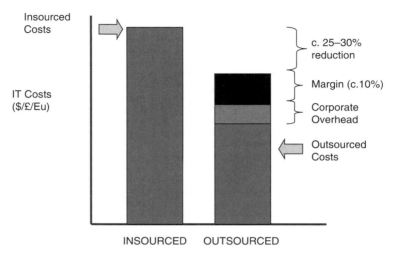

Figure 4.2   The Difficult Job of the Outsourcer

more accurate term "massive, risky loans", reached epidemic proportions. Money was lent to client organisations to fund outsourcing transitions. Some outsourcing companies even borrowed money themselves with the intention of paying it back from profits in the out-years of the deal. For my part, I am one of those simpletons who don't like loans. I also cling to the belief that you only recognise revenue when you have it in the bank. An outsourcing arrangement I once came across was mind-bogglingly complex in the financial engineering sense. Due to the labyrinthine nature of the financing, it seems the outsourcing supplier everyone thought they were using wasn't the outsourcer at all. A consortium of foreign banks, it turned out, was actually responsible for the contract. They had then sub-contracted the services to the outsourcer. The opacity of the arrangement was as bewildering and complex as it was unsatisfying. Everyone was happy once it was all over, although this did not happen until more than a decade had passed. Nobody on the client side understood what the contract was all about. Fortunately, the outsourcing side was just as perplexed, so as with all good local derbies, this one ended up as an ugly draw.

Contract Accounting and Runaway Trains

Perhaps the most dangerous financial engineering trick that lies in wait for you out there is the monster known as contract accounting. Mercifully, the financial crash of 2008 and subsequent financial hangover has also caused these types of arrangements to be seen much less frequently in the wild. But despite this, they are so dangerous that the diligent IT leader needs to learn how to spot them forming and stay well clear.

Figure 4.3 is a further development of the value proposition figures shown above. An x-axis has been added to show how costs are changing over time. In this model, a ten year contract is shown. The savings of the first few years (which probably represent losses to the outsourcing company) are made up in the out-years by elevated charges. This is so that the outsourcer makes a good profit over the full life of the contract. Big profits in the out-years cancel out the losses of the early years. The shaded boxes however show the level of profit the outsourcer is booking to their accounts each year. With cute financial engineering, clever accountants can show profits while money is actually going out of the door for the outsourcer. This leads to unpleasant concepts such as "unbilled" expenditure, where losses in the early years will need to be made good later.

These types of arrangements are usually long (and arduous) and I run into them more often than I expect. They often extend beyond the tenure of more than one IT leader, so there's plenty of time for the scourge of corporate amnesia to fog the situation. Indeed when such contracts move towards their end-game, it's entirely possible that everyone has gone. The situation

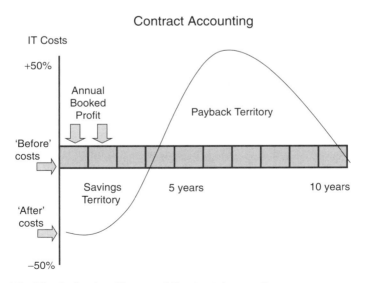

Figure 4.3 The Seductive Charms of Contract Accounting

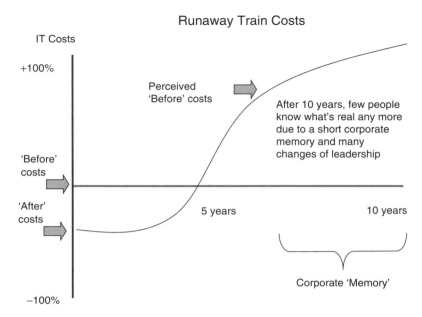

Figure 4.4   Runaway Trains and Corporate Amnesia

is exacerbated further because many heavily outsourced organisations suffer very high levels of turnover in their already scanty, in-house staff. The original rationale for the contract, all the complex logic behind it and any other agreements often get lost in the mists of time, particularly as generations of managers swing through the revolving doors of corporate employment. Incoming IT leaders who inherit such contracts must therefore be vigilant for a wide range of gotchas. The most common problem that flows from these types of arrangements is the "runaway train" contract. Figure 4.4 shows a further development of the contract accounting model described above. A runaway train has taken to the rails. The cost line never comes back to any sensible level, even at the end of the contract. Costs just keep on rising. And because corporate memory is so short, it is likely that there is hardly anyone left who knows anything about what was expected to happen. More often, incoming IT leaders just build their estimates based on last year's budget actuals and hope they can stop the train going any faster.

> **"This budget is like an Enron budget—smoke the numbers,**
> **cook the books, hide the truth and hope no-one finds out."**
> *Sen. John Kerry*

Faster than a Speeding Bullet ...

Before embarking on any new habit that can be addictive, it is often wise to stop and think about the reasons for doing it. By choosing to outsource, you are giving up work to other organisations because you think they can do it better than people on the company payroll. This can be checked by asking three good questions (the third of which I particularly recommend):

1. Can the outsourcer do it better than us?
2. Can the outsourcer do it cheaper than us?
3. Can the outsourcer do it better and cheaper than us?

These are tough questions to ask and they are even tougher to answer honestly. Should you ask your in-house team, then they will inevitably give you three big NO's. You have very little chance indeed of getting any positive views. It is a classic case of turkeys voting for Thanksgiving. These poor souls have mortgages after all. If you commission consultants, there is a danger that they will try to work out what "acceptable answer" space looks like. They may then give you a beautifully presented answer that conforms to those prejudices. If the CEO commissions consultants without including you, then the answer will of course be three big YES's. Your job will probably be the first to go.

So the best way to deal with this problem is to try to switch off your biases and carefully think about it from first principles. The three questions above essentially identify two major tenets of outsourcing. I submit that you either need a "capability" argument or an "economic" argument before you embark on such a journey. The answer will be different for each organisation. Large corporates may decide that they have sufficient mass and expertise to blunt or nullify capability or economic outsourcing arguments. Others on the other hand will relish the chance to offload non-core functions. Small or medium-sized enterprises (SMEs) may also have different views between them. Some will want to access outsourcing capability rather than build it themselves. Meanwhile, others, perhaps mindful of cash-flow challenges, may want to work with an in-house team that can be swiftly flexed in size as revenues go up and down.

The Capability Argument

Any home improvement activities I attempt end up going so badly wrong that they endanger both my personal safety and my marriage. As far as DIY is concerned my own capability levels are quite frankly, pitiful. So when it comes to home improvement, there is no cost equation here for us to explore at all. If I want a nice home, then my only option is to outsource all the wallpapering, bathroom fitting and any other decorating activities to someone who knows how to do it. As I learned from my exploits on the first house I owned, if I do things myself then what we get is both amateurish and unpleasant. I have learned that a professional wallpaper company for example, can do the job not only to a level of quality to which I could simply not aspire in a million years, but they also do it very quickly. And they only seem to do it the once (whereas it takes me many iterations). The comparison between this and the endless weekends of repeated applications of wonky wallpaper, cracked shower trays and the ever-present bleeding fingers is very stark. When my spouse sucks her teeth, composes herself, puts on her best poker face and finally says "It doesn't look that bad really", it feels a very poor reward for my endless hours of incompetent toil. The capability argument is simple. If someone out there has a track record of being really good at doing something and you need that same something doing really well then why wouldn't you make the call?

The Economic Argument

The economic argument for outsourcing is also simple. Basically, if the outsourcer can do the work more cheaply than you can do it yourself, why would you not use them? Doing so either leaves you with more profit or money with which you can do other good things. No matter how good you are at home improvements, you'd never bother to fabricate your own screws before you started to put up that shelf. It's much easier and cheaper to buy them from a hardware store. In IT, you do of course have to be careful that you are not being taken for a ride with financial accounting games as described above. However, it is possible for an outsourcing company to achieve significantly more efficient operations in a number of areas. This is usually possible for at least two good reasons.

(a) They will have learned how to do the job well because they are already doing it for a number of other clients and have been doing so for some considerable time.
(b) They may have industrialised the process so that they have found a way of doing the equivalent of "mass-producing" the service.

But it is tough for them. Remember that they have to make a profit and deal with their own overhead headwinds. This means that you should look closely at the economic arguments and satisfy yourself that the prices you are being quoted are real. But be aware of the perils of Financial Engineering. This is the place where you are likely to hear the first distant roar of this monster as it stealthily creeps through the jungle towards you.

Better Out than In?

I believe that you can get the best results from outsourcing if you think about it from an economic or a capability perspective. With this method you are at least applying brainpower to what you are doing and considering why you are doing it (which is more than can be said for many IT departments around the world). It is sometimes possible to build good business cases directly from either economic or capability arguments but more commonly you will end up with a mixture of the two. The various options can be boiled down to a shortlist of four rationales for outsourcing depending on the economic or capability mix. For me, the list is as follows and it gives four clear value propositions, all of which have worked for me in real-life situations:

- Commodity items
- Economy of scale
- Niche, specialist skills
- Well-controlled processes that can be tightly controlled remotely.

Commodity Items

Commodity items are those where there is a simple economic argument for outsourcing. Others can do the work more cheaply than you can do it yourself. Typically, these are fairly standard work packages. They tend to be mature, well recognised outsourcing tasks and lots of companies quite correctly indulge in this type of outsourcing. This means that there are plenty of suppliers available who could do this work. The suppliers will also vigorously compete between one another, leading to keen prices. Services in this category are usually very well defined and well understood (which of course makes them perfect candidates for commodity outsourcing). Commodity represents the lowest risk and probably the most successful types of contract in the outsourcing market. Examples of commodity items include computer operator services (backup and recovery), hardware support and local deskside support. Typically, commodity outsourcing areas are not the most technically or organisationally demanding to manage. You should also be able to switch supplier relatively quickly should you ever run into difficulty with a poor practitioner.

Economy of Scale

The economy of scale proposition is pretty much a 50:50 split between the capability and economic arguments. It works well when suppliers have industrialised their processes. In essence, they do the same stuff as you, except that they do it on a grand scale. This means you can be assured that they can not only do the work, but that they are also able to do it at a competitive unit cost. In these areas, standardisation, high levels of competence and a continuous improvement ethos can give an outsourcer an edge. These factors should have allowed the outsourcing company to comprehensively outperform any in-house cottage-industry solution that your own team could ever provide. Areas worth considering under this value proposition include wholesale management of data centres and provision of standardised service offerings (such as the office suite, email or standard application services). Indeed many of your infrastructure services might also usefully be dealt with by outsourcers who are able to deliver economies of scale (e.g. telecoms, networks, mainframe services, systems programming etc.). Large-scale standardised deployment programs, such as a new desktop operating system roll-out, might also fall into this category.

Niche Items

Outsourcing niche items is all about capability acquisition. The value proposition here is that you recognise that you need specialist skills, but you also realise that it is not worth keeping people on the payroll to do this work. This could be because the skills are only required for a short period, or perhaps because you only need small numbers of staff with those skills. Placing gurus in your organisation might be a fine thing to do, but if your gurus aren't any good, you can end up with very strange types of religion.

Niche items can be satisfied via hiring contract staff, traditional outsourcing or sometimes even by consultancy assignments. Consultancy engagements should of course be kept short to avoid excessive costs. Typical areas to consider here include deep systems programming expertise, specialist applications expertise (e.g. Materials Resource Planning (MRP), Customer Relationship Management (CRM) or some other critical application) or perhaps middleware layers such as exotic database languages. In all cases, there should be a demanding level of expertise which can't be satisfied by the generalists in your organisation. The downside of course is that niche skills usually attract premium rates. Someone who knows a leading MRP package inside-out, for example, can command exceptionally high day rates. It is always the case that if you want to buy some seriously heavyweight expertise, then you have to seriously pay for it. And take care. You must have sufficient expertise to know that you are truly buying expert advice. Be an intelligent buyer so that you can spot the stuffed suit with a silver tongue who isn't what you think they are.

Well-controlled Processes—Business Process Outsourcing

This area would fall into what the outsourced would recognise as BPO (Business Process Outsourcing). The concept of BPO got very hot indeed in the late 1990s and early 2000s, particularly when coupled with the concept of off-shoring. If you have processes in your organisation that are very well understood and you believe you can effectively manage them from afar, then there is no reason why you cannot consider outsourcing such processes—lock, stock and barrel. This outsourcing proposition critically depends on whether the process is sufficiently well understood, and whether your metrics management process allows you to control it with sufficient precision. You will not only need to keep things running smoothly, but your measurement system must be able to rapidly spot problems and deal with them promptly. The typical BPO outsource deal is mainly a commodity argument. This lends itself to off-shoring or near-shoring or any other kind of shoring where the costs of labour are competitive. Typically, BPO activities started off with very well understood processes such as payroll or accounts payable. More recently, it has become popular to outsource helpdesks and aspects of technical support and place them abroad. Other areas include human resources transaction functions such a hiring, firing, benefits management etc. In all cases, there have to be strong processes and high levels of standardisation or else it will all probably end in tears.

Protecting the Crown Jewels

Having decided that we are going to try our luck with a bit of outsourcing, are there any parts of the organisation which we should exclude? Are there any Crown Jewels out there that must be defended at all costs? Do we need to build a Tower of London and employ men and women (who apparently have to eat beef) to protect our most precious tasks? Once again, we spark a debate of demonic ferocity. Everyone will have a view.

In large corporates, most people's view of Crown Jewels will almost certainly be intensely parochial. People will worry about the trinkets in their own little velvet box rather than the massive diamonds, orbs, swords, rings, spurs, colobium sindonis, armills and of course the royal pall of the wider corporation. Such misconceptions do not occur because people are malicious. Rather, those engaged in the daily grind, competing to win budget money in their own little corner of the organisation, will simply be prepared to fight to the death for their small patch of turf. It's part of the DNA of being a middle manager in any organisation. Few (if any) may take the wider view.

I recall a great example of parochialism. It happened several years ago in a pharmaceutical company. A team was involved in developing a disaster recovery strategy for the corporation. The first task was to define the "mission critical" applications in the company. This would then be used to determine the order in which the applications would be returned should the data centre ever become the proverbial smoking crater. You know the traditional "disaster" scenario. The mangled remains of the building would be surrounded by ambulances and fire engines together with their blue flashing lights. Hordes of television cameras would be present while blanket-clad, shocked victims lay shivering in their tattered clothes. The initial approach in this exercise was to interview all the key stakeholders across the business. The team intended to gather the strength of the leaders' opinions as well as challenging them over the relative importance of their systems. They thought that this would allow them to build up a credible initial batting order for recovery. However, the outcome they ended up with was at once incredible, definitive, comical and sad (which were none of the adjectives they were hoping for). When the results were in, it turned out that the very first system the survivors of Armageddon would be bringing back was the "inter-library loan" system. Meanwhile, clinical trials systems monitoring patient welfare, critical company financial systems, control systems for pilot plants that were making nasty microbes and even databases of precious company secrets all appeared well down the batting list, together with many other worthy contenders. If you have ever met a set of intransigent librarians you will understand how it happened. Emotive topics such as disaster recovery can be all about the people and how strongly they feel. Happily, the team eventually swallowed a large dose of common sense tablets. They went back to the drawing board and restarted the whole exercise with a more sensible Terms of Reference. This led them to a more realistic list and the wheels were back on the rails once more. The one thing that united the team at the end of this project, however, was an overwhelming desire to outsource the library and everyone in it.

So, with more answers to this problem than there are people, things will be different for you. My advice is to follow the two mantras outlined below and then see what happens. If, by chance, inter-library loans systems pop up high on the radar, then you know that your work is not yet finished.

In terms of choosing what activities you should do yourself, I have learned that there are two important mantras you must follow. They are that …

- You should retain control of your destiny irrespective of how much outsourcing you have done.
- Anything the internal team can do better than an outsourcer should remain in-house.

With those thoughts in mind and the four value propositions for outsourcing (commodity, economy of scale, niche and well-controlled processes) you now at least have a framework from which you can build a strategy. From this you have a chance of making rational and defensible decisions. It's not an answer, but it is a start.

When I applied those criteria to my world, the top four "do not outsource" items on my list come out as follows

1. Business analysis
2. Strategy
3. Architecture
4. Project management.

You will almost certainly end up with a different list to this, but that doesn't matter. The solutions you define will tend to be more rational, sensible and defensible, though admittedly this type of approach is considerably less satisfying and a lot less fun than simply implementing large-scale change guided only by your own impulses, prejudices and despotic biases.

No. 1 Business Analysis

Top of my list is Business analysis. This would be the very last part of my organisation that I would outsource (and even then I would be kicking and screaming). Many of the outsourcing companies struggle to run their own businesses well so it mystifies me that they might think that they could provide deep and profound business insight into anyone else's organisation. Business analysis is all about understanding the business in great detail and being able to build requirements which will allow step-change improvement projects to be constructed. In fact, really good business analysts in my experience aren't IT people at all. They are business people who have as complete a grasp of your business processes as any mortal person could possibly hold. Weak business people who like to play with IT do not count! Indeed, if you are in what I would regard as the leading vanguard of modern IT leaders, you will have already gathered your process specialists together into competency centres, defining process-led change projects that will transform the enterprise. It's important to note that most IT applications projects aren't IT projects at all. They are business change programs. IT itself is at best a small (but nonetheless critical) component of most corporate change initiatives.

No. 2 Strategy

Strategy comes a very close second on my list. Identifying a vision for the future and defining a master plan to help you get there is not something I believe any IT leader should outsource. If anyone is to have a Bond-villain master-plan to take over the world, then it has to be you. The vision and the plan or strategy to carry you there are probably the single most important elements of an IT leaders role. If you do not feel this way, go directly to the bottom of the pile, do not pass GO and do not collect any money at all. That is because somebody else should be doing your job. By all means get specialist help from experts to help you formulate your strategy, but the strategy itself has to be yours and yours alone.

No. 3 Architecture

While Business analysis and Strategy vie for the top of my "must be done in-house list", there is clear blue water before Architecture appears. Architecture is something that outsourcing companies ought to be able to do well. However, many seem to struggle with it. I do not understand why this happens because it is very much in their interests to offer up architectures that allow a standardised, flexible framework to be built. Operating standardised services is a great way to make good profit. In almost every arrangement I have inherited, however, I have found an unholy mish-mash of trendy and ancient technologies. Each appears to have been implemented in an almost playground-like environment by capricious project managers who seem to have their own favourite ways of doing things. Some commentators have even referred to the resultant mess as a "hairball" (Kobielus, 2010; Feld, 2009). In one contract I managed, I found that fights had broken out between different factions within the outsourcer. My computing environment became a battleground where these people got to exercise their testosterone-rich and fact-poor technical hypotheses. Moreover, once the user community began to assert their own amateur biases, which bizarrely became mixed into the arguments, we ended up with a stunning number of incompatible point solutions. The mess was complicated by a bewildering blizzard of technologies. The completely disastrous muddle that ensued took years to straighten out. To avoid this happening to you, I would strongly recommend you define a multi-year architecture based around simple principles. Then make everyone stick to it—under pain of death (or whatever is appropriate and legal in your jurisdiction).

No. 4 Project Management

Successful project management is crucially important to CIO success. The thought of giving this critical area away to outsourcing organisations who have cheerfully spent hundreds of millions and sometimes even billions of dollars of hard-earned private or hard-taxed government money failing to deliver relatively simple administration systems doesn't make it to my "must do this morning" list. In the outsourcer's defence, many internal organisations are often no better. I have only been able to implement really massive large-scale change projects with high quality project managers who have been drawn from other areas of the business. The argument for project management is very clear to me, but in terms of value proposition it's all about managing the capability very, very closely indeed. It's much easier to do this with your own team and it's much easier to do it with people who (a) really know what they are doing and (b) don't give a stuff about the technology and all the mysteries within. Great project managers are people who make things happen. They are not generally particularly nice nor are they reasonable people; they're a teensy bit Stalinist in fact. That said, I think you need lots of them, you need good ones (preferably qualified with professional qualifications) and you need them on *your* payroll.

Everyone Needs to Win

Win-wins are not that hard to get into as long as you are honest with your outsourcer. At the end of the day, the outsourcer's needs are pretty simple to work out. They will want contracts that last as long as possible, they want to make good money and they'd quite like to have a happy customer who makes a good reference account. That means that they can go out and win more business on the back of their successes and start the cycle all over again. This is a good thing for all parties. The problem of revenue growth mentioned earlier might start to put them at odds with you at least in terms of spending levels. However, this can be countered if they can be made to understand the constraints you are under (and provided you have all the correct controls in place of course).

Here are some useful hints that might help you get into a better relationship with your outsourcer. I learned most of this from the "school of hard knocks", where things went very wrong before they got anywhere near being nearly right. Your organisation will doubtless be different, but you might just find one or two elements in here that look familiar enough to be transferable into your battleground.

- **Goal alignment**—Make sure you understand the outsourcer's corporate goals, their goals for the account and the way in which their staff are incentivised. If anything doesn't work for you, then get it changed. There's no point having the account team's variable pay (bonus) purely linked to growth in business if you are trying to cut back your IT budget. Cascading your own in-house management goals to the outsourcing team is something that is well worth considering. It has worked really well for me on more than one occasion.

- **Transparency**—Keep transparency levels as high as possible. This means you are going to (shock, horror) have to understand the true costs for running a service. You should aim to find out what the outsourcer's profit level targets are and also the level of corporate overhead they are expected to take from their masters back at Outsourcing High Command. This will help you to spot when you are being reasonable and when you are not. Listen to your dear outsourcing partner when he or she moans about all the problems they are enduring. Now is not the time to play the big bad customer. Darkly telling them that you are not interested in issues in their world isn't particularly "teamy". Such an action will only lead to a situation where you cannot be sure that anything that they are ever telling you from now on is true. Beating up a supplier is of course great fun, but it usually doesn't help you achieve your company's goals.

- **Incentives**—Don't be afraid to set the price book for your projects and services in such a way that it encourages everyone to follow your carefully prepared strategy. Once I stumbled across a simple trick in a recent outsourcing deal which turned out to be a stunning game-changer. The team was struggling with operational cost increases in a difficult contract. The solution turned out to be jaw-droppingly simple, though to be fair I certainly didn't realise at the time quite how powerful this method would be. The price-book in the contract was redefined so that all the operational costs would be serviced to the client at the cost price to the outsourcer. The balance of spending up to an agreed cap in IT costs would then be used for new investment which the outsourcer would source. Both parties liked this. The new investments would be carried out at higher margins on the one hand, while everyone tried to take out operational costs on the other. In essence, the more operational costs the outsourcer took out, the more projects were initiated and the more money they made. Within 24 months, the situation was stunningly transformed. Investment spending was rising at impressive rates. Meanwhile, operational costs were falling out of the trees and bouncing across the water-front like over-ripe mangos on a sun-drenched Caribbean beach. Within a three year period, the IT budget was reduced by nearly 40%, while investment spending had tripled against the baseline. The main problem with this little trick was that it fixed the situation so quickly that everyone was completely unprepared for the huge increases in investment that became available. As a result, both parties started running into hideous capability shortfalls in the projects area—both for the outsourcer and the in-house staff. The absence of any large, highly skilled set of project management shock troops that could be parachuted in to take on the projects ended up being a real problem for everyone. The only thing we all agreed on was that in the world of horrible IT problems, this was probably a good one to have.

■ **Skills**—Do push the transparency argument into the skills arena. Outsourcing companies are not stuffed to the gunwales with thousands of A-Team quality staff. Sure, you get to see the cream of the crop in the pre-contract mating dance. But this can't last. The outsourcer is going to have to play some members of their B and C-Teams into the game at some stage. It is unrealistic for you to monopolise their A-Team until the end of time (though it is certainly fun to try), so you should accept a mix as long as it does the job for you. Make sure you and the outsourcer are actively managing the people into and off the account together. Don't simply think this is the account manager's problem. His masters back at Outsourcing High Command are dedicated to making his or her life a misery. They will want to feed in as many weak players as they can get away with, jealously guarding their elite troops so that they can be used to shore up problems in contracts elsewhere. The account manager's problem is your problem. If you are a demanding but fair customer, then in my experience you stand a good chance of getting the best out of your outsourcer.

■ **External benchmarking**—In an engineering company where I once worked, one of my outsourcing partner's account managers was very worried about losing the contract. A re-tender was coming up for grabs in a couple of years' time and let us just say that everything wasn't exactly rosy in the garden. In fact there were few if any roses in there. Most of the garden was a wasteland filled with weeds, black-spot, manure and plenty of desperation. The answer we came up with was to implement a vigorous external benchmarking exercise. The rationale was quite simple. If the outsourcer could prove that the services and projects were being carried out at genuinely top-drawer levels of cost, quality and performance, then he would have an inside track when the renewal came up. Setting the bar high is never a bad thing as long as you give people a ladder and some time to train. Moreover, the benchmarking data also provide a sound basis for making decisions. If the incumbent was genuinely performing at top-class levels, then it became much easier to spot "loss leader" bids from their scheming competitors. If, of course, the outsourcer couldn't get to the highest levels of performance by the time of the renewal, then it was pretty obvious what was going to happen. They would have only themselves to blame. Outsourcing companies hate losing contracts to their competitors so it didn't take long before we heard the drone of Douglas DC3s, all converging on our city, Before long the skies bloomed with scores of billowing parachutes as "help" in the form of shock troops from Outsourcing High Command floated in. One other trick that can also work well is to ask the outsourcer to pay for half the benchmarking fees. This gives the benchmarking organisation permission to tell the client a few uncomfortable home truths. Feedback, as they say, is a gift. Finally, you should pick your benchmarking company carefully. There are only a few organisations that do this kind of work to the very highest professional levels and you need to know who they are.

"Relationships are like glass. Sometimes it's better to leave them broken than try to hurt yourself putting it back together."
Anon.

In Summary

As you've probably noticed, there is a great deal that can go wrong with outsourcing. However, arrangements can also work well. Nevertheless, many people are often not prepared to accept the very high level of work required on both the client and supplier sides of the fence. Managing a complex outsourcing arrangement can sometimes even take more time and effort than running an equivalent in-house operation. Outsourcing engagements never, ever go well when clients abdicate their responsibilities to the outsourcer so that they can get on with the more interesting parts of their jobs. This process—known as "dumping"—is far too common in the industry. Naïve outsourcers, keen to grab as much of the pie as they can, will often eagerly accept this unsatisfactory state of affairs without question. It isn't long, however, before they will become puzzled and disillusioned. For angry, frustrated customers will soon swan in with baseball bats and beat them about the head. This is not what they expected when they were taught about client relationships at outsourcing training academies.

Finally, any smart outsourcing client will look for experienced outsourcing partners with a successful track record. This is essential before he or she starts the mating dance known as the invitation to tender. It is also true that any smart outsourcer should be having a good look at the clients who are looking to tender for services. The outsourcer's needs are similar to the clients'. They need a client who is experienced in outsourcing with a successful track record of working with third parties. In short, it takes two to tango. So the best advice you could ever have is to make sure that you take lots of dancing lessons and learn all the steps before you clench that rose between your teeth and step out onto the floor.

CHAPTER 5

Chronic Consultancy Syndrome

"A consultant is someone who saves his client almost
enough to pay his fee."

Arnold H. Glasgow

Consultancy can be chronic—in all senses of the word. East Coast Urban Slang (Urban Dictionary, 2009), for example, curiously defines chronic as "high quality weed with red hairs on it". Such a delicacy is apparently often laced with cocaine, just to make it more appealing and enduring. Ugh. In more conventional dictionaries such as Merriam Webster however (Merriam Webster, 2013), less "streetwise" definitions are no less appropriate. Webster defines chronic as "marked by long duration or frequent reoccurrence", or else more prosaically as "always present or encountered; especially: constantly vexing, weakening, or troubling". I can certainly confess to suffering plenty of vexation at various stages of my career (both as a result of their fault and also mine if I'm perfectly honest). But I've also enjoyed successes which unlike Arnold Glasgow's quote above, have generated very high levels of goodness on whatever axis we were using at the time to measure it. Consultants it seems can be extremely useful, extremely expensive, extremely dangerous and extremely charming, possibly all at the same time.

Some of the skills that consultants are able to bring to bear still mystify me, even after decades of careful analysis. The most amazing story I can recall relates to a time when a selection process was underway for a global, game-changing, process-improvement initiative. Five corporate buzz-words in a row in the previous sentence, complete with two hyphenated platitudes tell you just how important it was in planet corporate. In fact, it was so important to the enterprise that the project team had a standing agenda item at each Executive Committee meeting. People would nod sagely when they were informed that someone somewhere had had a meeting and as a result had decided to set up a task force. This of course, as with many corporate bodies, had no clear task to execute and was comprised of people so weak that that no-one in their right mind would ever describe it as a "force". Newton would probably turn in his grave.

The changes in question were to be supported by a large and impressively expensive software package. Consultants had been active on all fronts to try and steer us towards their version of the "correct" answer, both from the client and the supplier ends. Juicy implementation contracts would follow. After exhaustive travails, the selection was finally made and the parties duly informed. The usual elation and despair followed. However, everyone was completely unprepared for the rear-guard action of one of the unselected vendors and their consultants. Somehow, someone managed to seat one of their account managers right next to one of the client company's most senior executives at a very large international sports event—a mere three days later. At the time, the team had presumed that the vendors were so desperate that they must have mugged the executive's wife and stolen her ticket; such was their need to make that last desperate pitch. But their plan was much more sophisticated than that. A senior consultant, who was also happily a former college friend of the leader, had somehow been found and briefed. His tactic was not to attack the package selection process, but to rather more insidiously attempt to undermine the credibility of the in-house team. He used a delicate blend of faint praise and gentle insinuations of amateur behaviour, garnished with a sprinkle of "questions about the process". This led of course towards the inevitable seed-of-doubt play. "Do you have confidence in your people?" So smooth was the operation that he had completed his task and quietly left even before the half-time whistle had blown. Happily, the seeds of doubt and uncertainty that the consultancy had attempted to plant failed to germinate upon the barren surfaces of strong process and management credibility. The decision was not revisited. This is just as well, for some years later the massive success of this venture achieved hundreds of millions in benefits for the company. It goes without saying that the necessary force of Stalinist project management and some spectacular upheavals needed to be brought to bear to achieve this end. And of course the early demise of any "task-force" teams and the inadequates who staffed them. But such spooky, insidious behaviour from a consultancy practice can leave a lasting mark, and most seasoned IT leaders I know well regard the art of consultancy with mixed feelings.

Consultants—The Hummingbirds of the IT Jungle

It's quite easy to poke fun at consultants (and to be honest, it is difficult for any IT leader who has been around a while not to pass up any good opportunity to do so), but these fine people do not have an easy life—at least the vast majority of them do not. Each consulting assignment may only last a matter of weeks. Some may stretch to a month or three, but long consulting engagements are generally rare beasts, despite the Olympian levels of persuasion a good partner is able to bring to bear. Selling coals to Newcastle or snow to Eskimos is an essential key "competency" for a partner (as our HR friends might say).

All of this means that things are tough and immediate. For a consultant, life mirrors that of the humble hummingbird. Hummingbirds (or *Trochilidae* to give them their proper name) are remarkable creatures. They hover in the air by rapidly flapping their wings up to eighty times a second. (Berne, 2013). A group of hummingbirds is called a charm—which might also be a suitable collective noun for consultants. At least it is more complimentary than the more common term of a "billing" or "charge" of consultants. Back in the fields, the tiny hummingbirds must flit from flower to flower seeking as much nectar as possible, lest starvation set in. If they do not keep moving then they will surely perish. Like consultants, they have a horrible dilemma. As they move they will expend energy which will ultimately drain their life-force. So how can they be efficient? To help deal with this problem hummingbirds have learnt to cleverly conserve energy. They go into a hibernation-like state when times are tough. When this happens, their metabolism slows to less than 10% of its normal rate. This is known as "torpor". I don't often meet consultants in between their assignments, so I am sadly unable to report whether they employ similar extreme techniques of energy conservation. This does however, conjure up a very vivid image of rows of glazed consultants all sitting in shiny "hot-office" accommodation on an industrial park near an international airport.

The hummingbird-like characteristics of the consultant mean that "time-sold" or the number of hours a year when each member of staff is earning revenue, therefore, is a crucial key metric for everyone in this industry. Whether you are the biggest big-wig at Big Firm High Command, a small, boutique niche player or a sole-trader specialist, everyone in this industry is obsessive about it. Eighty per cent time-sold means gravy and Ferraris whereas consultant utilisation levels of 60% or less probably mean that the partner isn't going to be a partner on Monday.

> **"Consultant—any ordinary guy that works more than
> 50 miles from home."**
> *Eric Sevareid*

As we've suggested, many IT leaders have something of a mixed view about consultancy (in much the same way views are polarised on outsourcing). Some see consultants as the god-like saviours of humanity. They believe a good firm is stuffed full to the gunwales with ethereal beings with gifted vision who possess an uncanny knack of spotting problems and solving them effortlessly. In short, the proponents believe that consultants are the people who show up with a load of paddles and the odd outboard motor when you are experiencing those difficult moments in the creek.

The fervent unbelievers out there, however, regard the common or garden "big firm" consultant as something of a parasitic shark with an over-active arrogance gland. This is possibly because the approach that some members of the consultancy industry take towards the business is rather intriguing to corporate eyes. For the small number of unscrupulous firms out there, good business does not seem to be about profit in the corporate sense, nor does it appear to be anything to do with added value. Some IT leaders believe that the bosses in the very worst consultancy partnerships are simply in it for personal enrichment. With no shareholders to please, no tiresome dividends to dilute your profits, and a small fixed cost base (which may not even involve renting premises), a partnership can be a perfect way to accumulate some serious wealth.

Survival of the Sharpest

In the biggest, sharpest, nastiest firms, it won't surprise you to learn that life is very big, sharp and nasty indeed. The charm of consultancy it seems is all about not being charming—at least to your peers. With an army of fellow consultants and only very few partners, it will not take long for the junior practitioners to work out that there is no such thing as a work-life balance. Indeed, work-life is just a cage-fight where only the survivors get on—a case of up or out. The astute underlings will also quickly work out that many of the partners are fantastically rich. Rookies therefore will vie for the attentions, affections and approval of the partner (or "Mr Big" as he may be known in discussions around the water-cooler). Their work ethic will be quite breathtaking, at least from the point of view of normal corporate mortals (aka clients). The rookies may sometimes even try to please the client, but that is often only a surrogate to get to the real customer—their boss.

As the weaker creatures are set upon by their colleagues, the field gradually thins. A vanishingly small number of the most assertive, determined consultants will metamorphose to "senior managers" (which being a good corporate word means that they are neither senior, nor are they managers). Then maybe, just maybe, the most lary, scary, thirty-something superstar— the kind you'd probably never want your son or daughter to marry—might be grudgingly admitted to the inner circle and ascend to the rewards of heavenly partnership. Fame and fortune beckon while their colleagues will cry into their skinny macchiatos. A terrible fate of wealth, infinite arrogance, silk ties and boundless conceit may now be unavoidable.

The internal workings of the meanest consultancies are intriguing because methods are practised that are not widely used in most other areas of the business world. The concept appears to be of a "Mr Big" who takes most of the cash. Meanwhile the voracious and somewhat downtrodden operatives are left to work off their socks (and most of the rest of their apparel and body parts) in a kamikaze haze. This is not an approach commonly found elsewhere in business (at least not since Victorian times). Indeed, examples of this behaviour can generally be found only on the darker side of commerce as well as in the mists of history. For example, in Charles Dickens' novel *Oliver Twist*, Fagin (who was one of the villains if you haven't read the book) used this business model to run a team of young pick-pockets in Victorian London. Admittedly, Fagin wasn't one of the best-dressed partners you might ever meet, but if he scrubbed up a bit, then his methods and techniques are so similar to those used by some of today's consultancies then I'm willing to bet a beer that he would be able to place some junior "consultants" on your next Windows upgrade project team.

Spotting Hummingbirds in the Wild

If you want to know whether you have any consultants on the ground in your organisation at any given time, then there are various ways to find out. The easiest method is to construct a "hide" in an open plan office somewhere in your empire. From here you can spend many happy hours with your binoculars waiting to see if any consultants come flitting along. A hide is quite easy to construct. Simply find a "hot-desk" in the area, plug in your computer and start "doing email". You will disappear into the background within minutes.

The first and most obvious clue to the presence of consultancy is the unmistakeable sight of a middle-aged gentleman breezing around the office (and these days it is sadly still all too often a gentleman). He will be wearing a suit which has quite clearly been created for him by James Bond's personal tailor. In the top pocket of his jacket, a scarlet silk handkerchief will peek out jauntily, possibly competing for your attention with a nearby red carnation. Hand-made shoes and a $500 haircut will be complemented by a whiff of cologne. But this is not any old cologne. This aftershave will be one of those glossy products that are only promoted at Christmas with big budget advertisements. Your partner thought it might make a good gift for you, but changed their mind when they saw the price tag. Its delicate scent will float pervasively across the gentle zephyrs of the office air conditioning, marking a territorial claim that a twenty kilo tomcat with a bladder problem would be proud of. Should you engage the gentleman in conversation, a beautiful hand stitched leather notebook will appear and he will make extravagant flourishes with a fountain pen the size of a beer-bottle. Congratulations! You have just met a senior partner from one of the large management consultancies!

The second clue which tells you that big-time consultancy is in town is less obvious, unless you know about the spectacles. To seek out the rest of the team you will need to gaze into the open plan areas and cubicles of your offices. As all good IT leaders know, consultants are not solitary creatures and they rarely work alone. Most often they prefer to group together and hunt in packs. This means of course that they can take on larger prey as well as push their colleague in front of any really nasty lions. Many of the litter will be young people, perhaps in their twenties or early thirties. All will be sporting hungry, yet earnest smiles. This is the rest of the team, otherwise known as the junior consultants. Consultants can usually be distinguished fairly easily from your own staff. While you might catch a tell-tale glimpse of a closely clutched clipboard which will give the game away, more often you will notice that each and every junior consultant will be wearing very smart clothes with conspicuous designer labels. The battle-dress will be as expensive as they can afford.

If for some reason you are still struggling to confirm the presence of any junior consultants, then you will now need to fall back on the spectacles test. Eyewear is always a smoking gun. A junior consultant in a big-name consultancy will always be in possession of what—to normal eyes at least—can only be described as the most outlandish designer spectacles. Many consultants I've met persist in sporting eye-gear even though the electric-ice-blue tinted contact lenses they are wearing obviate the need for any further optometric correction. The frames of their ocular oddities are a treat. They will be both minimalist, yet curiously complex. The arms of the frames will travel across the smooth temple of the incumbent at axiomatic Euclidian angles before settling gently on an ear which itself nestles neatly beneath a $200 haircut. But these are not just any spectacle frames. These are spectacle frames that are on the cusp of becoming fashionable. And you certainly won't be able to buy them in any shop.

If you still harbour any lingering doubts after all these good quality clues, then your next step is to talk to any one of the suspects. You will quickly discover that these youngsters will be alarmingly devoid of any significant industrial experience, but to compensate, each and every one of them will have a degree of self-confidence that will dwarf that of the most despotic, powerful, evil, world-domination-hungry dictator you could ever imagine. And as the junior consultant looks you up and down (as inevitably they will), he or she will immediately exude the one special thing that sets them apart from the rest of humanity—they are clever and you are stupid.

An Expensive Dose[1] of Aviary Assistance

It's quite possible that the previous sections might have led you to the conclusion that engaging a charging charm of consultants is a really bad idea. Indeed you may even have moved onto the next chapter by now. However, despite the

---

[1]Dose—a term broadly similar to "assignment"

trials and tribulations involved when hiring consultants, I submit that it is possible to get a great deal out of a well-organised consulting assignment, provided it is overseen by some strong management and when it is undertaken by good quality people from a reputable consulting firm. Despite the horror stories you may hear from your colleagues at IT symposia, there are plenty of good companies out there and many will have useful special skills. Some firms for example, will be good at helping you make acquisitions, while others will be really hot at showing you how to improve your company's operational performance. In my experience, specialist consultancies that are able to field people with superb domain expertise have generally delivered the most successful assignments for organisations I have led. And there are all sorts of specialists out there. Some consultancies, for example, are really good at helping you optimise the company's working capital (don't underestimate this unglamorous but nonetheless crucial bit of accounting), while there are others that specialise in benchmarking (which should be an essential part of any IT leader's armoury). Some I have worked with have even had great success building extremely niche businesses. For example, one company has made the repairing of broken relationships between clients and IT outsourcing companies their particular speciality. While this looks like a seriously niche business, it is a surprisingly rich seam to mine. This particular consultancy helped me with a very tricky asymmetric outsourcing arrangement and as it turned out, they were extremely good at it. And it was very valuable. Long-term outsourcing contracts often have the characteristics of a difficult marriage. After an early flash of infatuation and enthusiasm, things can then settle down into years of bickering and point-scoring. Half way through a long deal, any IT leader is going to need all the help they can get. Paying for a good outsourcing marriage counsellor is a very cost-effective alternative to years of trench warfare bleeding away your company's money.

So on balance, I think that it is possible to get great value from the good players out there. However, it certainly is not easy. Many pitfalls remain and one thing is very clear. If you do choose to engage a consultancy then you are going to have to play at the very top of your game and have a very clear idea of what you want the outcome to be.

Predator or Prey?

At the outset of any engagement, the best IT leaders know that the goals of the consultancy are not aligned with any of yours. Nor should they be. This should not come as a surprise. Your objective should be to get as much expertise and value out of the consultancy as you can—at the lowest possible cost. The good firms out there may not like it, but they will respond positively to this approach. They will want to do a good job and hopefully achieve their goal, otherwise known as the elusive follow-on contract. The nice guys will try to achieve this through the charmingly rustic, but nonetheless powerful, force we know as goodwill. The "hummingbird" imperative is unavoidable. For some other darker players, their objectives will be quite different, however. They may concentrate on wicked plots to administer addictive substances (such as doubt and uncertainty) that will have your organisation hooked on their ministrations for life and even beyond. The very worst firms have a very simple view. They are the predator and you are the prey (Craig, 2005).

So, if you find that your hummingbirds are slowly flying around you in circles, and that their eyes are curiously large and yellow and you notice that they are dribbling large gobbets of saliva onto the floor, then you should act quickly. You should dispel any such predatory notions as soon as you can. Early meetings with any consultant should concentrate almost entirely on the concept of "Me Customer, You Supplier" and the important second message "Me Happy, Me Pay Invoice".

"He who pays the piper calls the tune."
Proverb

Getting the relationship straight from the outset is crucial. But the fact remains, your organisation is the sugar-laden flower and if the hummingbird does not get enough nectar it will surely die. You should never forget this— because the consultancy certainly will not.

And so to the assignment …

What Consulting Isn't …?

No matter what work you end up doing with a team of external consultants, the fact remains that even middle-ranking practitioners in their organisations are probably taking home at least as much money as you are. Consultancy pays very well if the hummingbird can get its flowers in a line. You also know that the lackeys are almost certainly trumping your graduates' pay by a substantial margin. This means that the engagement process is going to be expensive no matter how you try to contain the costs. There is simply no way around this simple truth, at least none that I have ever found. However, the full scope of the costs will not be immediately apparent to the unwary, at least at the outset. Sure, the day-rates are eye-watering, but the length of the assignment will be carefully constructed to look both short and sweet. This will keep the number of billable man-days at low levels in the initial proposal. There is also the wonderful optical illusion of what is known to the wise as the "blended rate". This is achieved by hiding the spectacularly astronomic partner day-rates amongst the much more voluminous lower rates of Fagin's children, in order to create a much more palatable average day (or "blended") rate. This sleight of hand means that the total cost of "re-engineering" your organisation or whatever other grand title is man-ufactured for the assignment may actually look at first glance to be good value for money. At this early stage, the consultancy of course is still trying to land their fish (or more accurately, line up another border of nectar-laden herbaceous perennials). They won't want to scare you off, so they take great care to keep you well-soothed. If you are a new client, they may even choose to toss you a juicy loss-leader in your general direction first time around. For your part, and given the challenges surrounding consultancy, it goes without saying that it's really important to know why you are bringing consultants into the organisation. This means that you are the one who should take the time to define the requirements and scope as clearly and as fully as you can. Now is not the time for you to revert to the behaviour of your worst computer users and spit out whims and vague views. That works badly for the consultancy and it will work badly for you.

Let us start with some of the assignments that some IT leaders have cho-sen for their consultants, which in retrospect perhaps they wish they hadn't. They form some of the worst symptoms of Chronic Consultancy Syndrome. If you haven't ever seen these misadventures in the wild, don't worry, it won't be very long before you will. They happen with great regularity. Unfortu-nately, the only effective vaccination for these sorts of ailments is experience. Indeed without a seasoned IT leader to squash any misdemeanours, you will probably find that these scenarios and others like them will just keep on com-ing around again and again.

It Was Their Fault!

The "it was their fault" method is a very familiar scenario that I have seen more than a dozen times in my thirty year career. On average, it seems to pop up about once every two years. Curiously, each perpetrator of this method believes that they are the first person in the world to invent this particular wheel. The situation is simple. Weak IT leaders who want to make large-scale changes may be too frightened to do it for it themselves. Many will fear a backlash from staff, workers and their colleagues, not to mention labour union leaders and unbelievers amongst the company's leadership. Some believe that hiring in consultants to act as the fall guy is a great way of deflecting criticism. This method relies on pushing the consultancy team to carry out your wishes (as far as you are able to make them).When the final report is delivered, you wait until you see which way the wind is blowing. If everything is well-received and large crowds take to the street waving banners and cheering, then you immediately jump centre-stage and take all the credit. If all is not well and the mob start setting fire to flags, gathering in convenient town squares and chanting aggressively, then with this method, you simply step away, blame the consultants and ostentatiously fire them. All in all it looks like a good plan because on the face of it you get to win both ways. But be wary. Be very, very wary. If you choose to embark on this course of action, then you are almost certainly playing a dangerous game where you have little or no experience. Besides that, the consultancy is almost certainly fielding brighter people than you and your henchmen can muster. Many grizzled consultancies will have seen this technique all too many times before. At the first sign of trouble they will unleash their carefully prepared counter-attack. As you try and land them in the sticky stuff, you will suddenly and unaccountably find that you are playing chess with Bobby Fischer on one of his good days. Even before the first pawn is taken, predator and prey swap places and you will probably find yourself with a rapidly deteriorating situation on your hands. It might even degenerate into a dose of cuckoo consultancy (see later). So, if you try to behave in this fashion, then frankly, you deserve everything you get. Being disingenuous and spineless are not qualities that any world-class IT leaders should exhibit. The "it was their fault" method is strictly a spectator sport for the wise.

> **"Consultants eventually leave, which makes them excellent scapegoats for major management blunders."**
> *Scott Adams* **(The Dilbert Principle *1996*)**

The Magic of a Name

"The Magic of a Name" is coincidentally the title of a series of books written about a former employer of mine which I heartily recommend as a good read.[2] However, in this context we define "magic" as the instant credibility that the work of a highly respected consultancy house or "name" can bestow on any mailbox-busting PowerPoint presentation they deliver. Many believe that a name can carry the day, even if the presentation material could be better described as a "crock of …". This approach follows the time-honoured mantra that "it must be right because this famous consultancy said so". Again this is in my opinion, pretty weak leadership behaviour and while it is not particularly disingenuous, it is nonetheless shameful. This type of sad assignment seems to crop up about every 36–48 months in my experience, usually propagated by a leader who is beginning to fall out of the sky as a result of poor decision making or perhaps even management inactivity on his or her part. A surprising number of IT leaders have not yet worked out that there is more to their job than endless hours of emails and meetings. In my experience such sad cases don't stay the course. Since they bring down the average life expectancy of the IT leader, then I suppose it is good news for the rest of us that they are counted in our statistical bucket or pool or whatever other watery receptacle statisticians would expect us to live in.

---

[2]Peter Pugh, *The Magic of a Name—The Rolls-Royce Story*, Icon Books Ltd, ISBN 10 1840461519.

**"Consultants have credibility because they are not dumb
enough to work at your company."**
Scott Adams (The Dilbert Principle 1996)

The Consultant's Crutch

If I had a dollar or a pound for every time I have seen the "consultant's crutch" assignment, then I wouldn't be fantastically rich, but I'd certainly have enough coins to feed parking meters and vending machines for the rest of my life. The Consultant's Crutch (and make sure you spell that correctly) is how things manifest themselves on our side of the fence after the client succumbs to a case of what is known a "total consultancy dependency". This ailment is all about being gun-shy on a grand scale. For the afflicted, no decisions can be made before a "study" is conducted. A stamp of approval from the consultant is essential before anything can proceed. For some, kicking a habit of popping barbiturates or crack-cocaine would be easier. Sometimes, the client is so weak or so impressed with the brilliance of the consultancy that he or she simply cannot live without the wise and wonderful counsel that the dunderheads of their own organisation simply cannot furnish them with. Smart consultancy operators can keep these types of assignments going for years, shoring up the deficiencies of a weak internal management team. Before long the reasons for the original engagement (if indeed there were any) are long forgotten. It is sad to see once-proud leaders reduced to slobbering Pavlovian wrecks that believe that any and every utterance of a weirdly bespectacled, Armani-suited, twenty-something consultant carries a level of profound meaning that is right up there with the Word of God.

**"I come from an environment where, if you see a snake, you
kill it. At GM, if you see a snake, the first thing you do is go
hire a consultant on snakes."**
Ross Perot

But What Consulting Perhaps Should Be?

When it comes to thinking about consulting, there is no reason why we should ignore the normal laws of physics (or indeed commerce and capitalism). In my experience, there are usually only two reasons why anyone asks someone else to do a job for them:

- The first is because they don't want to do it for themselves.
- The second is because they can't do it for themselves (whether that is for reasons of skills shortfall or lack of time).

In both cases getting someone else to do the job is cheaper and easier than doing it yourself (at least from the perspective of the client).

Sometimes people don't want to do a job for themselves because they may think that they have better things to do with their time, or because the job in question might not be very pleasant. The "don't want to do" jobs therefore often tend to include lower-skilled activities. In corporate life you will find that non-core business areas such as cleaning, together with medium-skilled jobs such as mass catering/canteen provision fall into this category. The market hourly rates for such jobs are generally not stratospherically high, but outsourcing companies and even contracting individuals can still nonetheless make a good living from what for them is a low-margin business. The very best outsourcing companies take on huge volumes of it. When they do it well, delivering consistent levels of quality in a cost-effective fashion, everyone is happy. This is fine and we might all live happily ever after, but unfortunately consultancy does not fall into this category.

Consultancy is not a low-margin, commodity business.

So let's move to the second point. Things that people can't do for themselves are usually undertaken by people in highly skilled roles. Orthodontics, piloting a jetliner and open heart surgery, I would submit, all fall into this category. For these skills you generally hire an expert and you should expect to pay top dollar for the privilege. All the training the surgeon endured over many, many years, coupled with fine skill and a not inconsiderable professional indemnity insurance premium mean that his or her time and effort does not come cheap. Most people are happy to accept these prices, perhaps with the odd exception such as US attorneys. (I know this is true because when I once told our company lawyer that he was my second favourite attorney after Judge Judy, he declared me a friend for life). Clearly such a profession does not seem to engender large circles of friends or joyful clients. Sticking with the "high-skill" theme, though, you'd also be hard-pressed to find many parents who have tried to manipulate their own children's teeth with braces. Neither are you likely to come across many heart patients who attempt bypass surgery on themselves or their friends and family. Amateur brain surgeons are even less common.

So, as with all highly skilled jobs …

… Consultancy is a high-margin business (and yes, consultants should be highly skilled individuals).

A typical consulting assignment can cost a corporation many tens of thousands of dollars, possibly hundreds of thousands, and it is not uncommon for millions of the green folding stuff to be handed over. It is an expensive business. If you don't believe me, then could I suggest that you take a look at the final PowerPoint presentation deliverable from the most recent consultancy assignment in your organisation. Try taking the total fee you paid and divide it by the number of slides in the deck. Isn't it amazing to think that a

single slide of bullet points, motherhood statements and some fancy anima-
tion has cost you that amount of money? I've seen some assignments run up
bills of more than $10,000 per slide. And that's often all you get in terms of
deliverables. There's often no formal report and it's hard to find anything in
beautifully written prose English that you can cling to any more these days.
Sadly, to those of us of the old school, everyone now seems to uses "txtspk"
and has the attention span of a gnat.

> **"PowerPoint has a dark side. It squeezes ideas into a
> preconceived format, organizing and condensing not only
> your material but—inevitably, it seems—your way of thinking
> about and looking at that material. A complicated, nuanced
> issue invariably is reduced to headings and bullets. And if
> that doesn't stultify your thinking about the subject, it may
> have that effect on your audience—which is at the mercy
> of your presentation."**
> *Julia Keller, 2005 Pulitzer Prize Winner*

So when it comes to hiring consultants there should be no excuse. If you can
do the work yourself, then you are much better off hiring some temps at a
few tens of dollars a day, rather than paying thousands of dollars a day for a
designer consultancy engagement.

But what can the consultants offer you and can it help you solve that
problem?

To find out it is necessary to gaze into the singularity at the core of a black
hole in the centre of a consultancy. Only when you see past the event-horizon
of sales patter can you find the reasons why the whole industry of consultancy
deserves to exist in the firmament of IT. I once dared to take a brief glance. This
is what I saw … and I think that the assignments divide up something like this.

Forests, Trees and Spectacles

This section is not a guide on camping holidays for nerds. Rather, this type
of assignment is really just another manifestation of the good old-fashioned
"can't see the forest for the trees" idiom. Consultants are really good at spotting stuff that your own people cannot see. They are really, really good at
it. However, you should not think they can do this because they have keen
eyesight (they all wear spectacles remember?). Neither is it because they are
blessed with superhuman skills not normally bestowed upon mere mortals—
despite the best efforts of the partner to persuade you otherwise. No, one
of the major reasons why consultants are good at spotting things on your
patch that are going wrong or identifying possible inefficiencies and areas for
improvement is simply because they do not work there.

You however, are not so lucky.

For you and your staff, being mesmerised and indoctrinated by current work practices and customs is unavoidable when you spend eight to ten hours a day playing the corporate game. Even massive structural obstacles can fade into complete insignificance when you have to deal with them each and every day. One particular example that brings this point home to me happened many years ago. This incident took place in the days when even the computer department staff had to share their computer equipment—which some of you may recall were quaintly known as "terminals". I had recently moved jobs from a central London oil company to a pharmaceutical company which had two major sites in the suburbs. The sites were separated by thirty-five miles of hellish roads, which included the legendary M25 beltway. In London it is known as the "orbital motorway". This is great description because the only way you could get around it easily would be in a space-ship.

With these challenges to surmount, I found that one facility had been neatly built at the eight o'clock position and the other site was located in the one o'clock position relative to central London. Travelling between these sites was horrendous, particularly in the rush-hour (as you may have already gathered). Within days, I became frustrated with the fact that everyone seemed to spend endless hours travelling or more accurately "not travelling" between the two sites. It could take two hours to complete a few short miles on a bad day. I even made friends with one fish and chip shop owner whose premises were located next to a particularly hostile set of traffic lights (at least as far as you can develop a relationship through the medium of pained expressions, arm-waving and shrugging). However, I was not prepared for the stunning realisation that I seemed to be the only person in the entire company who saw this as a problem. Had I suddenly been gifted with divine powers and become a Messiah? Everyone else accepted that the travelling was part of the job, in much the same way that people today think that doing email is the same as doing work. I totted up the hours everyone was spending and showed my boss an unbelievable number with lots of noughts on it. He merely shrugged his shoulders. "If we don't continue to have frequent contact between the two halves of the department, then our projects will suffer", he added. Thankfully, it all turned out all OK in the end. After a few months, I had been "recalibrated". Once I had integrated myself fully into the "normal" ways of working I realised that what I initially thought was a shocking inefficiency was of course a perfectly sensible and reasonable way to carry out our business. Messiah? I think not, newby more like, even if I was a newby prone to catching group-think.

"Resistance is futile. You will be absorbed into the collective."
Borg recruiting script, Star Trek, the Next Generation (1987)

You Are not Alone on Planet Earth

While many of us regularly attend conferences and networking events, we probably have to admit to ourselves that we don't know diddly-squat[3] about what's going on inside our competitors' organisations and even less about what's happening in similar companies with whom we don't compete. Indeed, most IT leaders would gratefully settle for even a small but preferably coherent insight into what on earth is happening inside their own organisation. A surprising number of companies operate in splendid isolation from one another. Consultants on the other hand will probably be seeing lots of clients because of the hummingbird imperative. Stuff will be going on out there that you will have no idea about and more to the point you will also have no possible way of finding out. Competitors will lie to you and even partners and allies will spin you a yarn that is both rosy and strangely confusing. You may delude yourself into thinking that networking at conferences and symposia will provide this information. No chance. Any conferences you attend will be stuffed full of presentations by your peers, each of which will have exactly the same script. It goes something like **this**.

THE CONFERENCE PRESENTATION

1. This is my company, isn't it wonderful? And look at my impressive job title.
2. The last guy left a mess. My vision was to sort it out (and boy have I got a vision for you).
3. Through my leadership, we achieved unusual spiritual closeness with our user community/leaders/customers/suppliers (delete as appropriate) and gained rare insight not seen before in the modern world.
4. I initiated a project, the like of which you have never seen, which scaled untold heights of accomplishment. The project finished before it had started and we even spent a negative budget on it.
5. The wonderful new technology we had chosen performed so well that even someone's brother in the user community said something nice about it.
6. It was me that made it all happen. I am the one with the Midas touch. I am a minor deity.
7. We all lived happily ever after, reaping massive but curiously un-measurable business benefits.
8. I am looking for a new job (for unexplained reasons).

---

[3]Diddly-squat—Urban slang for "nothing", apparently much used by Emos, and other flightless birds.

Don't believe any of this, except the bit about the job hunting. And as for the software, I remain convinced that nothing ever works if it has shaky software in it. And even if you do by some chance have any relatives in the user community, they will certainly never say nice things about IT. Their life is far too precious to want to take the risk of being lynched and ritually disembowelled by their co-workers.

On the other hand, consultancies do get to see some of the horrible things that go on under the covers. Clearly their confidentiality agreements should preclude them sharing the most succulent details of the blithering disasters going on elsewhere, but they do have various clever ways of harvesting this value for their future clients.

Let me introduce you to the concept of the "client case study". Each of these stories will be beautifully embroidered caricatures of their previous experiences, but unlike the conference presentations of your peers (which are intended only to impress and intimidate), the consultancy may subsequently be asked to deliver on some of the things they have claimed. This means that there will have to be at least a smattering of truth in each of the stories.

The other method which some consultancy practices use is quite frankly, inspirational. It is a real favourite of mine and I never fail to be impressed by it. The cognoscenti call it Salome's dance, also known as The Dance of the Seven Veils. In this version there is a lot of dancing, wafting and waving, but disappointingly none of the veils are ever properly shed. I refer of course to the concept of the "Industry Best Practice" model.

This model is such a cunning wheeze—almost too cunning for words. Let's just say it makes the wiliest of foxes look gullible, kind, naïve and shy.

"Cunning… is but the low mimic of wisdom."
Plato

The "Industry Best Practice" model, as it says, is supposed to be a large database of business performance, lovingly built up over years so that the most wonderful things that clients might have ever achieved are recorded as a high-water mark of achievement. The consultancy will love to use the model to show you just how far short your organisation is of that mark. It serves as both a marvellous marketing tool on the one hand and a stick with which the client can be repeatedly beaten on the other. The model has an almost religious aura about it. No matter how much work you do, and whatever lofty heights you are able to scale, it simply won't be possible to achieve the perfection of "industry-best practice". And certainly not when there's more nectar out there in your rose-garden.

In a general consultancy, as opposed to specialist benchmarking consultancies, the crucial question is whether such a model does or does not exist. We can't be certain. However, we do know that every client assignment is different and the chances that the consultancy has built up a consistent database of information which is both relevant and current seem vanishingly small to me. They certainly won't be keen to do all that painstaking correlation work for themselves on their own dollar. When you ask to see the database, it cannot, of course, be shown to you due to client confidentiality concerns. On that basis, we can only conclude that it can't possibly be real. It could be that the model is simply a virtual vehicle which allows experience from previous engagements to be brought into play for new clients. It therefore might—intrinsically—be a good thing (which semantically, is pretty good going for something that doesn't actually exist). However, I would strongly advise for your own health that you do not drink coffee on your initial meeting with the partner when this is being discussed. I recently made that elementary schoolboy mistake. At a crucial point in our meeting the partner leant forward and in whispered and conspiratorial tones, he inevitably mentioned the towering "industry best practice" database that would be brought to bear on our current swathe of problems. As he continued, he conjured up a compelling image. Imagine the battery of all nine of the USS Missouri's 16" guns solely focussed on my troubles, backed up by the finest thermo-nuclear devices the world has to offer. They would simply blast our problems into oblivion. The timing was impeccable. I discovered to my horror that the apparently unrelated acts of laughing uncontrollably and drinking coffee at the same time could be life-threatening. In my case I got off lightly with just a small dry-cleaning bill and a nonplussed partner. Windpipe and oesophagus proximity is a major design flaw in human physiology, so watch out for it, at least where consultancy, coffee and other beverages are concerned.

Nothing New Under the Sun

One clear benefit of using consultancies can be described by the adage "there's nothing new under the sun". IT leaders do talk to one another. While many are secretive, some may boast about the massive levels of cash that they have decanted from their company's profits into the chateaux of the consultancy partners. I recall one organisation a little while back whose leaders were positively glowing about the fact that they'd made it onto one big firm's top ten client list.

I believe it is true that there is often a great deal of read-across from client to client, particularly if others are grappling with similar problems to you. In my own experience, I have found there are quite striking similarities between business sectors as diverse as oil exploration, medicine discovery and jet engine research. To be successful in each of these fields requires superior scientific or engineering skills, discipline, risk management, innovation, and a methodological approach, all underpinned by superhuman levels of Stalinist project management capability. At the highest level I reckon that these sectors look more alike than they look different. Consequently, there is a good chance that seasoned consultants may have seen similar problems to yours in one or more of their previous assignments, even if the client's businesses were quite different. Some consulting houses have even built up reputations (and the inevitable methodologies) for specific and niche situations. These include acquisitions, major technology upgrades and certain types of project delivery to name just a few. Sometimes this is just hype, but in my experience the best firms really do know their stuff.

However, the very best "nothing new under the sun" advice you will get—at least in my experience—is from a consultancy which has former leaders on its books who did once actually gird their loins to face the monsters and dragons you are now squaring up to. My own conviction is that it's not that hard to work out what to do when fireballs are raining down from above. Taking cover usually works. But people who have lived through the storms and worked out what it takes to cope and perhaps even flourish in the charred and smoking aftermath are worth a good daily rate. Provided that these people survived to tell the tale, stories of how they became singed by dragons and scarred by monsters will be of immense value to you. Even if their experiences are not directly relevant to today's problem at hand, it will certainly confirm suspicions that you may already harbour—that the life of a CIO is considerably tougher than any character in a fantasy horror movie.

Take the time to do the research to see if there is a consulting house out there that has expertise in the problem area you are addressing. Once you've found out that a firm has some real heavyweight grandees on their payroll then a call to the partner will be a very good idea. Just be careful with the coffee.

Hummingbirds Flap Harder than Cash Cows

The last item on my list relates to the work ethic of the consultants. We already know that the consultants will be killing themselves trying to impress their leader with their levels of commitment and revenue-earning potential. If you are smart, then you will have agreed a daily rate rather than an hourly one. There are twenty-four hours in a day after all. Consultants are creatures that won't be afraid of working into the night on your behalf. Just make sure that they are doing the stuff you need them to do. The pace that these young, ambitious, whizzy-kids can manage is truly impressive to those of us in the more pedestrian corporate world where project approvals may be measured in months. It is probably fair to say that we must look like dinosaurs to their hummingbird eyes. It's just as well that it's still the Jurassic Period in corporate life. Nonetheless, if you use your furiously flapping junior wisely and as directed on the prescription you might just get the outcome you wish for. A well-designed engagement based on a clear outcome and a sporty schedule that Hemon the Pyramid Builder (see Pathogenic Projects) would be proud of will perfectly harness the talents of the consultancy. Be reassured, for if any of the weaker members of the team do burn out, their colleagues will be positively energised by the prospect of less competition for that elusive prize of Partnership. Darwinism is alive and well.

How Hummingbirds Turn into Cuckoos

Within corporate life, the laws of physics can be suspended for long periods of time. It is not uncommon for the quasi-religious beliefs of messianic leaders to cause an organisation afflicted by group-think to willingly line up behind any number of "emperor's new clothes" projects. On rare occasions, strange things can happen to the laws of biology as well. Given the right set of circumstances, it is possible for hummingbirds to metamorphose into cuckoos. If you think of your empire as a nest, then you can probably guess where this goes.

The concept of fatal or cuckoo consultancy we briefly mentioned earlier may have grabbed your attention and perhaps it is even now gnawing away at the worry-centres of your brain and the all-too-thin lining of your stomach. Cuckoo consultancy can and sometimes does happen. It is frightening and you are right to be worried about it. Several colleagues I have known over the years have fallen 'fowl' of it. However, it is not common for bouts of Chronic Consultancy Syndrome to end this way and only a small number of firms set out to inflict this fate on their hapless clients. Most partners are smart enough to know that if they kill off an IT leader, then there's one less punter out there who could give them some business in the future.

The diagnosis of cuckoo consultancy is not usually too difficult for the wily IT leader to make. First, you must climb back into your hot-desk hide. Then you should grit your teeth, look busy and start reading email. Within an hour or two your camouflage will be perfect. You will know this because some kind soul will offer to bring you a coffee, assuming that you are just another co-worker or contractor drafted in to shore up another "challenged" project. Now you must sit, wait and watch.

Your goal is to see if you can espy any spotty junior consultants and rarer, lesser-spotted partners flittering around your empire.

If your investigations confirm that there is plenty of hummingbird game buzzing through your organisation and you know that neither you nor your trusty managers have hired them, then there's a good chance you are well into the primary incubation period of a cuckoo infection. Your career in this company might already be over. It's entirely possible that you might even be the last person in the executive team to know what is going on. In simple terms, if consultants are in your organisation and they do not belong to you, then they must belong to someone else. In traditional hierarchical organisations this means that someone more senior than you has probably hired them. And they haven't told you.

The stakes are now extremely high. You probably only have a few choices available to you. Of these, there are a few good ones and one bad one. Despite the obvious statistics here, for some amazing reason most people seem to always choose the bad one.

The bad option involves sitting things out and waiting to see what happens. Believe me, this is unpleasant. I've seen it several times. It is a bit like watching Smallpox or bubonic plague slowly ravage a small medieval community, house by house, except that this disease has a far higher fatality rate, at least in terms of careers. But if you are not the subject of this particular infection, then you might like to sit back and enjoy the show. It is a great spectator sport.

"Control your own destiny or someone else will."
Jack Welch

The cuckoo dose will start off pretty innocuously. The sun will come up in the morning as usual and a dapper consultancy partner will try to make an appointment to see you. Even if your assistant incorrectly identifies the partner as a "salesperson" and makes such a meeting difficult, the partner will remain quietly patient. He or she of course knows the final chapter of the story. The hectic busy schedule you currently enjoy will shortly be a thing of the past, but in the opening moves of this game the partner will always indulge you and respect the "important" work that you are doing. Meanwhile it is highly likely that under cover of darkness, charms of junior hummingbirds are already flittering their way into various corners of your organisation, each armed with a battery of clipboards and some pro-forma questionnaires that probably aren't relevant to the problem at hand.

When the day of the meeting comes, the partner will assume a kindly disposition and thank you profusely for taking the time out of your busy schedule to see him. He will treat you with simpering respect and may even toss in a few compliments about your "high standing" in the IT industry. For the unwary, the opportunity to be lulled into a false sense of security can be overwhelming. Then, after ten to twelve minutes of such pleasantries, the partner will sensitively yet purposefully detonate the thermo-nuclear warhead.

> *The CEO has asked us to conduct a strategic review of IT. We realise that you are doing a good job, but the CEO tells me that he (or she) has some concerns and he (or she) needs to be sure that the company is getting the best value out of IT. We are going to have a look at the operation for him (or her) and make some recommendations.*

As he sits comfortably back into his seat, awaiting a reaction, the situation is very clear—as clear as the clearest bell that is tolling on a perfectly clear day. The consultants are working for your boss because your boss doesn't like what's happening. It might be that he or she has never mentioned their concerns to you, or indeed they may have done so and you've not "got it". But as far as the future is concerned, it's almost certainly all over. That's all you need to know. Your CEO has taken this sharp-suited outsider into his confidence with the sole intention of investigating you and your happy band. All the hard schmoozing the partner had put in over many years now comes to a glorious and satisfying fruition. The CEO simply trusts the partner more than they trust you. From this moment on you are now at the mercy of the consultancy and you have, in effect, ceded control of your IT organisation. All that is certain is that the consultancy is going to win and you are going to lose. Moreover, if the partner who captured this piece of business is clever (and he or she usually is), then their share of the fees from this assignment and the inevitable follow-on work may enable him to upgrade that chalet in Aspen. Happy Days!

The naïve IT leader may nod, oblivious of the implications. "Yes, we could do with some help" they may muse. Sensing the possibility of an increased budget and perhaps the chance of a higher profile in the corporate pecking order, the IT leader may offer whatever support is required and let the consultancy team get on with it. The chances that anything good might come out of this work are of course absolutely nil. Such hopes are fanciful and misguided. Back at Consultancy High Command, teams of minions will be manufacturing PowerPoint slides which will gently damn the current organisation together with any management decision that the leader has ever taken (no matter how good they were). One of the big benefits of having devastatingly clever people working in your consultancy practice is that they could convincingly present even Mother Teresa as a tyrant in less than half a dozen animated PowerPoint slides.

The experienced IT leader, however, knows that something monumental has happened. The first cuckoo of spring has sung its plaintive song and even now the sound is echoing around the IT jungle. Those who know their birdcalls will be aware that there are probably only two good options available from now on.

The first involves immediate resignation. This "cut-to-the-chase" method works well and puts the leader in a strong position to negotiate suitable compensation. The play is simple. The consultants represent a vote of no confidence and the CIO gets the message.

The second method is equally drastic and it may take you to the same place. There is now a window of only a few short hours where you have a slim chance to recover the situation and get this bird out of the nest. This chance is known as the all-out, full-frontal, no-holds-barred counter-attack—also known as the "do or die" play. Simply put, the leader must immediately book a face-to-face appointment with the CEO and have a blazing row.

This "last-chance" counter-attack should be simple, primitive, clean and brief. The objective is to either call the CEO's bluff, or else to crystallise their complete lack of confidence in you and face the consequences that follow. Your discussion with your CEO should be short and binary. It's really simple. You should explain that either the consultants will work for you, or else you will no longer be working for the CEO.

At this point your leader will either back down, in which case you are now running your IT organisation once again, or he or she will not. In the latter case, you have confirmation that the situation is irrecoverable. You may now devote your efforts towards torturing the HR Department with an enjoyable and messy exit from the organisation as you plan your next career move. A grubby instrument known as the compromise agreement may now raise its ugly head from the bubbling, sulphurous pools of the legal department. But be not afraid. To experienced practitioners, this can be great sport. If the company offers to pay your legal fees, then you might like to see whether you can achieve seventeen or more iterations before finally agreeing the exit contract. Compromise agreements are considered by many to be unethical, unpleasant devices designed solely to protect the company when it chooses to dubiously dispatch its unwanted executives. It therefore follows that in the spirit of fairness and balance, it is not unreasonable for you to create a little grief for the HR goblins tasked to make you sign up (as well as making sure that the agreement contains enough of the green folding stuff to make you happy for years to come). Symmetry is a crucial ingredient in business. If they want you out, then you must make them pay for it in whatever currency you choose. Money and hassle are both legal tender in this game.

If for some reason however, you took the decision to let the situation run, then sit back and enjoy the ride. You'll get to the compromise agreement later and the terms won't be nearly as good.

First, the partner will schedule frequent "steering group" meetings with the CEO. These will be so frequent that the CEO will not be able to attend all or indeed any of them. This is of course perfect because we know who is running these meetings. The partner will then assign a project leader who carries the title of "senior manager". This individual is of course, neither senior nor a manager and of course, there will not be any client "steering" going on at any meeting. This deft move cunningly sets the pecking order for the game which follows. You are now matched in level to one of his lackeys (who might not even have ten years' postgraduate experience). More importantly, access to your leader is now controlled by the partner. You have become just a helpless passenger. You have been firmly and helplessly strapped to the commander's chair, and the controls have been set for the heart of the Sun.

A "Terms of Reference" or TOR will then be "agreed". The TOR of course will be the same one they used in the last assignment and the one before that. It will also be carefully constructed so that only one of two answers can possibly emerge.

Answer 1—The Cuckoo Consultancy End-Game Solution

If the consultancy has any form of outsourcing capability then the answer will be simple and straightforward. The IT division's services need to be professionalised. This can be accomplished through an outsourcing arrangement and the consultancy's outsourcing group will do it all for you—cheaper, faster, higher and better. There is of course an extremely protracted mating dance that has to be endured by all parties before that inevitable conclusion is made. For example, the partner will assert that he has the best interests of the client at heart. He will talk about a "transparent and open" process where the levels of "transparency and openness" will rival those employed by Joseph Stalin when he was busy purging the Red Army of any and every decent officer in the nineteen thirties. The partner will offer the services of his team to help the client write the contract to "best practice" standards. "Best practice" in this context means "a tender which is constructed so that we are the only ones who could ever possibly win it." Only later, as the massive expense of the complex tendering process they have constructed becomes clear, will the option be raised that it would of course be much quicker and cheaper just to let the contract to the outsourcing arm of the consultancy once the IT leadership have departed. This brings the end-game to a satisfactory and lucrative conclusion—the "cuckoo dose" has run its full course.

Answer 2—The Thin-Edge-Wedge-End-Game Cash Cow

If the consultancy does not have an outsourcing capability, then their leaders back at Big-Wig Supreme High Command will expect this "thin edge of the wedge" assignment to generate squillions[4] and possibly even zillions of dollars of repeat business. The antics of the locust-like numbers of clipboard-wielding adolescents who were billed to you as "senior consultants" now becomes clear. They have travelled far and wide around the whole enterprise spreading seeds of confusion and doubt as well as identifying multifarious exciting new opportunities for further work. The team now has a veritable feast of new assignments to chase. There are the more obvious follow-on opportunities, such as helping develop the IT strategy. This is often seen as pretty essential, since

---

[4] Squillion—urban slang for a large amount of money, though generally not considered to be as large as a zillion.

most of the IT leadership will have departed once the assignment is complete. Nobody likes a rudderless ship. Moreover, by completing and publishing the strategy before any new leaders arrive, the consultancy can promote a sense that they are part of the fixtures and fittings of the enterprise. This will almost certainly hobble any of the fresh ideas of the new leadership. That is also perfect for future business. Other opportunities will largely centre on neuroses which the foraging "data gatherers" will have picked up from leaders around the client organisation. Playing these concerns back to the CEO cannot fail to subliminally resonate. He or she will almost certainly already be aware that such problems have been bubbling away for years like a Mid-Atlantic volcanic fumarole, way beneath the apparently calm surface of the executive ocean. The CEO will therefore now believe that the consultancy has unique insight. Having sorted out their IT problems (which of course they haven't), they should now be allowed to fix wider and more extensive challenges across the enterprise. Ker-ching.[5] Life just doesn't get any better.

The happy ending to both of these options means many years of work for the consultancy and lots more cash for the partners. And so they live happily ever after. Or at least they do until the cost of IT becomes so high that the organisation decides to call in another set of consultants, so that the lifecycle can repeat itself once again.

To be fair, this sorry story happens only rarely. I have seen it twice in organisations where I worked (mercifully both times as a spectator) and a couple more times in organisations with which I was familiar. The root cause of the problem is firmly in the "stakeholder management" domain, so if you have worries in this regard, then you might like to re-read the Dislocated Stakeholders chapter. If your CEO trusts a consultancy partner more than he or she trusts you, then the ground is fully prepared and fertile for all this bad stuff to happen. You know what you have to do.

And Finally

So, having decided that you are going to proceed with a dose of consultancy and wisely putting yourself in a position where you are actually controlling it, you should also take care to make the assignments short and sharp. Each must have a definitive outcome that helps you solve the problem you need to solve. Words like "solve" and "outcome" mustn't be forgotten (which is why they are being written multiple times). And the outcome you want and problem you need to solve must be difficult ones to warrant this expensive assistance. Remember that each and every one of those PowerPoint slides you

---

[5] Ker-ching—sound of an old-fashioned cash register.

will endure during the final presentation is going to have to contain undiluted genius if you are going to get your money's worth. And while you are at it you might also like to ensure that a full report is delivered, even if it is considered by many to be a quaint old-fashioned deliverable. The report should be written in English (or the mother tongue of the organisation) with interesting novelties such as grammar and proper sentences, each contributing to an elegant piece of prose that clearly explains the method, analysis, recommendations and conclusions used. In my experience it only takes a few short weeks or months before the PowerPoint deck the consultancy has lovingly presented to you as its main "deliverable" will transform itself into incomprehensible gibberish that you'd need an Enigma machine to decode.

It is difficult to be prescriptive on areas where you should engage consultants. Each organisation has a different signature of problems in their patch. One company may be world-class in an area where the next company is positively Stone-Age. However, by keeping a close eye on what you want to do and the reasons why you want to do it, you should be able carefully to structure any engagement to deliver the answers you need, whilst playing to the strengths of the consultancy. Only then will you have a good chance of success.

Then, finally, as the work approaches completion, do ensure that nothing remains open-ended. You should take great care to make sure that each and every individual from the consultancy is taken off site once the work is completed. Any follow-on business should be carefully controlled—by you. As with antibiotics, when you are trying to get rid of any infection then you must keep taking the medication long after the rash has disappeared. This approach works well for both bacteria and consultants in my experience. Also be wary of secondary infections. Staff in your organisation may unaccountably think that you have a special place in your heart for the consultancy you most recently hired. As a result, they may even try to please you by initiating small additional assignments that address some of their own local concerns.

In one organisation where I once worked, I saw what I would describe as the most wickedly cunning method of chronic consultancy control. To constrain what appeared to be an ever-spiralling spend on consultants, the CFO in the company implemented a policy whereby any consulting assignments which totalled more than $80,000 had to be agreed and signed off in advance by him personally. After the initial seismic shudders of indignant managers had passed, the lazy, slow-moving Mississippi-like river of deep spending was eventually stemmed to the trickle of a Colorado mountain spring. Within months, the "professional services" line item in the company's corporate accounts had transformed itself from a levee-busting flood into a flat, dry lake bed in Nevada upon which you could (if you wished) attempt world speed records in jet-powered prams. Tumbleweed blew around the heaped piles of unused marker pens and clipboards that were left discarded in half-empty cupboards. But this bold leader had a price to pay. Within weeks, the poor CFO found long lines of people hammering on his door. Consultancy partners and middle managers alike were all desperately attempting to have their moment so that they could pitch their essential consultancy proposal. In his outer office, his assistant wasn't doing any better. She was plagued with persistent phone calls from both the consultancies and countless members of the in-house team. The CFO was jumped on, mobbed and mugged every time he dared to venture out of his office. He gave up visiting the canteen for lunch, for when he appeared, it was as though the whole world had tweeted that Justin Bieber and Johnny Depp would both be there. As a result he became a very grumpy man—which in fairness is probably not a bad attribute for a good CFO.

So, if all goes well and the engagement is successful, then you should congratulate yourself. It's rare that everyone gets to be a winner. If you've had your money's worth, the enterprise gets its problem solved and the consultancy has a successful assignment on their hands. Not only does the firm make a bit of money but it also has a happy client who may give them more work. The sun is shining on everyone. Business is about win-win, a point that should never be forgotten (even on rare occasions when suppliers have lowered their shields). If you win big and someone else loses badly, then they will usually just wait until they can get even. Some won't mind if it takes decades. The IT ecosystem is but a small village community, even if it is scattered all over the world. Integrity is all about being a good person, but there are also sound business reasons for doing it. People talk. It is tough to make consultancy work, but if you are streetwise and you approach it honestly then it can be extremely valuable. There are plenty of very good people out there who can help you.

CHAPTER 6

Strategy Schizophrenia

"In real life, strategy is actually very straightforward.
You pick a general direction and implement like hell."

(Jack Welch)

"Strategy" is one of the most wonderful corporate words. It can mean many things to many people because it is so wonderfully misunderstood by so many. For example, it is possible to create a fuzzy warm feeling amongst your acolytes just by lowering your spectacles, nodding your head in a sage-like fashion and quietly uttering the words "I have a strategy". In my experience, many people in the IT industry have absolutely no idea what "strategy" actually means, but they'll feel good if they think they've got one.

This type of ignorance shouldn't come as a big surprise to us in the IT industry. We are a community which eagerly consumes the latest fads and fashions. This has not changed across the decades. In the eighties, for example, we had our "CASE tools", which apparently was some sort of space-age concept that would ultimately render every programmer redundant. In this world, code could apparently "write itself". In the nineties, I recall the excitement about "object-orientation", and "structured methodologies" where everyone started to talk about Darwinian inheritance, data-flow diagrams and various other sexy terms. The noughties and twenty-teens have brought us terms such as "agile" and "cloud computing" (Bloomberg, 2013), (Kavis, 2014). Let's wait to see what history has to say about them. Certainly I can confess to having prototyped my way to disaster with agile methods on many occasions. I also feel that hard drives, preferably RAIDed[1] to extreme levels, seem so much safer than the vaporous, fluffy clouds of our much loved vendors.

---

[1]RAID—Redundant Array of Inexpensive Disks. The more RAID the merrier.

However, the main issue with all these new fads was that no two people ever gave me the same definition of what they meant. Strategy, for example, is often used interchangeably with the word "important" as discussed in the Pathogenic Projects chapter. Elsewhere, it can even mean "divine intervention". I have seen IT leaders look for such "strategies" when even full-blown miracles of wonder would not make the slightest difference to their hopelessly doomed predicament. But a strategy is none of these things. It is a plan. And it is not just any old plan. Strategies have to be big plans. Really good strategies are exciting, audacious, expansive and stuffed full of fine things.

A Beginner's Guide to World Domination

One of the best tutorials for strategic planning which you are likely to encounter can be found within the pages of the famous James Bond novel *You Only Live Twice* (Fleming, 1964). Here we learn about the strategy of an evil mastermind who sits atop a global organised crime syndicate. The anti-hero's name is Ernst Stavro Blofeld. He had a simple vision. He wanted to rule the world. However, he knew that this was not going to be a trivial task in the heady days of US-Soviet superpower shenanigans. Blofeld therefore decided that a bold strategic plan was needed. Hollowing out a volcano on a remote Pacific island, he developed his own space rocket programme (which doesn't sound too difficult if you say it quickly). He then blasted his spacecraft into orbit and cunningly arranged for his somewhat larger craft to capture any passing capsules from the superpowers of the day. He reckoned it wouldn't be long before blame games would shift to something more serious and World War III would inevitably erupt. After the isotope-fest, Blofeld could then step in to take control of what was left. Although most quality managers would doubtless be fretting about some of the more challenging entries on the risk register, it was a simple and clean approach which contains all the essential elements of a fine strategic play.

These being …

- **Vision**—the "to be" state. What you want it to look like when it's finished (e.g. I'm in charge of the world, even if it is a teensy bit more radioactive)
- **Strategy**—the "big plan" that gets you to the end state (e.g. volcanoes and spaceships)
- **Obstacles**—irritating things that prevent you executing your strategy cleanly (e.g. like secret agents)
- **Tactics**—small plans which allow you to overcome obstacles (e.g. killing secret agents and terrorising minions).

Figure 6.1 shows how these elements are related.

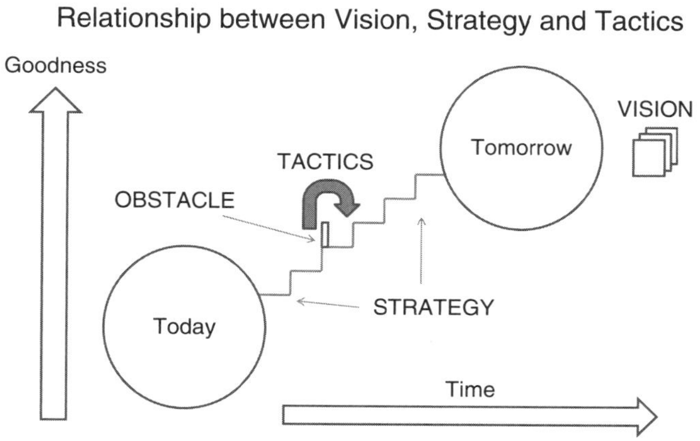

Relationship between Vision, Strategy and Tactics

Figure 6.1 The Strategic Landscape

The "Vision" in the top right of the diagram describes in detail how we want things to be at some stage in the future. It is always higher on the "goodness" axis than where we are today (even if Blofeld's view of "goodness" probably wouldn't attract universal acceptance). Also, the vision always lies on the right side of the time axis. This is because no matter how loud we shout or how hard we stamp our feet, it always takes time to do things.

The lower circle marked "Today" shows us where we are at the moment. Meanwhile the higher circle, marked "Tomorrow", shows us where we want to be. Like the vision, our tomorrow is both later in time than today and it exists higher up the y-axis in a more desirable place, at least in terms of our notion of "goodness". We are, after all, trying to make the world a better place.

Finally, the stairway (or plan) that leads us from our "Today" to our desired "Tomorrow" will form the basis of our "Strategy".

It is possible that we might be blocked by obstacles along the way (such as the intervention of an irritating secret agent). This we attend to with a helping of "Tactics". Blofeld found that terrified, expendable minions who aren't assigned to any critical path activities are perfect for this task. Indeed, if you want to add a dash of style to the proceedings, you can even kit out your secret base with an artificial pool filled with piranha fish spanned by an amusing retractable bridge. What fun you can have with those who fail to complete their tasks on time.

> **"Strategy without tactics is the slowest route to victory. Tactics without strategy is the noise before defeat."**
> ***Sun Tzu, The Art of War***

Types of Strategy

Some believe that there many ways of developing a strategy, but in my experience, there are essentially two main approaches by which you can arrange for the future to happen in the way you want it to:

- First, you can look at the problem from the perspective of today, taking note of all of today's issues. Fixing most or even all of them will certainly give you a "Better Tomorrow".
- Alternatively, you can forget about all today's troubles and instead you focus your energies on building a vision of how you want things to look in a utopian, unconstrained future of ultimate goodness. This is the main tenet of what is known as a "Grand Plan".

Most good strategic approaches will contain a mixture of elements from both of these two extremes. Depending on your circumstances and the level of risk you are prepared to enjoy or endure, you can choose which basic approach suits you best and then mix and match the most appropriate pieces from each. Bond villains are usually in the Grand Plan camp, but there's no shame in being a little less ambitious. Not everyone is a megalomaniac after all.

Let's look at the two methods in their purest forms and consider their relative merits.

The Better Tomorrow

The Better Tomorrow philosophy looks at strategy with the assumption that you are pretty unhappy with where you are today and that you need to fix a whole bunch of problems really quickly. With this approach, the present-day areas of dissatisfaction that everyone is persistently emailing you about become the powerful engine that drives the changes. The process is relatively simple and although it can sometimes be time-consuming to complete the exercise comprehensively, it can create great successes quite quickly for you and your organisation.

The essential elements of the Better Tomorrow strategy are:

1. I'm pretty unhappy about where we are today …
2. … but I need to understand where I am before I can go to a better place …
3. … so I therefore need to document my "today" state as thoroughly as I can in order to understand it (the "as-is" position)
4. Now I must identify the areas of dissatisfaction and difficulties

5. For each of these areas, I will build a "get well" plan
6. Now I can execute a prioritised set of "get well" plans to take us from our "today" state to the better place tomorrow (the "to-be" state).

The Better Tomorrow method is by far the most common form of strategy development I've seen used in Information Technology in global corporates. It works well because no matter how good the people in the IT function may think they are, there never appears to be any shortage of things that an adoring, computer-using public feel unhappy about.

The Better Tomorrow model has several significant fine attributes to recommend it. These include the following:

- It addresses areas of unhappiness. There is a promise that life is going to get better and what's more, the better tomorrow you are promising isn't very far away. This is never a bad thing. Punters like this.
- The approach is highly data-orientated and so it is appealing to logical, rational managers. Happily, you will probably find lots of these types of people in your IT organisation.
- Resistance to the proposed changes will generally be much more muted compared to many other change program. This is because the compelling logic of the approach can easily be grasped and the likelihood is that the changes you are about to make will be perceived as beneficial by most. Indeed, such strategies are unlikely to be too radical and threatening to your employees and your stakeholders (which is something they will be grateful for).

The philosophy has similarities to the Japanese continuous improvement ethic. It is also highly concordant with the Six-Sigma methodology and the concepts of Kaizen (Toyota, 2013). In this regard, if you are in a company that operates the Six-Sigma martial arts system, then you can gather together a series of small, so-called "green belt" projects or larger, "black belt" projects to help you achieve your strategic ends. The Better Tomorrow approach is a perfect vehicle for coordinating squillions or even zillions of Six-Sigma improvements into a coherent program of change for good. If your company is into Six-Sigma, this strategic approach also offers a great way of communicating and securing buy-in from your senior business colleagues. If you really want to cut a dash, you can even align your projects with the seven Mudas of Waste (Lean Manufacturing Tools, 2013). Your stakeholders will understand exactly what you are trying to do—which in the IT world is a rare and beautiful thing. Within hours you could be engaging in a spot of communal Hoshin Kanri and enjoying playful banter around the Kanban Board.

> ### THE BASICS OF SIX-SIGMA
>
> Six-Sigma is a business strategy, originally developed by Motorola back in 1986 (Tennant, 2001). Today it enjoys widespread application in many sectors of industry. Six-Sigma seeks to identify and remove the causes of defects and errors in manufacturing and business processes. It uses a set of quality management methods, including statistical methods, and creates a special infrastructure of people within the organisation ("Black Belts" etc.) who are experts in these methods. Each Six-Sigma project carried out within an organisation follows a defined sequence of steps and has quantified financial targets (cost reduction or profit increase). To learn more explore *Lean Six Sigma for Dummies* (Morgan & Martin, 2012)

The Better Tomorrow approach is also favoured by many consultancies, not least because it offers a great chance to sell a client a pleasing number of billing hours documenting the "as-is" and "to-be" states. Indeed, the process to record the full details of the "today" state can be made as large and extensive as you wish. With all this effort, you can certainly build up a humungous array of interview notes. So if you do want to impress anyone with the volume and extensivity of your diligence and hard work, then this is a great way to do it. The final report will have a serious "thud" factor to it. When it's done, you will find that it is also relatively easy to demonstrate the improvements to your masters because you have—of course—been addressing all the biggest bugbears of the day. What's not to like?

> **"I have a plan so cunning, you could put a tail on it and call it a weasel."**
> **Edmund Blackadder** *(Curtis, Elton, & Atkinson, 1983–98)*

The relatively conservative nature of Better Tomorrow strategies means that the scope for you to create disasters of biblical proportions is greatly reduced compared to many other methods. There will be no plagues of locusts, boils or frogs. The only major downside of this approach is that it often ends up providing only incremental improvements to the "today" state. The fact that you've spent so much time trying to understand the "today" state means that little if any effort has been expended in developing a wholly unconstrained "tomorrow" view. Nonetheless the process has worked very well indeed for many people and it has a very important place in the armoury of any good IT leader.

There are two specific situations where the Better Tomorrow approach can offer unrivalled salvation to any beleaguered IT leader:

- If your IT function is in a terrible, terrible state then it's a smart idea to address the major issues as quickly as you can through a Better

Tomorrow strategy. Indeed, if you get it right, it might not be long before the lynch mob that is currently baying for your blood and threatening to set fire to your intestines is magically transformed into an adoring band of lifetime supporters. Before long flags and flattering posters of you may adorn the office walls (well, you can always hope!). Such successes will give you a platform of credibility from which you can make further gains. You might even want to risk using this platform to try something a bit more ambitious later.

- If your IT function is in pretty good shape after years of diligent continuous improvement activities, then you may only need a small push to achieve those world-class, upper quartile levels you are aiming at. You do not need to take high risks with other, more radical approaches—so don't. Cruise over the finishing line, benchmark your successes and sit back and enjoy the spoils of war.

Figure 6.2 shows a schematic describing the Better Tomorrow method. Note the length of the strategy staircase. It is neither long on the time nor on the goodness axes. This means that the plan should not take long to implement and as such it will tend to carry lower levels of risk than other methods. As we've discussed, you will create a "to-be" state (or vision) which should enjoy a high level of buy-in from your stakeholders. This approach might seem to fly in the face of the "big plan" definition of strategy, but while the details of your plan will probably contain many zillions of minor tasks, nobody could deny the strategic value of your bold goal to fix everything that the enterprise is unhappy about.

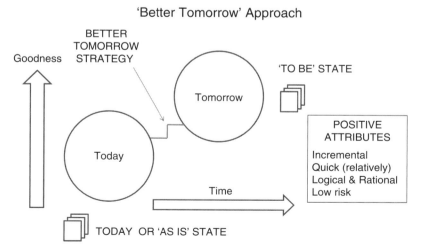

Figure 6.2 The Better Tomorrow Strategic Landscape

The Grand Plan

The Grand Plan on the other hand, is quite a different beast. Grand Plans are all about bold strokes and dramatic visions. For students of the Grand Plan approach, the more exciting and daring it is the better. These people aren't just interested in better tomorrows. They want to go much further into the future and to drive the corporation towards ever heightened levels of corporate ecstasy. Grand Plan advocates will be into full-blown "promised land" messianic visions of the future. For these reasons the Grand Plan is usually the method of choice for any good Bond villain. Incremental improvement isn't generally considered to be the fastest method of achieving world domination (unless you are a Japanese automotive company).

The main tenets of the Grand Plan are:

1. I don't care where I am today. That is just an accident of history.
2. I want to be (delete as applicable)
   (a) upper quartile
   (b) the best in the industry
   (c) transforming my company so that it can wipe the floor with the competition
   (d) eliminating poverty
   (e) any other wild and hairy goal you may wish to choose
   (f) all of the above.
3. I need to clearly figure out exactly what tomorrow looks like and document it thoroughly.
4. Once all the stakeholders agree on the shared vision, then I need to build a strategic plan to deliver it.

The major focus of the Grand Plan isn't the "today" state, nor is it interested in all the day-to-day problems you are currently wrestling with. In this type of strategy, all the early effort is directed almost exclusively into defining the target end state—your vision of the future. And since you are building your own personal version of Rome, it is unlikely that you will be able to accomplish it in a day. Grand Plans are rarely executed in less than a year. Some may take five years, but on average, a good Grand Plan in Information Technology has a two to three year execution horizon.

Once you have a clear vision which has the buy-in of your stakeholders, then you can collect your $200, pass GO and proceed to the next stage. Now you turn your attention to the construction of the bridge (or strategic plan) that will carry your organisation towards the vision. Grand Vision strategies are much, much, much higher risk than most Better Tomorrow plans. Your chances of success are therefore correspondingly much reduced, but in compensation for this, the rewards should be much higher should you succeed.

And there is always the possibility that you will capture the imagination of your audience who may even choose to join you on your quest. JFK's iconic moon vision statement is probably the best example of a grand vision you are ever likely to hear:

"I believe that this nation should commit itself to achieving the goal, before this decade is out, of landing a man on the moon and returning him safely to the Earth."
President John F. Kennedy

While this vision was undeniably tough, the boffins at NASA somehow managed to overachieve on this goal. These fine folk actually managed to get twelve men on the moon and then bring them back. They even got to play a spot of golf and bring back some seaside rock. How cool is that?

Back on the Earth, if you are enlisting external help for a Grand Plan approach, then you will need to satisfy yourself that any consulting team you engage is appropriately staffed with heavyweight players. These players will need to have an excellent track record both in forming Grand Plans and in shaping the complex and the difficult strategies that flow from them. Such people and such teams are rare. You will need to look beyond the marketing platitudes. It's never as easy as the gushing consultancy posters in airport departure lounges would have you believe.

Figure 6.3 shows a schematic of the Grand Plan approach. There are several differences between this and the Better Tomorrow method.

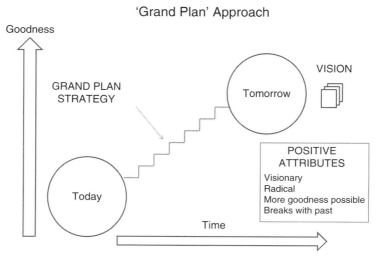

Figure 6.3   The Grand Plan Strategic Landscape

First of all there is a long strategic staircase. Grand Plans usually take much longer to implement than Better Tomorrow strategies, though you do of course get a plan that potentially can deliver much higher levels of "goodness". However, both these attributes render the Grand Plan more vulnerable to obstacles and to the unwelcome intrusion of external events. As you move into the execution phase, you will also quickly find that any shortcomings in your organisation in terms of project management or business transformation capability will surface very quickly. Then, just as you start to make the changes, you will also probably discover just how much of that "shared vision" that you took so much time to lovingly create is really "shared" by everyone (and whether it has sufficient detail to allow you to develop a coherent strategy).

The Grand Plan is therefore a bold, often multi-year approach that is effectively a large-scale business transformation program. It is often deployed in the following circumstances:

- If you and your C-level colleagues are visionary leaders and you want to make a step change in performance.
- If you are involved in a merger or major acquisition and the current operating model from either merger partner will not work for the new company.
- If you're the kind of person who loves doing risky things (whom uncharitable friends might call a megalomaniac).

Advocates of the Grand Plan approach will tell you that this is the strategic approach preferred by great leaders (Alexander the Great certainly was a Grand Plan man), whereas the Better Tomorrow model is better suited to managers and less visionary people. This is harsh. But idealists and scientists out there who believe in concepts such as "truth and beauty" will find the seductive qualities of the Grand Plan irresistible, even if the journey to utopia is an exercise in crawling over broken glass.

Grand Plans, Better Tomorrows and all shades in between, however, are equally valid approaches to the problems at hand. As with all calculated gambles, this game is all about picking the right horse for the right course on the right day. At the beginning of the race it is not always obvious what you should do, though there will be no shortage of people with an inside track who will share their "hot tips". My own post-race experiences suggest that corporate landscape, environment and above all, appetite for change are the best pre-race "form" indicators.

Figure 6.4 shows one model to help you decide which method to use and when.

The left hand side of the diagram shows a place where all is not well. You may be in a swamp wrestling with alligators or perhaps drifting aimlessly in

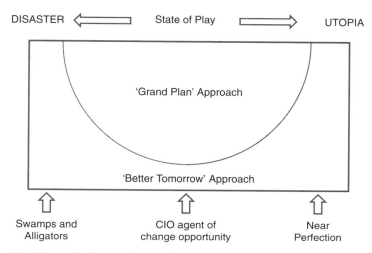

Figure 6.4   Strategic Approaches: Which to Use, When and by How Much?

a fetid brown creek without a paddle. Your corporate patient may possibly be bleeding to death. Here the Better Tomorrow techniques can stabilise the situation until you can order a load of swamp-draining pumps.

In the middle ground between disaster and corporate utopia, the ground is fertile for the CIO to emerge as the change agent for the business. Here an IT leader can not only execute their Grand Plan, but they may also be in a position to seize an opportunity to genuinely lead the business through process-led technology change. The sunny uplands of a better future beckon. The middle ground is a great place for visionaries.

On the right hand side of the diagram, we find those fortunate enough to already be performing at genuine world-class levels. Final delicate Better Tomorrow polishing within the context of a continuous improvement ethos is probably the best course of action for them. New, risky, radical approaches can wait until circumstances dictate. Now is not the time to snatch defeat from the jaws of victory.

Strategy Schizophrenia—Balancing the Unbalanceable

When you have summoned up enough courage to decide which kind of play you are going to make (Better Tomorrow, Grand Plan or more likely, some hybrid of the two) you will quickly become aware that there are a large number of forces acting on you. Different stakeholders will all seem to want something quite different. Some will continue to see themselves as your customers (even if you refuse to follow the discredited internal customer/supplier model described in the Dislocated Stakeholders chapter). Some with an agenda all of their own will probably be doing all that they can to influence, cajole or even bully you to do their bidding. Meanwhile others will simply assume that you are telepathic. They will expect you to deal with all the things they haven't talked to you about together with a range of things they haven't even thought about themselves. Balancing the needs of your internal stakeholders is enough to drive anyone crazy.

In addition, there will be range of external factors acting on the IT organisation. There may be a coherent business strategy with which you must align (which would be nice, but don't hold your breath). And of course, the perennial pressure of external budgetary constraints will be bearing down on you. Accountants are never far away from the action at least as far as the cash is concerned. You can also look forward to dealing with the challenges of your IT industry suppliers, including all the trends and latest fads, and of course the never-ending pressure to upgrade—the unfortunate side-effect of Moore's Law that we unearthed in the Seriously Shaky Software chapter. Finally, you will obviously want to factor in your own views once you have taken the rest of the world's prejudices into account. In short, there are many, many people and lots of different circumstances pushing, pulling, constraining and crushing an IT leader. Sir Isaac Newton himself would probably have struggled with all the conflicting forces you have to deal with. With such impressive tidal gravitational energy in play it is therefore not surprising that many IT leaders can act in distorted ways. Irrationality and schizophrenia are but a short step away, when everything looks like an image in a fairground mirror. One psychiatrist summed it up like this:

> **"The experience and behaviour that gets labelled**
> **schizophrenic is a special strategy that a person invents in**
> **order to live in an unliveable situation."**
> **R.D. Laing, British Psychiatrist (1928–1989)**

So, in summary you will find plenty of heat, noise and light out there and most of it will be directed at you. But if you are strong enough and able to deal with the "unliveable situation" without descending into the horrors of Dr Laing's "special strategy", then you will probably have worked out that this is a game that's all about balance. Think of it as if you were crossing Niagara Falls on a tightrope in a gusty gale. Only those with good balance, nerves of steel and incredible determination will survive. Others will wobble alarmingly as they make their trepidated way across the wire. Before long, the unfortunates will succumb to the Newtonian forces of wind, wibble, wobble and mental stress that are all conspiring to hasten their doom. The crowd will gasp as the ropewalker's arms flail and finally the victim will plunge earthward towards the foaming waters of failure where they will be dashed on the rocks of ruin. And then, as with those who have suffered the fate of Pathogenic Projects since Egyptian times, their remains will be swept out to sea (or a great lake in this particular case). Put simply, this stuff is not easy and the stakes are terribly high.

While on the face of it, there appear to be many different stakeholders pulling in different directions, when you look at things closely, many of them are curiously lined up behind one another. Indeed, they will often pull you one particular way—a tactical way. At least that's how it always was for me. Your users and middle managers and even some of the senior leaders are often intensely parochial in their outlook. These are the savvy beasts in the corporate jungle who will expect you to satisfy them and accede to their whims. They will be more concerned about hygiene elements such as quality of service, helpdesks, local support levels and the modernity of the desktop devices. The demand for small-scale projects from their acolytes will also be intense. In my experience, demand for new projects in Western companies typically runs at between two and four times the available investment budgets. This means that poor IT leaders are confronted with crushing black hole-like forces dragging them towards an event horizon beyond which infinite numbers of projects are spawned. Demands are usually overwhelmingly in the "keep me happy" category. As a result, loud and vociferous stakeholders in the business usually enjoy disproportionate levels of project and operational support from battered and bullied IT departments. Here the average size of IT projects is often quite small, while the number of initiatives is voluminous (tending towards infinity in fact). The overall impact of such a fragmented program is highly questionable in terms of moving any of the needles at company level, but many IT leaders will feel that they lack sufficient support and gravitas to risk executing any other agenda. So if you are a Grand Visionary, then your life suddenly looks very difficult indeed. For those of the "Better Tomorrow" school, the situation may be little better. Your problems are going to be all about controlling the large number of disparate, wriggling strands of a very complex plan. And of course to make sure that this plan is not leading you to a bad place.

Looking down from on high, some mature CEOs and Board members, however, will want a very different type of program (Figure 6.5). They have specific and lofty responsibilities. When you appear in front of them at that first frightening Board meeting, they will not unreasonably expect you to be doing work that is in line with how they, the leadership, are directing the company.

Figure 6.5   The Conflicting Requirements of Stakeholders and the Consequences of not Dealing with Them

Board responsibilities vary between countries, but they all have the same general thrust. The UK Institute of Directors Factsheet (IoD, 2010) gives a good summary. In general Boards are worried about things such as:

- Defining strategic objectives
- Tracking progress against the objectives
- Appointing senior management (possibly including you)
- Being accountable to the shareholders for the company's activities.

They will also be very, very concerned about risk, both to the company and to their ability to control what's going on in the company. Directors are personally liable to both civil action and criminal prosecutions up to and including corporate manslaughter. Making sure that you keep yourself out of gaol is a pretty good incentive for staying on the ball as these things go.

Summary

Resolving this amazing array of different opinions into something meaningful is immensely challenging. If you do try to implement an exclusively high-level agenda that is linked closely to the strategy of the company, then you can expect huge levels of resistance at all other levels in the organisation. I can confess to having made this major blunder at least once in my career. Guerrilla warfare is a much cherished and finely honed art in corporate cultures. Most middle managers must have read Che Guevara's famous book (Guevara, 2006 (originally 1961)). Otherwise, how could even relatively junior managers in such a company effortlessly slow down, stop or derail major change programs in the way that they do? You may even be treated to a dose of the delightfully unhelpful "malicious obedience" (Urban Dictionary) which is every bit as terrifying as it sounds. Finally, your actions may incur the wrath of the many. Transformational endeavours tend to upset people, particularly if parts of the program threaten their job security, their responsibilities, their location, their ways of working or if it means they will have to pay for their coffee from now on. Most people are only happy with the concept of change when they are the ones doing the changing or if it is happening to someone who they don't like. What's worse is that if most of your efforts are devoted to the large-scale, there will be little time and money left to deal with IT hygiene or any small-scale local demands. This will further enrage your audience of computer users. None of this is going to be easy.

Hopefully, the macro-level strategic models shown above can help you find some kind of shape for your program. Since strategy and budgets are closely interlinked, we are now fast approaching the time when you will have to fit a budget to your chosen strategic approach. As you've probably already guessed, this is not in the slightest bit straightforward. Now we need to move a little further down the course to find out how we can avoid bleeding all our money away for little gain to the enterprise.

CHAPTER 7

Bleeding Budgets

"Don't tell me what you value, show me your budget,
and I'll tell you what you value."

(Joe Biden)

Hobbits and Elves get very excited about "rings of power" and "ring-bearers" in the world of myth and fiction (Tolkein, 1954). But in corporate life the true source of earthly power and influence is an ancient, mysterious resource known as the "budget". If you are fortunate enough to be a "budget-holder", you can be sure that you will never be short of friends (or enemies for that matter). Indeed the bigger your budget, the more power you will be able to wield and the more followers you will acquire. Many elves and goblins who live in the realm of the corporate world regard the budget as a crock of gold at the end of their rainbow. With lots of glittery stuff potentially lurking just beneath the surface, it's not difficult to see why people get so excited. Many believe that budgets are not only wondrous things, but they also believe that the treasure is curiously infinite (at least for their purposes). As a result there are always hordes of pilgrims to be found chasing these rainbows with their metaphorical spades and shovels (otherwise known as project proposals). But there are challenges for any who tread this path. Budget-holders, no matter how powerful they may be, will know that once their precious cash has been dissipated, their strength will fade as fast as Samson's on the day he decided to visit his barber.

If your strategy is *the* plan which shows the way towards your ultimate vision, then budgets are the crocks of gold that fund the activities in your kingdom. Budgets and strategies are inextricably intertwined. It is written that one can have no substance without the other. Unbelievers who dare to scorn or scoff at this ancient truth will be doomed to haemorrhage their budget to the tune of something altogether more sinister. It is known as either "spending the money on any old thing that takes our fancy", or its darker twin, "stuff you get bullied into doing by angry users". Neither of these options is likely to lead you to any good outcome. The day of reckoning will arrive when the grey-suited, stony-faced accountants of your organisation close in to tot up the scores at the end of the game (or the "accounting period" as they prefer to call it). For them it will come down to the simple assessment of whether you've ended up with something valuable, or whether you've just been spraying the company's life-blood all over the office. It's easy to spot whether you've been a bad boy or girl. Everyone will look very anaemic when the auditors show up.

One IT leader I knew some years ago fell afoul of this awful fate. He spent lots of his company's money trying to keep his users happy. When he explained this to his boss, there was a long, uncomfortable silence. Eventually he was told in no uncertain terms that this was a very bad idea. The boss, who had something of a dry sense of humour, told his manager that if he wanted to spread lots of happiness and engender undying loyalty from his user community, then he should instead try selling crack-cocaine instead. This method, he explained, is much more effective and it is certainly more satisfying than initiating hundreds of IT projects that would probably never finish. Disclaimer— for those intending to try this at home I must point out that the crack-cocaine approach is not generally in the list of "best practice" IT management tools. It is also considered illegal in most jurisdictions in the world.

Making the right decisions on which items you should include in your strategy and, probably more importantly, which you should leave out is in effect a series of bets. IT leaders who attempt to please everyone please no-one. Besides, there is never enough money to keep all the rainbow pilgrims happy. One very good way I have found to set up my betting approach is to start with the Board's view and then to work my way down. This is a good place to start, because it gives you the best chance of enacting your organisation's major strategic goals. The alternative where you ask fifty thousand people in your company for their views will probably generate more than a hundred thousand opinions, especially if they are engineers or scientists. As you shape the budget around the strategy, you can use the models presented here to check how the conflicting forces that are acting upon you all balance up. The compromise you end up with may not look very pretty, but it's not prettiness you are after. You want something that will work.

So let's get to the task of working out how to share out all this lovely money.

A Beginner's Guide to Building a Roulette Table

How Much Are You Going to Spend?

I have been extremely fortunate in that I have had the opportunity to work with some outstanding Board members with perhaps one of the best Chairmen you could ever wish to serve under. These august people and my executive colleagues were highly instrumental in helping me develop this approach. I have found it indispensable to help me develop a coherent framework for my work plans. Early on in our relationship we discussed two questions that at once were breathtakingly simple, yet devastatingly profound. They were:

- How much money are we spending on IT?

... and

- How much good are we doing?

I was not able to give a clear answer. It was a goldfish moment. I felt like an idiot, but it seems I am not the only one to have ever fallen into this particular elephant trap. I take some comfort from the fact that many CIOs from all over the world are wriggling around on the same nasty spike at the bottom of this particular concealed pit. However, the situation moved forward in a constructive way and led us towards a helpful discussion on the size of the total IT budget (which included all the clandestine stuff done outside the control of the IT thought police) and how it related to overall sales. The equation for this first question is very pretty in all respects. It is pretty simple as well as being pretty useful:

$$\frac{\text{IT Spending}}{\text{Total Company Revenue}} = \text{Percentage of Revenue spent on IT}$$

This result now allows meaningful comparisons to be made with other companies (assuming you can find the data). When I completed this exercise the first time we arrived at a shocking conclusion. We discovered that our company was spending nearly 4.2% of its revenue on IT while our competitors were spending less than 3% on theirs. And what's more our closest competitor had recently embarked on an IT cost reduction program that would open up an even bigger gap. This horrible finding could only mean one of two things:

1. If our company was charging the same price for our product as our competitor, then we were probably making less money than they were.
2. If we were building our IT cost disadvantage into elevated prices for our product then we would probably start losing sales in a competitive environment really soon.

This led us to the simple "percentage of revenue" metric (Figure 7.1). It defines the size of your pot. It also facilitates rational discussion at budget time. If, for example, you have an absolutely magical project which everyone believes will transform the future of the whole company with spectacular benefits, then you can start the process of justifying the proportional increase in your budget.

This allows us to create the first main metric and it is the lynchpin of our budget model. How much are we planning to spend as a percentage of sales? Your playing piece is now firmly on the board and you can start rolling the dice.

Figure 7.1   IT Budget as a Percentage of Sales—the First Board Level Metric

How Much Goodness?

The second question they asked relates to goodness. We initially puzzled as to how we could prove how much goodness we were adding. This led the debate to the first macro-level breakdown of the budget. How the budget breaks out is obvious when you think about it, though when you see the answer it will probably send shivers down your spine:

- How much money are we spending on new IT investments (and what value are they adding)?
- How much money are we spending on everything else?

This led us straight away to the next two key metrics in our stack. The first we defined was investment as a proportion of the total IT budget. We defined the second category as "everything else", though most of us felt it needed a better name. We eventually decided to call it "operations" (Figure 7.2).

Looking at the whole IT function through this new prism immediately started to shape our behaviours and attitudes. For example, these metrics immediately generate an expectation that the proportion of the budget allocated to investment should be as high as possible. Meanwhile the percentage allocated to "everything else" should ideally be as low as we might dare to reduce it ... at least if we want to create the maximum levels of goodness for the corporation. Now I was beginning to realise why only certain people make it to Board level. Leadership really isn't about answers; it's all about the questions you ask.

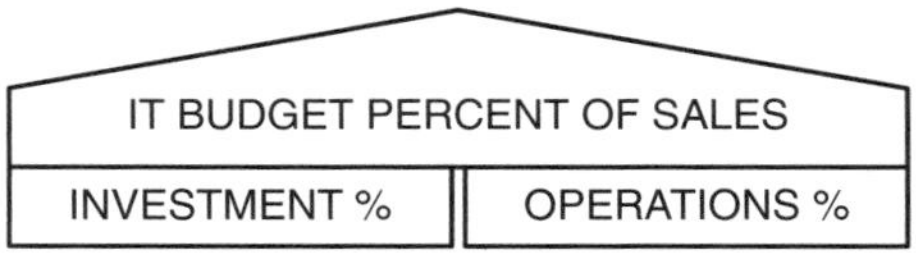

```
        ┌─────────────────────────────────┐
        │  IT BUDGET PERCENT OF SALES      │
        ├────────────────┬────────────────┤
        │  INVESTMENT %  │  OPERATIONS %   │
        └────────────────┴────────────────┘
```

Figure 7.2   Investment versus Operational Costs—the Second Main Board Metric

We continued working this trail of logic and further broke out elements of the investment and operations budgets.

Operations

For the operations element, we could see that some of our operations work was planned. This included operating system upgrades, scheduled maintenance and an array of other housekeeping tasks. Unsurprisingly, these tasks were being carried out as projects with the same kind of processes we used on our investment projects.

> **"There are two kinds of people in this world: Those who believe there are two kinds of people in this world and those who are smart enough to know better."**
> **Tom Robbins**

However, the lion's share of the operations money was being spent on unplanned events. This category of support spending covered everything over which we seemed to exert little or no control. In the data centre these included dealing with major systems failures, bug fixes, and backup failures together with any crisis management activities that were required. They also included external problems such as those on the voice or data networks and even the antics of wayward Internet service providers. We were also struggling to keep abreast of in-house application failures and bugs, not to mention vendor packages that didn't do what they should be doing. Finally, there was the tricky question of how to keep on top of the plethora of desk-side support issues that were trying the patience and sanity of the helpdesk team.

While office-based equipment enjoys impressive reliability levels, statistics works against those who dare to run IT functions in large organisations. Mean-time-between-failures metrics of around 20,000 to 30,000 hours are not uncommon, but if you are servicing 100,000 or more computer users, then you are going to have your hands full. At these reliability levels you can expect to see up to five PC failures an hour (or about 10,500 a year). Then there are the helpdesk calls you have to deal with. Metrics from organisations I have managed suggest that, on average, a typical user calls the IT helpdesk twice a month. For the 100,000 person organisation mentioned above, this would translate to nearly two and a half million helpdesk calls a year. In some organisations, the human race would become extinct before the caller struggling with his or her spreadsheet macro ever got to the front of the queue. "Your call is important to us. Please continue to hold until the end of time."

This level of demand soaks up impressively large volumes of time and money. If you have the misfortune to be managing a complex, unreliable IT environment then this category of support spending can turn into an insatiable monster that will swiftly consume your entire budget. You will be left naked to face a disappointed, hostile user community. IT Operations is not a sport for the faint hearted (Figure 7.3).

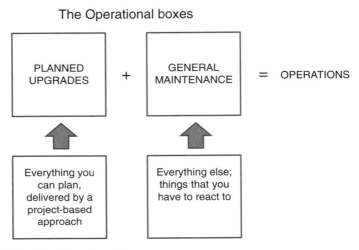

Figure 7.3   The Operational Boxes

Investment

Over on the investment side, things were not much better. We found that the £20m of investment money we had allocated in the current year's budget was being spread across nearly 700 projects. The persistent demands of an angry user community seemed to have resulted in a showering incandescence of small projects. Nothing was happening quickly. The benefits from this cacophony of unfinished trivia were extremely difficult to calculate. We quickly realised that it was almost impossible to prove whether any benefit had been delivered. Because the progress of the portfolio was so slow, few if any of these projects were being completed. Meanwhile new projects were being shovelled into an ever-expanding hopper of insatiable project demand hopelessness. For me this was the moment when I recognised the full and unabridged horror of the internal-customer/supplier model. The ugly goblin of realisation stared at me with contempt, jumped out, grabbed me by the throat and spat in my eye. We had arrived at the hostile buyer/captive supplier end-game. The angry middle managers' demands were never going to be satisfied. This left the IT function only two options. We could respond aggressively and refuse to play in this game of Bleeding Budgets or else we could curl up in a ball and surrender. As with many IT organisations all over the world, this team was made up of nice people who were keen to please and so they initially chose the second option. They could now look forward to a future of bullying, bad press, torment and suffering. The more projects they did, it seemed, the less benefit would accrue. The overwhelming majority of the projects turned out to be what we dubbed "keep score" applications. Many were designed to make the lives of managers a little bit easier. Few if any were automating critical business processes or disrupting the market with competitive new innovations. Few if any could be traced through to meaningful business benefits which meant that once we totted up the score we found we had a net-negative portfolio on our hands. We were dishing out the equivalent of crack-cocaine to keep our users happy, only no-one was getting high. This realisation led everyone to a new place. Other critical new metrics needed to be quickly identified.

They were:

For Investment

- **Average project size** ($, with internal manpower metrics converted to money)—We figured that the bigger the project, the more chance that it could make a positive impact on the enterprise or our market position. We decided that we should try to make this number as big as we could.
- **Benefits minus costs**—Big benefits for low costs across the project portfolio. This wasn't hard to sell as a concept. We decided that we'd try to make this number as large as we could. Crucially, someone came up with the idea it should be independently verified by Internal Audit once the project is in full operational use. Project sponsor and senior IT leader would be held jointly accountable. Everyone would be now sacrificed on the altar of genuine business benefits. This made us all very honest, but at the same time very uncomfortable.

For Operations

- **The ratio of planned work versus general support and operations activity**—We decided that we wanted to get as much of this work into a planned state as we could. This would give us the best chance of creating a controlled environment.
- **Cost per desktop**—This was an interesting metric that emerged after long days and nights of debate. We worked out that if we kept this number low, then we could use any savings to fund more investment projects. Moreover, it would also be a driver to help our standardisation efforts which would in turn also help reduce the unplanned "general" operational costs.

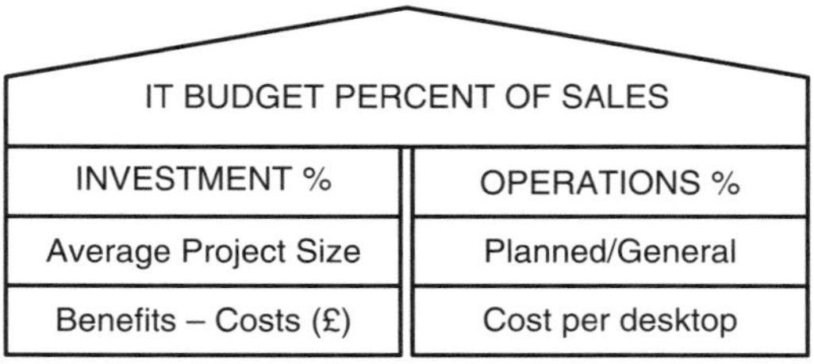

Figure 7.4   The Third Incarnation of the Metric Model—Investment versus Operations

All this led to the third incarnation of the Board metrics diagram (see Figure 7.4).

With this model dictating a very different shape to the budget allocation process, we could now turn our attention to the investments. How could we make our investments create the biggest bang for the buck? We realised that up to now we had effectively been following a "Better Tomorrow" strategy, where there wasn't any better. Maybe now was the time to think about something a bit more radical. This led us to another question. Which investments give us the right goodness profile for our enterprise?

Which Investments?

There is no shortage of management tools out there to help you refine your investment strategies within the world of IT. The first and most widely used was originally developed in the 1970s. It takes its name from Boston Consulting Group who pioneered the use of this fine weapon of mass destruction. It is also known as a "growth-share matrix" (Stern & Deimler, 2006). Originally, the Boston Grid was used to help companies decide on appropriate investment strategies at the macro level. It was originally constructed by plotting the growth of the market on one axis, versus the current market share of the company on the other axis. In Figure 7.5, various roadmaps are shown indicating how investments can change over time. Further work by others such as McFarlan and McKenny whose widely cited paper "The Information Archipelago—Plotting a course" (McFarlan & McKenny, 1983) developed the concepts further in the IT world. Other work using similar concepts (Warr, 1990) together with new techniques such as "balanced scorecards" are also now widely used in enterprises across the globe (Kaplan & Norton, 1996). Today, almost every consultant you come across will be brandishing glossy PowerPoint slides stuffed full of two-by-two matrices.

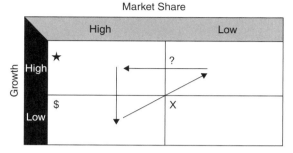

Figure 7.5 An Example of a Boston Consulting Growth Share Matrix, Showing the Success Sequence (Stern & Deimler, 2006)

Many of these models will be used to judge your organisation. The method for the unscrupulous out there is simple. In a two-by-two matrix there are four boxes. One is really good, one is really bad and the other two are OK in the sense that they are not really OK. Guess which one your organisation fits in?

Having started to put together a series of metrics that made sense to us as far as percentage of sales etc. was concerned, we decided to continue with this process. While there were other techniques out there, we resolved to stick to the first principles method we had started in the previous sections. We felt that this would help us define a set of investment categories that would work for our organisation. We looked at processes rather than organisational functions or IT systems themselves. Our organisation had a fairly mature process model which had been operating successfully for some years. From this model it was possible to identify many of the key or core functions of our business.

"Core Business" Processes

To identify the core processes we asked "what's important around here?" We felt that this would enable us to identify the business processes that defined our business and allow us to triangulate the results against the process model. For a pharmaceutical company for example, core business processes might include the design of new chemical entities or the operation of clinical trials. For an aerospace company, it might include CAD/CAM design methodologies, manufacturing and supply chain activities as well as the important after-market functions. And in an oil company, core business processes will include such things as oil reservoir modelling in the upstream part of their business and oil refining processes at the downstream end. Our definition for these processes was:

> *Core business processes are the elements that you need to run your business. They are generally unique to your sector.*

Each of the competitors will also be operating similar core business processes. This should be no surprise.

"Supporting the Business" Processes

The next step was to try to classify everything else. This was initially easy, largely because we decided that we would use the "everything else" category once again. Clearly, as well as our core business processes, the company will also be carrying out activities which every other company of a similar size and scale would also have to do. We decided that our "everything else" processes would be those that supported our business. Since they are not core, then they were never going to be specific to our company or indeed any sector. We decided that they are generic necessities—and you generically have to carry them out whether you generically like it or not.

> *Supporting the business functions are those which are not core to the business. However, every company of your size and complexity will need to carry out these processes.*

Sometimes "supporting the business functions" may be necessary due to government legislation. Sometimes they exist because you have to provide your business with administrative or various other forms of support. Examples of supporting the business functions include activities such as HR and Payroll. Accounting processes such as financial analysis and reporting will also fall into this category. Finally, we noted that processes such as cleaning, catering and facilities management, together with any administrative computer systems, also belong in this box.

This, we felt, defined our business rather nicely. It looked like this (see Figure 7.6). Having worked out what was core and what was supporting, we realised that what went on in these areas reflected the "today" state of the organisation.

It was time to stop and draw breath. Good progress was being made and it was clear that each step was moving us to a place where we could more objectively assess where we should be spending this precious budget of ours.

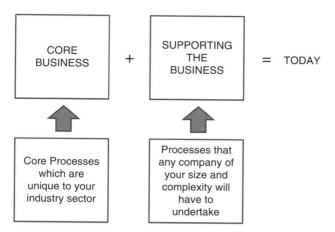

Figure 7.6   Our Business as it is Today. Core Functions Together with Everything Else that Supports the Business

But What about Tomorrow?

Despite many employees' best efforts, companies and public sector organisations do not stand still. In a competitive and fast-moving world, you have to move forward to survive. If you do not, then someone will usually show up and start eating your lunch. Before long you will be discovering just how unhappy people can get when you have to tell them that they no longer have a job.

We turned out attention to the future. What should we be doing to make sure that our company would be successful in the future? We all agreed that we wanted to enjoy a pension when we retired, so we figured that working through a process to create a viable future for our company was a fine and noble thing to do.

"Competitive Advantage" Processes

If you sit in the Boardroom as a member of an executive team, it is usually not long before the words "competitive advantage" crop up. Companies are quite rightly obsessed about it because it is this and only this that will allow them to improve their position in the market place. Whether it be improved profitability, increased sales or greater market share in a difficult geography, everyone wants a piece of it. And guess what? The world of IT is actually well-placed to help. This led us to the concept of working with our business leaders to identify new processes that would give our enterprise definitive and verifiable competitive advantage. In these highly connected, technological times such opportunities often lend themselves to being easily supported by IT systems. In some cases, the technology might itself be used as a weapon of strategic advantage. Everyone liked the sound of that.

We had to be hard and honest about this category, because it was so potentially important. Clearly everyone wants their piece of the action to be the game-changer, but for many this is simply not possible. So, for processes in this box, we defined them as follows. In simple terms, they must create competitive advantage which will *definitely* lead you to one of your company's visions or major *short-term* goals.

> *Competitive advantage processes are those which will lead to definitive competitive advantage within a short period (typically 18 months to 2 years).*

Given that competitive advantage processes have to deliver their advantage within a relatively short time frame, they must have attributes of a game-changer for your industry or your markets. You are therefore unlikely to have a long list of these investments. This is truly the realm of disruptive technology and innovative processes. IT teams get excited about these opportunities. And so they should. This work is much more fun than the more usual fare of delivering a macro-laden database to track and alert a junior manager that his expenses need to be submitted.

"Future Opportunity" Processes

We were now starting to get the hang of the method of classification we had unwittingly devised. It should come as no surprise that every other future-looking business change fell into the "everything else" category. The only major difference between the "competitive advantage" processes and our "everything else" category turned out to be the level of expectation. "Everything else" did not guarantee a definitive competitive advantage within a short period.

We dubbed the "everything else" bucket "future opportunity" category, a more palatable term (we were getting really good at metaphors by now). These candidates are often the "good ideas" for doing new things. Some opportunities that fall into this cell might be completely whacky, blue-sky notions. Others for example, could be hard-headed ideas that might have just failed to make the "definite competitive advantage" criteria. All the ideas in the "future opportunity" box can be regarded as medium to long-term, both in terms of time and also in terms of odds.

Future opportunity processes are those which may lead to definitive competitive advantage over a longer period (typically 3–5 years or even longer).

While it might be easy to place new ideas in the "future opportunity" box, deciding how to fund those ideas can be difficult. We thought that an impact/probability approach was probably the best way to think about these investments. You can never have too many 2×2 matrices after all. For example, if you like lots of risk, you could choose to support all high impact-low probability items. It might only take one of these bright ideas to change the world. On the other hand if you have little appetite for risk you could choose to finance the ideas that offer much less benefit, but perhaps with more certainty of outcome. Fierce debate with live budget ammunition is a great method to find out what everyone thinks.

One other way in which you can look at the "future opportunity" box is by taking the view that it is a Research and Development fund. We found that this category is a good place to spend relatively small proportions of your budget in "proof of concept" projects so that you can determine the viability of the new ideas. Any successful projects can be moved into other categories such as the "competitive advantage" or "core business" boxes, while those that have failed can be quietly forgotten. This is broadly congruent with the methods used in the Boston Consulting Growth Share matrix (Stern & Deimler, 2006). Given the uncertainty, there is no shame in failing in the "future opportunity" category. However, few if any felt that we should move successful items on into the "support the business" category, no matter how well they went. If we were conducting R&D on our "support the business" processes such as cleaning, catering or rubbish removal then we reckoned that we were probably in the wrong company.

If the "core business" and "support the business" functions represent your "today" state, then, logic suggests that the "competitive advantage" and "future opportunity" categories represent the "tomorrow". They are the candidate projects and processes that are hopefully going to change the way that everyone works. We also felt that if we could generate a good pipeline of ideas in the "future opportunity" box, then they could potentially form the feedstock of the company's competitive advantage further out into the future. They may even be the driving force that might help us reinvent your business. Despite the attractive nature of the "tomorrow" boxes, we were struggling to deploy meaningful resources into these areas. For us, the pressures of "today" were just too immediate and too powerful to resist.

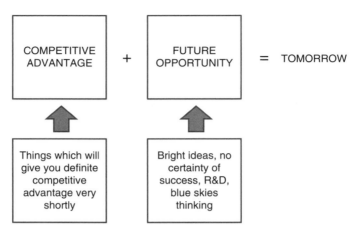

Figure 7.7   The Opportunities We Have to Change our Business Tomorrow

With these two categories now clearly defined, our "tomorrow" state investments now looked like Figure 7.7.

Putting Today and Tomorrow's Investments Together

When we put all the investment categories together, we found we were left with a 2×2 matrix resembling a Boston Grid. Now that the categories were grouped together, it became clear that the emerging model had other properties.

In the combined model, we placed the "competitive advantage" and "core business" processes on the left hand side of the diagram. Meanwhile on the right hand side we placed the "future opportunity" and "support the business" functions. This reflects the notion that these two groupings demand different types of funding approaches. For example, you probably don't want to spend large volumes of your precious budget on "support the business" functions unless you really have no other option. You also may not want to spend all your money making big bets on blue-sky projects in the "future opportunity" box, especially if they only have relatively low chances of success. So for the right hand side of the matrix, we decided that the best-practice watchword is "to contain our spending". Consider carefully just how much you want to bet on the risky initiatives and keep a lid on the demands of the ever-escalating support process costs. Do you really need yet another shiny new HR database?

Over on the left hand side of the matrix, the situation is rather different. Since these activities are critical for business success both for today and

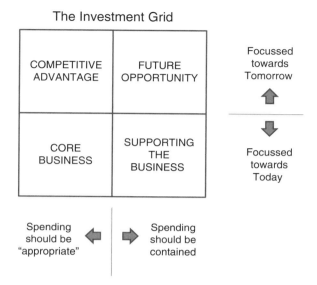

Figure 7.8   The Completed Investment Grid

tomorrow, the spending approach we felt we should adopt for these activities should be different. A great key word we invented for investment strategies in these areas is "appropriate". You clearly need to keep your business processes effective and efficient and you may also want to spend significant amounts of money on your sure-fire competitive advantage opportunities to get ahead of the opposition. These two different spending approaches should now condition us into thinking about how the projects in the boxes should be funded and how the competing demands for money can be balanced. We had in effect created yet another investment grid. Ours looks like Figure 7.8.

Putting the Final Touches to the Roulette Table

Now that we had defined pretty much all the areas of our budget, we decided to put the various investment and operational boxes together. This created our final "roulette table". The main body of the board will contains budget allocations from which the derived metrics at the bottom of the table are calculated. Allocating money (or betting) was now only a short step away. The IT Budget roulette table looks like the diagram in Figure 7.9.

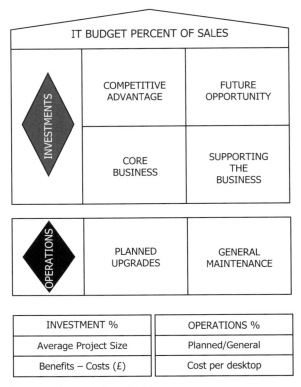

Figure 7.9   The IT Budget Roulette Table

Placing the Chips

It is now possible to start populating the table. This can be done in one of two ways. The first is really good fun, but very scary. The second is far more sensible and practical, but much less entertaining.

1. The first method broadly supports the Grand Plan type of approach. Here, you explicitly allocate percentages of your budget to each of the boxes in a top-down fashion. Then you choose which projects and which support activities are worthy enough to be allocated pieces of your precious budget. This is dangerously radical but very exciting. My own recommendation is to carry out this activity in a sound-proof room in an off-site location. When we first attempted it, the high emotion it generated—with associated shouting, stamping and periodic walk-outs—terrified everyone else in our building. Passion is a rare and beautiful thing. As the final box is filled, and the last chips appear on the table, the blue touch-paper of the firework is lit. You would be best advised to retire to a safe distance and wait for the show to start. What you think you need to do in an ideal world compared to what you are actually doing rarely coincide. For this reason, top-down allocation is only recommended for those with a strong constitution, a visionary outlook and a wicked sense of humour. That said, this approach has great value in providing long-range vision options. Not least, it can be a powerful brake to the ever-increasing demands of the all-consuming operational boxes.

2. More commonly and for those who are executing "Better Tomorrow" strategies, an alternative method recommends that you take your current portfolio of project and support activities and allocate them to the boxes in which you believe they most comfortably reside. While this may appear relatively tame compared to the previous method, the exercise can nonetheless create quite a shock the first time you try it. Many organisations will discover to their horror that they are spending disproportionate amounts of money on unplanned support activities. We certainly did. Any remaining slivers of cash not consumed by operations are probably being exclusively spent on the "today" areas of their business. They may be dismayed to learn that the strategic impact of what might be quite impressive levels of spending is minimal. You might be running your railroad on time, but there's a good chance that nobody is setting any money aside in the "future opportunity" box to fund a couple of brothers from Ohio who are experimenting with powered gliders.

As you progress through the allocation process, you will need to take care to ensure that every part of your budget is captured somewhere on the table. You also need to take care to ensure that you don't end up with an enormous cast of slaves building you another Egyptian pyramid. This allocation process should be carried out quickly and easily, ideally in a group session with your management team. Complications can confound. For example, accurately working out staff costs is not easy. Brevity should be your measured response. It is perfectly acceptable to take your fully loaded people costs (which are typically about 1.6 times the salary bill), then break the workforce up into leadership, managers and workers before proceeding with the allocation using a the much loved concept of a blended rate for each of these three categories of staff member.

As word gets around, it won't take long before others get wind of this exercise. They may try to use the model to get the answers they want. There is nothing sinister about this. In corporate life managers want stuff. Some-times it's because they sincerely believe that it is the right thing to do for the corporation and sometimes it's because they want to do it to further their own career aspirations or for the benefit of their own teams. Corporate politics is simply a game which plays out each and every day in each and every company in the world.

However, the relatively short life expectancy of an IT leader, for example, means that some cynical unbelievers in the workforce may be simply "waiting you out". Those who may have topped out in their career might reasonably expect to be doing the same job in five years' time. They also know that if your shelf life runs true to the form of most IT leaders, then they will be working for your successor's successor at the end of those five years. Faced with such circumstances, even normal, well-intentioned people will be reluctant to pledge much allegiance to your revolutionary new ideas, particularly if they are controversial. Who can blame them? It is entirely possible that those who do so will be branded witches by the leaders of the next regime. No matter how sensible the current leader's strategy may appear, the prospect of being ducked in a pond, or burnt at the corporate stake isn't a pleasant one for a grizzled mainframe programmer who is hoping that the creaking technology they are supporting will just keep going long enough to see them safely through to a grateful retirement.

Our Transformation Journey

It took us nearly three years to make sufficient changes to provide sufficient momentum and impetus so that we could travel towards a better place. The first base position was to bring our escalating costs under control and then to reverse those changes. The medicine was brutal and highly unpopular. However, it was possible to extract more than £50m of annualised operational cost reductions and these were passed through into profit so that the percentage of sales metric started to fall. With a large proportion of our work being handled by an outsourcing company, a great deal of work was required to recondition their team to align to our new goals. Communication is key to this type of change. This, together with the willingness of our partner to play ball, made sure that we could travel the journey together. Trust is a valuable commodity. More than eight years after this particular transformation program started, the outsourcing partner at that time still enjoys substantial levels of business with the company. With the costs falling and the estate standardising, the next step was to add impetus to our competency centres which were attempting to drive large-scale process and IT change. Increasing levels of resource were applied to these "competitive advantage" programs. The number of projects fell and the average size of projects increased. After five years, we had built enough capability to be able to deliver global projects across tens of countries and we had a clear idea of the value that our investments were generating. In terms of those Board level questions, we now at last had answers to both. We knew that we were spending 2.8% of our revenue on IT, while our benchmarking studies suggested that two of our competitors were in the 2.9% to 3.2% range. We in IT were at least not being a drag on our business.

In terms of benefits, investment had grown to half of our total IT budget. This was largely due to a ruthless exercise in standardisation over the five year period. This exercise had drastically reduced our operational costs. The internal audit assessment suggested that the average returns on our projects had improved. There had of course been some hits and plenty of misses, but two large successful projects skewed the results in our favour. They had delivered significant benefits, each running into hundreds of millions of dollars. This left us with a good story to tell when we finally had the courage to give definitive answers to our Board. The liberation of operational cash also had a few positive side-effects for those who are traditionally unloved. There was even enough cash left for the HR organisation to standardise on a single solution worldwide. They got their shiny new database after all.

Figure 7.10 shows the two roulette tables from our "before" and "after" states.

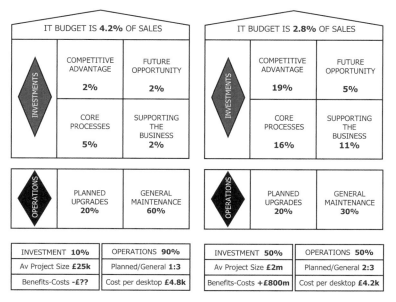

Figure 7.10   The "Before" and "After" State of our IT Function

Other Funding Profile Examples

There are plenty of strategies you can employ when you visit the budget casino. In fact there are an infinite number of options and opportunities. There are also many interesting side-effects to be enjoyed. You can have hours of fun with your managers and staff arguing about the merits of your funding choices and debating what a "good" shape looks like. Provided that the discussions do not descend into physical violence or lifelong feuds, then robust discussion is probably a good thing. Since this model is showing you a highly "zoomed-out" version of your IT empire, it is an invaluable and perhaps rare opportunity for you to discuss the whole picture of the battlefield with your trusted generals. You can also use it as a useful communication vehicle to explain your plans to your stakeholders and staff, though as we've already discussed, the appearance of yet another management model and its associated religious book of truths isn't going to set the hearts of many of your journeymen aflame. Here are a couple of extreme examples, where the roulette table spending choices give you an idea of what the organisation is trying to do (whether this is conscious or unconscious!).

Funding Choice 1—The Support Organisation

In the example shown in Figure 7.11, over 80% of the budget has been allocated to operations, with 60% being consumed by ad hoc general maintenance activities. The team have been able to dedicate significant amounts of their effort towards upgrade activity, suggesting they are working hard to keep the estate current. The cost per desktop metric is quite low. This, together with the upgrade program, suggests that the estate may be well standardised.

Investment spending is largely confined to today's problems with the "core business" and "support" boxes receiving similar levels of funding. Little if any spending is allocated to the "competitive advantage" box and only a modest amount to the "future opportunity" category (perhaps evaluating the impact of new technologies). Average project size is small. Many initiatives are in flight at any one time. The benefits-costs metric is negative. This implies that overall portfolio planning is absent. The overall spending is given as 2.0% of sales revenue. All these data suggest that this is an IT department which is fighting to standardise a complex estate with the backdrop of a demanding set of users. There is no Grand Plan strategy here and it is possible that this department is either executing a Better Tomorrow plan focussed on reliability and cost, or else it is operating without a clear strategy of its own. IT may be seen as an overhead. Such a spending profile is not uncommon in beleaguered western manufacturing companies.

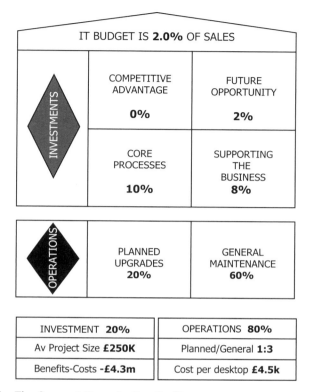

IT BUDGET IS **2.0%** OF SALES

| INVESTMENTS | COMPETITIVE ADVANTAGE **0%** | FUTURE OPPORTUNITY **2%** |
| | CORE PROCESSES **10%** | SUPPORTING THE BUSINESS **8%** |

| OPERATIONS | PLANNED UPGRADES **20%** | GENERAL MAINTENANCE **60%** |

INVESTMENT **20%**	OPERATIONS **80%**
Av Project Size **£250K**	Planned/General **1:3**
Benefits-Costs **-£4.3m**	Cost per desktop **£4.5k**

Figure 7.11   The Support Organisation Profile

Funding Choice 2—The "Go for it" Organisation

In Figure 7.12 we see an extreme example of an IT function's scary strategy. It's completely different to the previous example. A huge percentage of the budget has been placed on game-changing projects. The average project size is large, but the expected benefits are enormous. Modest amounts are being spent on "research" and "support the business" processes, while the "core business" processes enjoy significantly higher funding levels than the organisation above.

Operational costs are relatively low suggesting that high levels of standardisation are in the plan. Architectures are probably simple and technical diversity is well controlled. Nearly half the operational spending is planned, suggesting that good controls are in place here too, though it is likely that the user community may not feel it is getting adequate support. The cost per desktop seems high but this probably reflects the way in which IT seems

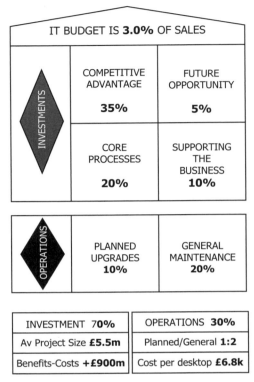

Figure 7.12 An Extremely Aggressive Strategic Investment Profile

to be integrated as a business enabler. The overall IT spending levels are proportionally higher than the previous example, but this, together with the high project costs, particularly in strategic initiatives strongly suggests a bold Grand Plan is being executed by a leader with some kind of daring vision for the future.

Summary

There are no right or wrong answers when it comes to budgets and strategies. Some answers can be very right or partly right and some can be downright disastrous. What's more, organisations evolve and what worked well last year may not work at all well in future years—particularly if you have had a change in leadership or the company has suffered (or enjoyed) a change in fortunes.

For example, rapidly growing companies will usually require a high level of internal entrepreneurship as they seek to build market share. However, once they have secured a large slice of their market, the strategy and tactics that supported them in the fast growth phase may no longer be relevant (and may even be a positive disadvantage).

As far as the IT leader is concerned, there are some significant choices to make. Bold Grand Plans or conservative Better Tomorrow choices should ideally be made early in the decision-making process. However, do not be afraid to change tack if you need to. You might have a bold vision, but it might not be the best answer at that time for your organisation. Facing a major trauma, most surgeons will tell you that they will prefer to stop the bleeding and stabilise their patient before attempting any major surgery. You might just have to do the same if you are starting from somewhere you'd rather not wish you were. Like crawling out from under a bus.

The relationship between the IT organisation and the business community is also critical. As with Plate Tectonics, large corporate companies need to experience very large seismic shocks before major changes in the landscape can come to pass. The most important thing for IT leaders in this context is to understand what the organisation needs (especially your CEO's view of this) and then to work out how you and your henchmen should service those needs. Unlike Blofeld, you may not be in the business of starting World War III. Who would want to rule a world of radioactive desolation anyway? But as we've considered, the wide and fearsome forces acting on you as a leader are capable of tearing you and your organisation apart. However, salvation is possible. A clear set of long-term goals together with a set of defensible processes upon which you can build your strategy are essential CIO leadership components. Such an approach will almost certainly help you extend your shelf life as an effective leader. Better Tomorrows or Grand Plans, underpinned by a coherent roulette table of budget choices, give you a solid and defensible framework which can help you make the best decisions for your organisation. It will also help engender helpful debate. Rationally discussing the relative priorities of the business is definitely preferable to an emotional shouting match where toys are ejected from prams and bullies get their way. If you can rapidly achieve agreement on the "what" aspect of your plan, then all your energies and those of your stakeholders can be exclusively directed towards arguing about the "how". This, in my experience, is infinitely more productive and more enjoyable—for everyone.

CHAPTER 8

Epilogue—What Might Overcome You?

"Dying is easy, it's living that scares me to death."

(Annie Lennox)

I f for some reason you are ever curious about which real-world show-stopper is likely to be the one to shorten your life, then there is a myriad of statistics available with which you can cheerfully depress yourself. The World Health Organisation datasets are particularly extensive (World Health Organisation, 2013). You can spend a long, miserable morning mulling over their macabre mysteries. Even surfing LeDuc Media's comprehensive world life expectancy website (LeDuc, T., 2013) probably won't make you feel any better. You can for example, find out which is the biggest killer in the Cook Islands (it's coronary heart disease if you were wondering). Most "Premier League" biological diseases are fairly easy to spot. The same old culprits tend to crop up again and again, year after year, all over the place. For example, even though Nepal is about as far away from the Cook Islands as you could imagine, this beautiful Himalayan kingdom (where we sought project enlightenment earlier) also sadly sees coronary heart disease at the top if its killer list. And disappointingly, being eaten by a Yeti doesn't even make it onto the bottom of the Nepalese mortality list. Or anybody else's list for that matter.

It's Always the Same Culprits, Except When it Isn't

While there are depressing similarities in the mortality statistics of different countries, geography still has an important part to play in biological demises. It is true that in western countries, such as the USA, UK and Germany, coronary heart disease, stroke and lung disease are all amongst the biggest killers. It is also true that they aren't just rampant in the western hemisphere. Together these three ailments also kill more than 3 million unfortunate Chinese citizens each year. However, in Brazil, whilst heart disease and stroke may also jealously guard their privileged position at the top table, the dark horse of diabetes has galloped in to claim the bronze medal position. And as we move deeper into the developing world, the profile of pathogenicity changes quite markedly. In many of these countries, it is the local bugs and parasites that generally hasten one's journey to the next life. In Sierra Leone, for example, malaria, influenza and various unpleasant diarrhoeal diseases top their "bad things" list. This pegs the average life expectancy to just 46.5 years—one of the shortest spans you are likely to find anywhere (LeDuc, 2013). And it's not just the same old bugs and parasites we have to be careful about. Viruses and bacteria seem perfectly happy to move between species. As we have seen in West Africa in 2014, a beast of a disease has quite literally emerged from the jungle and devastated communities with ruthless efficiency. Ebola Haemorrhagic Fever, first seen in Yambuku near the Ebola River in the Democratic Republic of Congo, is thought to be carried by the humble fruit bat. It is not only deadly, but it also causes symptoms that are truly terrifying. As the victims succumb to uncontrolled internal and external bleeding, relatives can only watch, for any contaminated fluids will quickly infect anyone nearby. The World Health Organisation (WHO, 2013) tells us that the mortality rate can be up to 90% and concludes bleakly "There is no treatment of vaccine available for either people or animals." And Ebola probably isn't the worst of the newcomers. Even as you read this, various strains of the influenza virus are assiduously replicating and mutating ready to jump another species hurdle. With the current level of global connectedness, preventing deadly aerosol viruses from wiping out most of humanity may end up being mankind's biggest challenge for the next century.

One other major factor which influences how you will climb into your box is of course your age. However, in the USA, where very good statistics are available, there are some surprises to be found. Those in their teens or younger years who fail to make it to adulthood are generally afflicted by congenital problems, low birth weight or injuries—which may not be unexpected. However, for the 15–24-year-old age range, road traffic accidents top the list, followed disappointingly by suicides, although for young men, homicides are also uncomfortably high up the table. As you progress into your thirties, poisonings and suicides seem to become more common. It is only when you eventually make it into your forties that Mother Nature reasserts herself over the deadly combination of free will, depression and bad driving. Middle-aged women begin to fall prey to breast cancer and by the mid-forties to mid-fifties, the big C becomes the biggest female killer in the US. Meanwhile, their male partners are not faring much better. If the men didn't commit suicide or re-enact a male version of the final scene of the Thelma and Louise movie in their thirties (which involved a car and a cliff if you've not seen the film), then their hearts may well give out as they pass into their forties. But as the decades fall away and you reach your sixties and beyond things become more predictable. Coronary heart disease, strokes, lung disease and Alzheimer's line up as the heavyweights at the top of the US mortality leader board and they remain stubbornly at the top of the list thereafter until everyone is dead (LeDuc T., 2013). Even if your ticker has ticked away flawlessly as you Zimmer your way into your nineties, it is still the most likely thing that will grind to a halt and send you shuffling off this mortal coil. In effect, if you do not kill yourself or get yourself shot, run over or poisoned as a young adult, then it will be a failure of your blood pump, a malfunction of your air pump or a blockage or burst in the plumbing in your head that will most likely send you to the afterlife. Who other than a plumber would ever have thought that pipes and pumps were so important?

While all these data may appear to be very depressing, the reality is that things have never been so good. Not only do you have the best chance of living your life to the full, but you will probably be living it a good deal longer than anyone from years gone by would ever dare believe. Today, those who live in Japan can expect on average, to celebrate their eighty-third birthday. In Europe, the Anglo-Saxons of Britain and Germany will make it to just beyond eighty, while those in the US are closing fast with an impressive average age of 78.6 (WHO, Retrieved 29th May 2014).

"Let us be frank about it: most of our people have never had it so good."
Harold Macmillan, British Prime Minister, 1957

Only one of the historical figures we have studied managed to get close to these levels of longevity. It was Joseph Stalin. Our comrade with cap and moustache is believed to have capitulated to a stroke at the age of 74. Sadly, our heroes from further back in time only enjoyed much shorter spans. Nostradamus, Rembrandt and Leonardo made it to 62, 63 and 67 respectively, while Henry VIII and Caesar both called it a day at 55. "Early retirement" really meant it in those days. The historical data for our pyramid-makers are somewhat incomplete. Nonetheless it looks as though Pharaoh Khufu may have made it into his forties or fifties before he took up the occupancy of his grand pyramid (together with his healthy but almost certainly seriously disgruntled staff). The most unfortunate hero we have studied, however, was poor old Alexander the Great. After only ten years or so of campaigning where he achieved the most remarkable conquests and achievements, his life was tragically terminated at the tender age of 32. There is still plenty of scholarly debate as to how Alex actually died. Many believe it was due to malaria (as we suggested in a previous chapter), while others think he may have been poisoned (Skelton & Dell, 2009). Neither of these should be a surprise. For if Alex had been living today, there would still be a good chance that a thirty-something male who spent a fair bit of time in Africa would end up meeting his maker in one of those same two ways. There is nothing new under the sun it seems.

Failure and Folklore

Unfortunately, statistics charting the demise of the careers of IT leaders are not anything like as comprehensive as biological records. The world may be filled with train-spotters, librarians, introverted statisticians together with bewildering numbers of audit teams and various other people who compulsively count things, but there appear to be no convenient websites which can show us the really important dataset we are interested in. Which horror of horrors will likely kill our IT careers? There is no World IT Health Organisation. Moreover, it is incredibly difficult to sort out the facts from the folklore when leadership changes ever do take place in the IT firmament. Anecdotes quickly exaggerate themselves before becoming apocryphal. After more time has passed, they finally metamorphose and become full-blown fairy stories that the Brothers Grimm would be proud of.

I recall one messy CIO exit from long ago. The tales became impressively more extravagant with each passing year. Today, some storytellers would have you believe lurid tales of garishly-coloured company limos. Others talk of management teams persistently inebriated on gin who initiated public executions in front of the coffee machine. All of this was happening while a policy of "long-march" indoctrination introducing the stern religion of "structured methodologies" was force-fed into the snaking lines of the hapless serfs of this particular IT unit. I arrived on the scene as part of the "rebuild" team a little while after the fall of the emperor. From what I could see I suspect the truth may have been much more mundane. It's not difficult to guess how an IT leader with rather too much self-importance, self-confidence and a spectacular deficiency in tact will fare. When they also deliberately upset everyone they come across—every single time they meet them—it shouldn't be a surprise that nobody rushes to help when that first, major flagship project is fatally holed below the waterline and starts its slow, graceful journey to a final resting place in the abyssal depths of the ocean.

> **"Be nice to people on your way up because you'll meet them
> on your way down."**
> *Wilson Mizner*

So, in the absence of any good databases and with only fairy stories out in the public domain, compiling any league table of IT challenges is going to be tricky. What's more, as with their biological counterparts, you will probably find that the epidemiology of IT diseases will also depend on a wide range of factors such as geography, the maturity of the IT function, the state of the business, HR cultural expectations and the market the company is operating in—just to mention just a few.

This means that we are now forced to look to our own experience and that of people we trust. This makes for a small and imperfectly-formed database. Witness accounts from anyone with a family name of "Christian Andersen", or any fans of P.L. Travers, should be taken strictly with a pinch of salt (or perhaps a spoonful of sugar) (Travers, 1934). Stories about ugly ducklings, mermaids or any songs about feeding birds or other wildfowl should be similarly discarded (Christian Andersen, 1870). But the exercise is nonetheless valuable and it can be great fun. Guessing which unpleasantness might infect your organisation is a bit like standing on the bridge of the Titanic looking for icebergs. It can be very fruitful if you call it right, but you can expect to get very cold and very wet if you get it wrong, though you can console yourself that there's always a slim chance that in the years to come someone will make a movie about your epic plight.

IT Leadership Morbidity Tables

My own database of despair spans a time from the early eighties to the present day. It started in the times of paper tape and punched cards. Even full-time programmers had to share a "terminal" in those days. While Margaret Thatcher and Ronald Reagan commenced their ideological love affair, I was struggling in my formative IT years in a University Department. Later, just as Mr Reagan first met Glasnost Soviet Leader, Mikhail Gorbachev, I moved on into corporate life to endure the horrors of programming in FORTRAN for a pharmaceutical company and later for a global oil company. Then, as communism and the Berlin Wall fell, it was time for me to return to Pharmaceuticals for another decade and a half. Later, with consummate bad timing (immediately after 9/11) I tried my luck with a jet engine manufacturer. In all this time, I reckon I've seen nearly three dozen IT leaders come and go, together with quite a lot more who blew up before they achieved the destiny they craved. Without apology, here are my thoughts on how trials and challenges play their part in the real IT world. The observations may match up with yours or perhaps they may not. They are at least a set of data points even if they come from yet another unfinished database.

First Tier—Dislocated Stakeholders

Without doubt, the very topmost item on anyone's IT morbidity list, in my opinion, is the whole notion of "Dislocated Stakeholders". If the leader of the free IT world becomes detached from everyone or anyone else, it's only a question of time before everything becomes their fault, particularly when anything bad happens (which it inevitably will). For this reason, I believe the "Dislocated Stakeholder" challenge should sit alone on the first tier of the "bad things" table. There is clear blue water between it and all the other items on our list.

If you are the kind of CIO who is keen to implement a "Grand Plan" Strategy, then complete and utter, unblinking air-cover from your senior stakeholders is utterly essential. Grand Plans can upset thousands of people (or possibly even tens of millions if you are working in the public sector). Without a king and a powerful army to protect you, you run the risk of being pursued across the plains by an angry mob and their dogs. To avoid this, the smartest CIOs always fly in close formation with their CEO, their COO and their CFO. They will also execute the agenda of their leaders, rather than one of their own (that would be an elementary schoolboy mistake). They will also need to expend infinite amounts of energy trying to build relationships with their business peers, despite the apparent futility of this task. If by chance you can squeeze just a few drops of blood out of those particular stones, you will find that they will be more valuable to you than any amount of fabulously expensive gold or printer ink.

The trump card that the Dislocated Stakeholders' ailment can play is a cunning one. This is because this particular disease can switch from acting as predator and quickly become scavenger when circumstances are right. Rather like a vulture swooping down on an unfortunate piece of still-warm road-kill, it is quick to pile in when other bad things strike. Dislocating yourself from your stakeholders is a poor lifestyle choice. It's a bit like eating, drinking and smoking too much throughout your life. It might have been good fun at the time, but when all that morbid obesity, emphysema and a wrecked liver start to make their presence felt you have set the scene for the next act. And it isn't usually very long before Mother Nature steps in to restore equilibrium. She rarely disappoints and the forces of Darwinism chalk up another point. Similarly, if you are suffering dislocation of key stakeholders in the IT world, and you fail to promptly do anything about it, then you can expect a similar grisly fate. Almost any project failure, botched software upgrade, major service fault, budget over-run, outsourcing disaster, disappointing consultancy assignment or indeed any combination or perhaps all of them (ouch) will precipitate calamity. The end result is usually the same. You are left with the inevitable sobbing personal assistant, a cardboard box and a few head-hunters' phone numbers. In short, you must keep the stakeholders that matter firmly on board. It's simply not possible to conduct a long and successful career from the cold solitude of an air-lock or a dingy office in a distant province of a sprawling empire. Of all the IT leaders I have worked with over the years, every single one who found themselves unceremoniously dispatched was afflicted by this problem either as a primary or a contributory cause. It's very common and it happens at all senior levels in an organisation.

Second Tier—Money and Strategy

If you are successful at keeping your adoring public on board, then in my experience, the next most likely things to potentially get you shot are the intertwined horrors of Bleeding Budgets and Schizophrenic Strategies. It's not difficult to see how this can come to pass. If for example, you start spending a lot more money than people are expecting you to spend, then that will probably get them worried. And if you can't tell people why you are doing it, then it doesn't take a PhD in psychology to work out that even reasonable people might just start getting a teensy bit uncomfortable. Before long your judgement is in question and dark forces will start to assemble. The executive committee will meet without you and shortly afterwards you will be called out of a meeting to receive an important phone call.

Some years ago, I came across a major IT function in a large corporate company that was suffering from this haemorrhagic cash problem. The total spending on IT had risen alarmingly. Such lofty levels of spending might have been justified if a "Grand Plan", game-changing, future profit enhancing change program was being cunningly executed. But in this case there was no strategy and unfortunately, a great deal of cash was being consumed on operations and maintenance. In the Schizophrenic Strategy chapter, we briefly discussed the concept of the "stuff you get bullied into doing" problem. This is exactly what was happening here. The IT estate was complex and a bewildering number of small projects were all in flight. None of them were moving quickly and many were not even moving at all. When it became clear that the competitors were spending much less the Board suddenly became very interested. When the grandees also learned that one of these competitors was executing a coherent series of major improvement projects which was supercharging their business performance, then the Board became very stern. Consultants were called in and the scale of lost profit and lost sales as a result of the bloated IT budget was calculated. Seismic changes followed, accompanied by a tsunami that washed many of the senior IT players away.

> **"A goal without a plan is just a wish."**
> *Antoine de Saint Exupéry*

The take-away message for the second tier ailments is quite clear. If you have a great set of relationships with your most senior colleagues then that's a good start. But to avoid falling at this second set of hurdles, you must make sure you know what you are doing. You need to have a great strategy and you must communicate it well. And, just as important, you must keep your hand firmly on your wallet while you are doing it.

Third Tier—Projects and Software

Many will be surprised to see that problems with projects only scrape onto the winner's rostrum with a joint bronze medal, at least in terms of IT mortality. Many will know that a really good "black death" IT project that has "gone seriously viral" can cause untold damage to life, property and careers. But I think there is a distinction to be made between projects that should never have been started, which belong in the "failed strategy" category on the tier above and projects that you and your team just screwed up, which are the rightful members of the "failed projects" grouping.

If your IT strategy demands that you assemble an unimaginable number of kettles so that you can get down to the important task of boiling the Pacific Ocean, then this to me is a strategy failure rather than a project failure. You are clearly deep into "undoable" Stonehenge, Pyramid or Moon Landing project territory. Even if your project team is initially successful, you will be disappointed to find that all the other oceans are inconveniently connected to the Pacific and your travails at best will end up with a luke-warm outcome. There are plenty of clues out there to warn you that you are embarking upon strategy-led disasters. Terraforming a planet is one, as is developing an elixir of eternal life and beauty (hint: never go for twin goals). More commonly, asking the question "who's not done one of these types of projects before?" will give you the answer you need. When I was responsible for a nuclear power station controls unit, this was always the first question I asked. But these issues happen all the time. Who, for example, would ever start a multi-billion pound or dollar public sector IT project when pretty much all the previous projects had gone supernova? Most politicians and senior civil servants it seems.

In addition to projects, software also deservedly gets a podium place. In my experience at least, this is mainly due to that disappointing quality of human optimism that we discussed in a previous chapter. Optimism and software make poor bedfellows. Software doesn't work unless you and your vendors have expended an inappropriate amount of your life force into making it work. If you ever do manage to get your Frankenstein up and running (though it is much more likely to be staggering), then don't keep mucking with it, because the moment you change anything it will promptly fall over in a heap and refuse to get up.

"If it ain't broke, don't fix it."
Bert Lance

Fourth Tier—Outsourcing

Some might also be disappointed that outsourcing does not warrant any kind of silverware in the "bad things" league tables. Certainly outsourcing can create lots of damage. That's why an entire chapter has been dedicated to it. Some in-house IT leaders certainly see outsourcing companies in a very dark light, particularly if they were a victim of it in their earlier careers. But this is not a time for blaming the tools. In terms of outsourcing, lots of organisations do not get what they want, but on balance it's probably fair to say that they usually get what they deserve. Most outsourcing organisations I have worked with over the years were not bad people; indeed many were rather good at what they do well (sic). Successive disasters have quelled the 1990s pretentions of grandeur and bad behaviour that characterise the "mega-outsourcing" deals and as a result, most outsourcers have developed pretty good levels of expertise. They have even realised that if their own businesses are not going well then they have no business taking any of yours and running it themselves.

As far as outsourcing is concerned, evolution is an amazing thing. There's virtually nothing that can't be fixed by a few decades of steady improvement. Perhaps it will occur through phyletic gradualism or via the punctuated equilibrium of major contract failures (Mayr, 1988). The simple message is that if you fall foul of any of the Obsessive Outsourcing Compulsions and—critically—fail to plan in meticulous detail, there is nothing that even the best outsourcer can do for you. No matter how cheaply they may quote.

Fifth Tier—Consultancy

Chronic Consultancy Syndrome is the ailment which completes the line up (Figure 8.1). Consultants should exert no "executive" control on anything they do for you. These demi-gods may be suggesting where you should travel, but if you are wise then you will not let any of their hands get close to any of your tillers. Also do not let them pack any parachutes unless they are the ones doing the jumping. Listen to what they have to say and then decide what you are going to do. Besides, it's much more fun when all the mistakes are your own.

Things can and do of course go wrong when consultants become involved. If you have a dumb IT leader, he or she may appoint a bunch of dumb consultants. It's entirely possible that they will come up with some dumb recommendations. Should the organisation then dumbly implement the dumb recommendations, then it is entirely possible that a dumb outcome will result. This can create the illusion of a consultancy-led disaster unfolding in front of you, but in reality it's a case of too much dumbness in

The Premier League of CIO Challenges

Position	Challenge
First Tier	Dislocated Stakeholders
Second Tier	Strategy Schizophrenia Bleeding Budgets
Third Tier	Pathogenic Projects Seriously Shaky Software
Fourth Tier	Obsessive Outsourcing Compulsion
Fifth Tier	Chronic Consultancy Syndrome

Figure 8.1   One View of the Relative Priorities of CIO Dangers

the system. Happily, the leaders of most of the top consulting houses aren't dumb and they won't generally deploy dumb people to work for you. So if you do set up a well-defined assignment and you get some good people who understand a great deal about the area they are working on, then you can look forward to a potentially interesting and possibly even useful final report.

Any who may have fallen foul of the "cuckoo" consultancy problem (mentioned in an earlier chapter) may be wondering why this particular risk does not propel chronic consultancy further up the table. My defence is that cuckoo consultancy (where the consultants usurp the in-house leadership) is now fairly rare in the second decade of the twenty-first century. I have only seen it successfully come to pass when IT leaders have made the lifestyle choice we know as "Dislocated Stakeholders". In my own experience I have fallen foul of an attempted cuckoo consultancy coup on two occasions, both instigated by the same firm, more than half a decade apart. Both attempts happily failed. This experience leads me to the conclusion that you might also see it attempted on your organisation perhaps once or twice in your career.

The Unknown Unknowns

And finally, while a good working knowledge of the most common problems can potentially save your career, you should always be mindful that there are even more problems out there. There are many parasites in the jungle and viruses in the bloodstream as well as sharks in the corporate sea.

You might have the misfortune to run into the chaotic, squabbling horrors of a "Toxic Team". Here, deficient man-management skills allow vicious personal agendas and malicious point scoring to flourish. Making a colleague miserable or being unpleasant to an outsourcing partner can become the main reason for going to work. The world of IT for some reason often engenders strange behaviour. Normally sane, law-abiding professionals can rapidly become religious zealots. This can lead to a World-War-I-style trench warfare scenario. You can get all the mud, muck and bullets you could ever wish for. In this environment if your team hasn't already declared war on their suppliers or their vendors, then it won't be long before they start digging trenches and lobbing howitzers towards the poor souls over on the other side of the office.

Also, in these days of cyber-warfare and cyber-crime, you might even be unfortunate enough to suffer a bad dose of "Security Seepage". Here you may be expected to commit career hara-kiri to maintain your honour. This can happen after all your company's important data have somehow found their way into the databases of a competitor or foreign power.

One unfortunate CIO I once knew woke up one morning to find that several of the servers in his company had been hacked. If this was not bad enough, he was horrified to discover that the company's computers were being used to spam most of the free world with various "medicinal" offerings. Further investigation of the email traffic revealed more exotic mysteries. It seems that a large number of impecunious African princes—who were apparently suffering from cash-flow problems—had also hacked the servers. They were using his computers to send distress messages. Good samaritans were being encouraged to supply small amounts of cash so that the substantial but curiously inaccessible assets of the princes could be unfrozen. The samaritans would of course be richly rewarded for their time and trouble. Just send money.

As the investigation widened and deepened, so did everyone's incredulity. Interesting new websites had appeared inside the firewall. Many of these sites offered a match-making service pairing lonely western men with impoverished young women from former Soviet satellite states. Even if the lives of exotic princes and poverty-stricken damsels in distress were going to be improved, the CIO realised that even he could not pass off these laudable but highly illegal activities as "corporate social responsibility". It turned out to be a poor year for management bonuses in the IT Department. But there was a silver lining. The newly-appointed Security Director was surprised and delighted to see the size of his new budget.

Perhaps the final words as far as challenges are concerned should be left to a couple of military leaders who wielded great power in their day. In February 2002, Donald Rumsfeld, The US Secretary of Defense, was leading a news briefing where he made what many of us believe to be one of the greatest quotes of all time.

> **"... there are known knowns; there are things we know
> that we know.**
>
> **There are known unknowns; that is to say, there are things that
> we now know we don't know.**
>
> **But there are also unknown unknowns—there are things we do
> not know we don't know."**
> *Donald Rumsfeld, 2002*

So in the spirit of this unassailable piece of logic, I hope that this book might have provided you with some small insight to help you deal with some of the known knowns that lie in wait for you. It might even be that some of the unknowns out there are now known to you—which would be a great thing. As for the unknown unknowns, we have to look to the words of the great French leader, Napoleon Bonaparte. He knew what kind of people he needed to deal with this particular problem.

> **"I know he's a good general, but is he lucky?"**
> *Napoleon Bonaparte*

And don't forget to panic slowly.

ACKNOWLEDGEMENTS

"Always acknowledge a fault. This will throw those
in authority off their guard and give you an opportunity
to commit more."

(Mark Twain)

It has been thirty-five years since I first came into contact with the world of IT. Much of the material in this book owes itself to experiences I have enjoyed and endured with some wonderful people. After being imbued with the importance of education by my parents, Peter and June, my first fleeting encounters with the rudiments of programming were made on an undergraduate training course at Exeter University in Southern England. They were perplexing and unfruitful. At the time I decided that this "computing thing" was all too hard as it seemed to be filled with insurmountable challenges. Many decades later I still feel much the same way about it, though I have at least made a few friends along the way. I cannot remember the name of the bearded lecturer who led the course. But if you are still alive and you know who you are—then the bespectacled student in the Pink Floyd T-shirt at the back of the class who kept falling asleep says "thank you".

Other seminal moments require appropriate acknowledgement. I owe thanks to Robert Ash and the team at the Aberystwyth University computer suite for their patience during my research years. If they were ever wondering why the university mainframe seemed to curiously crash so often during the night, I fear that on some occasions at least, it might have been due to me and my incomplete understanding of multi-dimensional arrays. At the same time Dr Andy Barnicoat achieved the twin objectives of being a great supervisor for my doctoral thesis work while relentlessly teasing me for the devastatingly poor quality of my FORTRAN and Pascal code. The notion I championed,which is best described as "if you don't GOTO, then you don't get to", was probably not best programming practice even then. He also taught me how to make a Sirius personal computer play tunes on its variable speed disk drive—a true highlight of academic research.

Dr Dave Burwell at BP introduced me to the first rudiments of rigorous project management from which the Stalinist doctrine developed, while John Hearn at Glaxo kindly picked up the pieces as I applied early versions of this exciting new approach to the innocent project teams I was assigned to lead in medicine discovery. Also at Glaxo, I am grateful to Dr Philip Loftus who mesmerised us with his mastery of the whiteboard and theoretical models which have conditioned my thinking ever since. The global data centre and infrastructure management team also merit mention. Here amongst others, Lee Duncan, Janet Benn, Neville Brown, Karen Alexander, Peter Abbott and I jointly learned about fortitude as the mind-bogglingly unmanageable complexity of global data centre hell was somehow gradually made manageable. We found that it is possible to change-control your way out of anything with sufficient determination and an unlimited supply of coffee. However, I was unaware that my confidence in their abilities was higher than their own until they physically carried me out of the computer room as the Y2K clocks ticked over. Halon is nasty stuff apparently.

I am very grateful to Sir John Rose for the opportunity to join his transformational leadership team at Rolls-Royce late in 2002. Working closely with John Cheffins, John Rivers, Mike Lloyd, James Guyette, Paul Butler, Mike Terrett and Colin Smith amongst many others, we struggled with outsourcing and process improvement challenges. At the same time, Ken Duncan, Joanna Ledington and I learned how hard it is to effect swingeing cost controls across an unwilling enterprise. However, it was at Rolls-Royce that I truly saw just how transformational business process change and IT could be as we genuinely globalised our supply chains and made great strides to structurally improve the whole process of engineering products at the very edge of physics. I even learned to respect engineers. In hindsight it can't have gone that badly. The Rolls-Royce share price increased nearly eighteen times during that decade. It's hard not to be proud of the value delivered to customers and shareholders together with the security of employment for the workforce that followed no matter how insignificant my own contribution may have been.

The book took some considerable time to write. This is the third full incarnation of the manuscript and an overflowing waste paper bin dutifully measured the tortured progress. I am immensely grateful to David Roberts for his honesty, wise counsel and guidance in this regard. He gently advised me that the first version was too dry and academic while the things he said about the second version are best left in the London pub where we first discussed it. Hopefully, this third attempt has a few more "Goldilocks" attributes about it, perhaps balancing the need to provide enough meat, but nonetheless being sufficiently digestible. Of the quarter of a million words in the three versions, you have been reading the best eighty thousand. I'm afraid that's as good as it ever got.

A large number of industry heavyweights have selflessly given their time and provided me with their most valued opinions on the manuscript. Some have offered expert advice in their specialised areas, while others looked at the whole book. In the early days, Simon Branch-Evans at HP thoughtfully reviewed the Outsourcing section. As the Rolls-Royce Account Manager at the time I suspect he may have hoped that the chapter might give him some insight into where I was coming from as a rather erratic CIO. Unfortunately, his learnings were instead confined to the adage that people do not necessarily practise what they preach. Meanwhile in the consultancy area, Bob Fawthrop, as both a respected consultant and as a CIO in his own right, was horrified to discover that early drafts of that chapter had defined members of his guild as nasty demons with added greed. I am still not sure how our friendship has endured, but at least that chapter is now rather more balanced. It certainly taught me that it's a bad idea to write original material after enjoying a bottle of red wine on a Saturday night.

Denise Plumpton, one of the leading female CIOs in the UK, who also has invaluable experience in leading both private and public sector IT functions, helped me with a number of chapters. David Chan, of the Cass Business School, a fellow warrior in the religious war that we are waging to improve the quality of IT leadership, provided vital insight and support in many areas. Dave Bell, formerly of Logica, gave me his best professional technical authorship advice, while Simon Lovegrove, my long-time coach, continued to provide his subtle blend of refined, people-orientated advice which enhanced the clumsy material he was handed.

In some of the more specialised areas, I was fortunate to obtain advice from some genuine world-class experts. Jonathan Hale, the former Strategy Director at Rolls-Royce, understands how to shape company strategy better than pretty much anyone you could wish to meet. I thought I understood this area until I met Jonathan and Sir John Rose. In the projects area, Martin O'Dowd's skills were invaluable. While his chapter reviews were very helpful, it was while I watched him manage an extremely large transformational nightmare-from-hell project that I was able to refine the Stalinist project management doctrine. I remember vividly asking him how his project was doing. "We are just under two years behind the schedule" he replied. While I was gurgling incoherently, he added "Yes, that's nearly 2.7 days in elapsed time." When it comes to projects you are either in control or you are not. Martin simply doesn't understand the concept of "not being in control". Martin's Loughborough University MBA group also provided helpful feedback and I hope this book will help them in their studies. I am also grateful to Doug Tracy, my respected CTO and more recently a CIO of various major US corporates in the automotive and IT Services industry. Doug's dry insight on the perils of outsourcing is the kind of thing that will keep any leader sane on a bad Friday afternoon.

Moving on, I am most grateful to Gemma Valler, my commissioning editor at John Wiley, for her patience and persistence over many months. Her rapid and positive response to the manuscript I sent her was a huge surprise.

Rather than simply dropping the material in the "round filing cabinet", she read it and told me that she liked it. This is not how I expected commissioning editors to behave, at least after the briefings I received from other aspiring authors.

I must reserve the greatest thanks to my wife, Anne Mitchell. She has read and corrected the manuscript more times than either of us would care to guess. She is now capable of reciting large sections of it from memory with the accuracy of a nineteen sixties primary school class chanting out their "times tables". I have never met anyone with such a blend of patience and optimism, neither of which remotely score any points in my psychological profile. She also reads and corrects wider aspects of my life. I am very lucky.

Despite the efforts of these fine people, there may well still be many mistakes in the text and blunders in the presentation of the material. Since most of my favourite mis-spellings somehow found their way into the system dictionaries, you should find plenty to choose from. The fault for this of course all belongs to me.

Finally, a big thank-you is due to you, the reader. First of all I'm grateful that you not only bought a copy of the book but that you had the stamina and fortitude to read it this far. If by chance you were given a copy, then why not repeat the crime by buying another one and giving it to a trusted friend or mortal enemy (depending on whether you liked it)? I earnestly hope that at least something between these pages will have been useful to you in your task of succeeding as an IT leader. If not, then I apologise and hope that you nonetheless found it an enjoyable read. IT is a most powerful force for goodness. It can change people's lives, effect business transformation and do lots of other positive things for humanity. But it does need good people to make it happen. You are almost certainly one of them. I hope you stay the course.

BIBLIOGRAPHY

Abdy, J. (2012). Feudalism: Its Rise, Progress and Consequences, Lectures Delivered at Gresham College. Forgotten Books.

AdventureStats.com/Explorersweb.com (2013). Everest 1922–2006 Age, Success and Fatalities. Adventure Stats.com Keeping Track of Adventure History (web source).

Bell, A. (2006). *Great Leadership: What It Is and What It Takes in a Complex World*. Davies-Black Publishing (a division of CPP Inc).

Berne, E. C. (2013). *Hummingbirds—Faster than a Jet!* The Rosen Publishing Group.

biography.com (2013). Alexander the Great Biography—Facts, Birthday, Life Story. biography.com.

Bloomberg, J. (2013). *The Agile Architecture Revolution: How Cloud Computing, REST-based SOA, and Mobile Computing are Changing Enterprise IT*. John Wiley & Sons.

Boeing Corporation. (2013). *787 Propulsion System*. Seattle: Boeing Corporation.

British Battles. (2013). *The Battle of Hastings*. britishbattles.com.

Business Dictionary. (2013). Definition Stakeholder. Business Dictionary.com.

Christian Andersen, H. (1870). *Hans Christian Andersen: The Complete Fairy Tales and Stories*. Copenhagen: Anchor (1983).

Cobb, R. H. (1990). Engineering Software under Statistical Quality Control. *IEEE Software*, 7(6), 44–54.

Craig, D. (2005). *Rip-Off!* London: The Original Book Company.

Curtis, R., Elton, B. and Atkinson, R. (1983–98). *Black-Adder: The Whole Damn Dynasty*. Penguin Books Ltd.

da Vinci, L. (2006). *The Complete Works*. David and Charles ISBN-100715325535.

Daily Mail (2011) £12bn NHS computer system is scrapped (retrieved 14 April 2014).

Eadline, D. (2011). May's Law and Parallel Software. *Linux Magazine*.

Feld, Charles (2009). Blind Spot: An IT Leader's Guide to IT-Enabled Business Transformation. New York: Olive Press.

Financial Times (2012). *London's New Airport Held to Ransom by Folly* (7 November).

Fleming, I. (1964). *You Only Live Twice*. London: Vintage.

Fortuna, M. (2013). *Invention of the Wheel*. eHoW.

Franck, R. (1658). *The Meridian of Scotland to which is added The Contemplative and Practical Angler* (1821 edn). Edinburgh: Archibald Constable and Co. & Hurst, Robinson and Co.

Friedman, T. L. (2005). *The World Is Flat* (1st edn). New York: Farrar, Straus and Giroux.

Goodall, W. (2005). *Why Great Men Fall: 15 Winning Strategies to Rise Above it All*. New Leaf Press.

Guevara, C. (2006 (originally 1961)). *Guerrilla Warface*. Ocean Books.

Hammill, M. and Goševa-Popstojanova, K. (2009). Common Trends in Software Fault and Failure Data. *IEEE Tranactions on Software Engineering*, 484–496.

Harris, Hannah (2012). How Climbing Mount Everest Works. How Stuff Works-Discovery.

Hartsfield-Jackson Airport. (2014). Operating Statistics (www.atlanta-airport .com/Airport/ATL/ATL_FactSheet.aspx). Atlanta: Atlanta-Hartsfield Airport.

Hartshorn, P. (2011). *Lincoln Cathedral: A Journey from Past to Present*. Third Millennium Information.

Herald Tribune (2012). How broccoli became America's most hated vegetable (10 July).

Higgins, G. (1994). The operation was successful, but the patient died. Reflections on health care costs and social support cuts. *Canadian Family Physician*, 421–428.

Hirschheim, R. A., Heinzl, A. and Dibbern, J. (2009). *Information Systems Outsourcing*. Springer.

IBM (2002). *IBM Global Services—A Brief History*. IBM Internal Publication.

IoD (2010). *The Duties, Responsibilities and Liabilities of Directors*. London: The Institute of Directors.

Jalote, P. (2005). List of Common Bugs. ww.iiitd.edu.in.

Kakabdase, A. K. (2002). *Smart Sourcing International Best Practice*. Palgrave McMillan.

Kaplan, R. S. and Norton, D. P. (1996). *The Balanced Scorecard: Translating Strategy into Action*. Harvard Business School Press.

Kavis, M. J. (2014). *Architecting the Cloud: Design Decisions for Cloud Computing Service Models (SaaS, PaaS, and IaaS)* (1st edn). John Wiley & Sons.

Kobielus, J. (2010). THOSE NASTY "HAIRBALL" ANALYTICS PROJECTS: USUALLY THERE'S A DATA WAREHOUSE AT THE CORE. Forrester Research Blog.

Lean Manufacturing Tools. (2013). The Seven Wastes—7 Mudas. http://leanmanufacturingtools.org/.

LeDuc, T. (2013). WorldLifeExpectancy.com.

Lincoln Cathedral. (2013). *Lincoln Cathedral History* (lincolncathedral.com). Lincoln: Lincoln Cathedral.

Livius (2013). *Alexander the Great and Aristotle. Livius, articles on ancient history* (retrieved 14 April 2014).

Loades, D. (2009). *Henry VIII: Court, Church and Conflict.* London: The National Archives ISBN 9781905615421.

MacNamee, G. (2012). *Did Nero Fiddle As Rome Burned?* London: Encylopaedia Britannica Blog.

Macro-Business. (2012, 5 15). *How much does Greece owe?* Macro Business (Australia) Economy, Houses and Holes in European. Australia.

Mayr, E. (1988). *Toward a New Philosophy of Biology.* Cambridge: Harvard University Press.

McConnell, S. (1993). *Code Complete: A Practical Handbook of Software Construction* (2nd edn). Microsoft Publishing.

McFarlan, F. and McKenny, P. (1983). The Information Archipelago— Plotting a course. *Harvard Business Review.*

Merriam Webster Dictionary (2013). New York: Britannica Publishing.

Merriam Webster (2013). Pathogenic Definition. Encylopaedia Britannica.

Morgan, J. and Martin, B.-J. (2012). *Lean Six Sigma for Dummies.* John Wiley and Sons.

Naimark, N. M. (2011). *Stalin's Genocides.* Princeton: Princeton University Press (Reprint edition).

Nostradamus, M. (1555). *The Complete Writings of Nostradamus, Prophecies of the World's Most Famous Seer.* Paris: Kindle Edition, Amazon Media 2013.

Pickering, D. A. (2013). *Witch Hunt—The Persecution of Witches in England.* London: Amberley Publishing (reprint).

Read, H. H. (1975). *Introduction to Geology.* New York: Halsted.

River, C. (2013). *The Pyramids and the Great Sphinx of Giza: The History and Mysteries Behind Ancient Egypt's Famous Monuments.* CreateSpace Independent Publishing Platform.

Rolls-Royce plc (2013). *Large Aircraft Engines (RB211).* London: Rolls-Royce.

Romer, J. (2007). *The Great Pyramid: Ancient Egypt Revisited.* Cambridge, England: Cambridge University Press.

Sauer, C. and Cuthbertson, C. (2003). *The State of IT Project Management in the UK 2002–2003.* Available online, http://www.computerweeklyms.com/pmsurveyresults/index.asp accessed 7 May 2005.

See-Larsson, K. G. (2010). *A Cookie Cutter Introduction to FMEA and FMECA: A Practical Example from Theory to Implementation.* LAP Lambert Academic Publishing.

Skelton, D. and Dell, P. (2009). *Empire of Alexander the Great.* New York: Chelsea House.

Smith, B. E. (2010). *Laptops for the Older and Wiser: Get Up and Running on Your Laptop Computer*. John Wiley and Sons.

Soxlaw. (2002). *The Sarbanes-Oxley Act*. www.soxlaw.com.

Spartacus Educational (2013). *Henry VIII*. http://www.spartacus.schoolnet .co.uk.

Stern, C. W. and Deimler, M. S. (2006). *The Boston Consulting Group on Strategy*. John Wiley and Sons.

Tennant, G. (2001). *Six Sigma: SPC and TQM in Manufacturing and Services*. Gower Publishing Limited.

The Argus newspaper (2012). Park benches removed in Crawley after "absurd" health and safety ruling (6 September).

Tolkein, J. (1954). *The Lord of the Rings*. Harper Collins.

Toyota. (2013). *Kaizen*. Toyota-forklifts.co.uk http://www.toyota-forklifts .co.uk/EN/company/Toyota-Production-System/Kaizen/Pages/default .aspx.

Travers, P. (1934). *Mary Poppins*. Reynal and Hitchcock.

Trow, D. L. (2010). *The Tudors for Dummies*. John Wiley & Sons.

Urban Dictionary. (2009). Chronic. High quality weed, often laced with cocaine, sometimes with red hairs on it.

Urban Dictionary. (n.d.). Malicious Obedience (Definition).

Warr, A. (1990). *Strategic Opportunities and Information Management*. Cranfield School of Management Journal.

Weir, A. (2002). *Henry VIII: King and Country*. London: Random House.

WHO. (2013). Fact Sheet 103 Ebola haemorrhagic fever. World Health Organisation.

WHO (Retrieved 29 May 2014). Global Health Observatory Data Repository. World Health Organisation (http://apps.who.int/gho/data/view .main.680?lang=en).

Wilson, E. (2013). *Star Trek: Exploring the Original Series*. CreateSpace Independent Publishing Platform (ISBN-10 1490345264).

Wirth, N. (1995). *A Plea for Lean Software*. IEEE Computer Society Press Los Alamitos, CA, USA, 64–68.

Wood-Harper, D. J. (2008, 6). A study in project failure. BCS: The Chartered Institute for IT: Research paper. London.

World Health Organisation. (2013). Global Health Observatory Data Repository. http://apps.who.int/gho/data/node.main.1?lang=en.

Index